A Synopsis
of the Four Gospels

in a New Translation

Arranged according to
the Two-Gospel Hypothesis

and

Edited by
John Bernard Orchard
osb

Mercer University Press

All Mercer University Press books are produced on acid-free paper
which meets or exceeds the minimum standards set by
the National Historical Publications and Records Commission.

Library of Congress Cataloging in Publication Data

Main entry under title:

A Synopsis of the four Gospels.

Includes index.
1. Bible. N.T. Gospels—Harmonies.   I. Orchard, Bernard, 1910-
BS2560.S93   226'.1   81-18753
ISBN 0-86554-024-1   AACR2

Table of Contents

Dedication

Genetrici
Dei
Nostraeque
Matri

Foreword

Ancient Synopses. To the Christian every single saying and deed of Jesus is important, no matter whether it has or has not a parallel or parallels in the other Gospel texts. Hence it is not surprising that the practice of paralleling the similar texts of the Four Gospels goes back at least to the 3rd century when Ammonius the Alexandrian put the similar pericopes of the other evangelists alongside their Matthean parallels. Ammonius's Gospel parallels seemingly did not commend itself to many contemporaries of Eusebius of Caesarea (ca. 260-340 A.D.). Eusebius accordingly invented a new system of section numbers, recorded in marginal references, for which he compiled the key in his "List of Ten Canons" (see Eusebius's letter to Carpianus). Eusebius thus offered a detailed system of references not only for all parallel passages but for all pericope-units throughout the Four Gospels, without the demerit of splitting up the Sacred Text into visually distinct units. Eusebius therefore avoided offending the susceptibilities of those who considered the Ammonian sections to be an illicit form of tampering with the Scriptures.

Our modern practice of parceling out the Gospels into a large number of pericope-units is in fact a rejection of Eusebius's plan and of its medieval practice, and is a return, so it would seem, to Ammonius's scheme for the sake of its usefulness for study purposes. For such a scheme enables the scholar/theologian to recall and visually compare at will the many similar passages that throw light on one another, and so to gain a clearer insight into the minds of the evangelists. The great Origen himself in his *Hexapla* paralleled the Old Testament in a somewhat different way in order to check and if possible to remove corruptions in the current text. Today the scholars parallel the text, pericope by pericope and word by word, not only in order to recover the original text where it still remains uncertain and to elucidate its meaning, but also in order to establish the exact literary relationships between the Four Gospels. Scholars now recognize this paralleling of the text to be the necessary preliminary to fixing the text and to attaining its inner meaning.

Modern Synopses. Source criticism did not command the attention of the Ancient Fathers, however, for at that stage of investigation everyone unquestioningly accepted the traditional order (Matthew, Mark, Luke, John), together with Augustine of Hippo's dictum that the writer of the Second Gospel knew the First, that the writer of the Third knew the other two, and that the writer of the Fourth knew the former three. Nevertheless, from earliest days there has existed considerable evidence for supposing that the traditional order of the Gospels is not in fact the actual order of their literary composition and that the real chronological order of composition and so of literary dependence is: Matthew, Luke, Mark, John. The first person to suggest this in print was Henry Owen, in a work published in London in 1764 entitled *Observations on the Four Gospels.*

Owen's theory, it seems, was taken up by J. J. Griesbach between 1784 and 1789, and the latter's advocacy succeeded in winning wide support for it during the first half of the 19th century until it yielded place to various theories of the priority of Mark. It was Griesbach too who, in 1776, produced the first "Gospel Synopsis" in its modern form in order to aid his text-critical researches, and he has since had countless imitators.[1] Most of these synopses have been constructed according to some theory of synoptic literary relationships, and the currently popular synopses—those of Aland, Huck-Greeven, and Throckmorton (based on Huck)—are fundamentally influenced by the hypothesis of Markan Priority. During the past decade, however, Owen's theory, more generally known as the Griesbach Hypothesis, has enjoyed a revival; and now, in the opinion of an increasing number of scholars, it offers a more plausible explanation of the literary phenomena than any other current theory. This revived hypothesis has now been restated in modern terms and given a new and more explicit title—the Two-Gospel Hypothesis—and argues that our Greek Matthew is a main literary source of Luke and that both Luke and Matthew are the two main literary sources of Mark.[2] The present Synopsis, then, for the first time presents the *four* Gospels arranged according to this hypothesis in support of that part of the tradition which holds that the true literary order of composition is: first, our Greek Matthew, then our Luke, then our Mark, and finally our John. Since the Gospel tradition is "fourfold," a synopsis ought always to include all four Gospels in full, as is done here.

---

[1]See H. Greeven, "The Gospel Synopsis from 1776 to the Present Day," in *J. J. Griesbach: Synoptic and Text-Critical Studies, 1776-1976* (Cambridge: Cambridge University Press, 1979).

[2]See J. B. Orchard, "The Two-Gospel Hypothesis," *Downside Review* 98 (October 1980):333

Origin. The present Synopsis has grown out of the process of preparing a new *Synopsis of the Four Gospels in Greek*, now due for publication in 1982 by Messrs. T. and T. Clark Ltd of Edinburgh, Scotland, my original intention being to accompany and to face the Greek text with this English version on the opposite side of the page. But various factors, including those of cost and bulk, together with the insistent request of the Mercer University Press to publish the English version separately as a special contribution to the ongoing research into the Synoptic Problem, finally overcame my reluctance to seeing it appear independently of the Greek text to which it is so closely bound. On the other hand, the separate publication of this text offers a number of advantages: now a much wider public will be made aware of recent new thinking about the Gospels, and of the existence of an important new tool for synoptic research that opens up fresh perspectives for understanding the Gospels.

Purpose. The aim of this Synopsis therefore is to provide college and seminary students, and other students of the Gospels, with a viewpoint, both new and yet traditional, by means of a simple, concise, and unencumbered presentation of the Gospel parallels, a presentation that will enable those with little or no Greek to grasp the fundamentals of the literary relationships between the Four Gospels. To this end, this new and intentionally literal translation has been provided, together with a short and simple list of the major textual variants of special synoptic interest.

Text. As the text printed here is the English rendering of the above-mentioned Synopsis in Greek, it is in order here to note the main principles upon which the latter has been constructed. Since there is today, in certain professional circles, a growing doubt about the correctness of many of the radical departures of twentieth century text critics from both the Vulgate and the Textus Receptus, I have thought it best to construct my own text on the principle that for the source-critical purpose of this Synopsis it is preferable to retain in the Gospel text itself a considerable number of words and passages which modern critics either reject outright or about which they have serious misgivings, rather than to relegate them to an apparatus at the foot of the page or elsewhere. For it seems safer as well as more accommodating and liberal to mark the doubtful passages with an asterisk and then leave them on view in the text, and so allow the reader himself to decide whether to retain or to exclude them.

These asterisks should be warning enough for those who might otherwise want to use doubtful passages in support of one source theory or another. Of course it is inevitable that every editor's own source theory will have a substantial influence on the text he decides to print, and the editors of both the United Bible Society's third edition and Nestle-Aland's twenty-sixth edition reveal the influence of the Markan Priority hypothesis in their texts. Consequently, the Two-Gospel Hypothesis will also be found to have had its influence upon the present text. Nevertheless in practice I have preferred the reading which logically follows from my theory of synoptic relationships only where a real choice seems to be open and the arguments for and against appear evenly balanced. Two other criteria have occasionally influenced my decision to include a text: (a) where a Gospel has no synoptic parallel, I have for the most part marked with an asterisk only those variants that notably change or add to the meaing; and (b) a few readings, such as John 5:4-5, which are generally held to be later additions, have been retained either because of their intrinsic interest or their theological importance.

Unique features. This Synopsis possesses a number of new features never before incorporated together in a single presentation. Thus it breaks new ground in the following ways:

● The order of the columns adopted here—Matthew-Luke-Mark-John—appears now for the first time in the 200-year-old history of synopses. The Gospel of John, an integral part of the fourfold Gospel tradition, is presented in full in its relationship to theSynoptic Gospels.

● Each Gospel can be read in a new and more complete manner in its natural order, and in its own column. Duplications are printed in italics.

● This is the first English version to be made expressly for synoptic purposes, that is, the translations of all parallel passages are as far as possible fully coordinated with the Greek original.

● The Parallel pericope-units are broken down into separate phrases, clauses, and sentences in order to clarify the pericope structure and so to permit the student to perceive the development of thought and expression from one Gospel to the next. Hence gaps in the text are allowed only where they occur syntactically, that is, only *between* one phrase or clause or sentence and the next one, and never within them.

● This Synopsis is also the first ever to be specially designed to illustrate the Griesbach or Two-Gospel Hypothesis; thus it becomes the essential counterpart to the other current synopses, all of which have been planned and executed by editors who have accepted the hypothesis of the priority of the Gospel of Mark, and whose judgements in the course of their presentation have been necessarily and properly colored by the assumptions of that hypothesis.

• This Synopsis is also unique among modern synopses not only in frankly declaring the principles on which it is based, but also in explaining the manner of its construction (see below).

• The 396 pericope-units into which this Synopsis is divided are of course influenced by, and dependent upon, the editor's own understanding of the Gospel relationships. The pericope titles also reflect this understanding.

The Construction of a Vertical-Column Synopsis. Recent work by Professor David L. Dungan, and others, has proved that it is impossible to construct a "neutral" synopsis, as has been generally believed and stoutly asserted.[3] This means that every synopsis must necessarily reflect the synoptic views of its constructor, if it is to be of any use for the study of the Synoptic Problem. And since all existing synopses, whether Greek or vernacular, inevitably reflect in their construction the Markan Priority hypothesis of their constructors, no further progress can be made towards the solution of the Synoptic Problem until we possess a synopsis or synopses based on other hypotheses, and in particular one based on the theory diametrically opposed to Markan Priority, namely, that of the Griesbach or Two-Gospel Hypothesis. Hence a sine qua non for progress in synoptic studies is for students also to have in their hands a synopsis that visually presents the case for the opposing hypothesis. The present work is in fact the first of its kind to do so.

Method of Construction. There are in fact just three distinct ways of constructing a vertical-column synopsis (even if we ignore the possibility of the primacy of Luke). It can be done either (1) by applying the text of Matthew to that of Mark and then adding Luke to suit, as is basically done by the Synopses of Aland and Huck (including the new thirteenth edition), both of which in fact are based upon synopses constructed long before by other editors; or (2) by applying Luke to Matthew, then adding

Mark to suit both; or (3) by an eclectic application of both (1) and (2) to different portions of the text. Both Aland and Huck are good examples of (1), and Aland also bears traces of (3). But the present Synopsis is the first example of (2) to see the light. In the case of (1), Mark is the *mean* between Matthew and Luke; in the case of (2)—that is, of this Synopsis—Luke is the *mean* between Matthew and Mark.

The Impossibility of a "Neutral" Synopsis. To the question, Does it matter whether we adopt (1) or (2) or (3)?, the answer is that it matters a great deal, and in fact it makes all the difference. For to use a synopsis put together according to a preconceived theory (as one must) is to enter into a presentation that favors and illustrates that theory at the expense of other theories, while a synopsis put together by combining opposing theories merely induces confusion and perplexity. The considerable difference between the arrangement of the material in this Synopsis and its arrangement in all the others provides ocular demonstration that this is so. For the adoption of pattern (1) is really the equivalent of assuming that Mark is prior to Matthew and Luke, while to adopt (2) is to assume that Matthew is prior to both Luke and Mark. To mix the two procedures is to produce a hybrid pattern (not immediately recognizable) which leaves the student with no guide to the method of composition at any particular point and therefore with no understanding of why the parallels need to be arranged exactly as they appear in the text. Furthermore, the desire to be "neutral", that is, impartial, though in itself praiseworthy, is yet in this connection quite impossible of realization; for the synopsis-maker is forced to opt for one pattern or the other, or else to vary it from pericope to pericope without any indication to the student.

Value. It follows from what has just been said that the procedure adopted in this Synopsis is the one best calculated to indicate the advantages and the disadvantages of the Two-Gospel Hypothesis. And since it is now being generally agreed that the theory of Markan Priority is no longer adequate, a synopsis setting out the pattern of relationships according to the new hypothesis is scientifically valuable, if only because it applies a new technique to the four Gospels for the first time. In fact, the pattern of this Synopsis is based on the research incorporated in my *Matthew, Luke and Mark*[4], to which the student is referred

---

[3]See Dungan's article, "Theory of Synopsis Construction," *Biblica* 61:3 (1980): 305-29.

[4](Greater Manchester, England: Koinonia Press, 1976).

for further details of the construction.

In conclusion I should like to express my deep gratitude to the Rev. H. K. Moulton, for his indefatigable help and advice in improving both my translation and my use of the English language. I also want to record my thanks to the director of the Mercer University Press, Prof. Watson E. Mills, for his initiative, encouragement, and assistance at all stages.

Ealing Abbey   John Bernard Orchard osb
London W.5   Feast of St. Augustine of Canterbury, 1981.

Note on the Arrangement This Synopsis

Each Gospel is presented in its entirety in its own column from beginning to end in its own natural order, and is printed in Roman type. There are gaps, of course, here and there to allow for another Gospel to intervene. Italic type is used only to indicate parallels found in a different order in one or more Gospels. Thus in the Great Sermon (Matthew 5:2—7:27 = Luke 6:20-49), wherever Matthew and Luke run parallel in their natural order both are printed in Roman type, for example, in the Beatitudes, Matthew 5:2-12; Luke 6:20-23; 24-26. But where Luke has a parallel to the Sermon elsewhere in his Gospel, the parallel is printed beside Matthew in italics in order to indicate that it is not in its right place in the order of Luke, for example, Matthew 5:14-16 = *Luke 11:33*.

The pericope arrangement of the four Gospels of course has been made according to the Two-Gospel Hypothesis, that is, by assuming the order of composition and of dependence to be: Luke dependent upon Matthew; Mark dependent upon both Matthew and Luke, with John following his own independent tradition, yet aware of all three and shaping his own Gospel in the light of this awareness. This arrangement is fully outlined in the Conspectus of Parallel Passages below (p.xv), but the following table may help to clarify the over-all pattern. To avoid over-elaboration, some of the pericopes peculiar to one Gospel or another have been omitted, but the omissions do not substantially affect the presentation.

Matthew	Luke	Mark	John
3:1—4:11	3:1—4:13	1:2-13	
4:12-22	4:14-30	1:14-20	1:19-4:54
	4:31-43	1:21-38	
4:23	4:44	1:39	5:1-47
	5:1—6:16	1:40—3:7a	
4:24-25	6:17-19	3:7b-12	
5:1		3:13-19	*6:1-5*
5:2—7:27	6:20-49		
7:28—8:4			
8:5-13	7:1-10		
	7:11—8:3		
		3:20-35	
	8:4-21	4:1-34	
8:14-22			
8:23-27	8:22-25	4:35-41	
8:28-34	8:26-39	5:1-20	
9:1-17			
9:18-26	8:40-56	5:21-43	
9:27-38			
10:1-15	9:1-5	6:7-11	
10:16-42			
11:1	9:6	6:12-13	
11:2—13:58			
14:1-2	9:7-9	6:14-16	
14:3-12		6:17-29	
14:13-21	9:10-17	6:30-44	6:1-71
14:22—16:12	9:18-50	6:45—8:21	
		8:22-26	
16:13—18:35		8:27—9:50	
19:1-2	9:51	10:1	
	9:52—18:14		7:1—11:54
19:3—20:34	18:15—19:28	10:2-46	11:55-12:19
21:1—25:46	19:29—21:38	11:1—13:37	12:20-50
26:1-75	22:1-71	14:1-72	13:1—18:27
27:1-66	23:1-56	15:1—16:1	18:28-19:42
28:1-8	24:1-12	16:2-8	20:1-10

As stated in the Foreword, the number and size of the pericope units reflect the editor's own understanding of the Synoptic Gospel relationships. The criteria used to distinguish these pericope units are as follows:

- adoption of the hypothesis that Luke depends upon Matthew, and that Mark depends upon both Matthew and Luke, and that John depends upon Matthew, Luke, and Mark;
- that each pericope must be an "idea-unit," that is, a complete sentence or a complete story that can stand by itself;
- that these "idea-units" can in most cases be identified by comparing the parallels; and
- that "parallel-units" are ones which have either a considerable number of words in common or some common syntax; which treat the same topic (in most cases in a similar way); or which as a rule appear in the same overall context or order (though not invariably); or which enjoy several of these factors at once.

The pericope units of the Gospel of John present a somewhat different problem since they appear to belong to a diverse literary tradition. The presupposition here is that John is subsequent to and aware of all three Synoptic Gospels. John's points of contact with them are limited, however, because John appears to presume the story of all three in order to provide further material which generally fits into the overall framework of the Synoptics, thus filling up some of the gaps in the Synoptic story. Compare, for example, the story of the Judean Ministry before the opening of the Galilean Ministry, and the insertion of several visits to Jerusalem not recorded in the Synoptic accounts. Since there seems to be no means of establishing a precise chronology for these extra visits to Jerusalem, an editor has no alternative but to place them at points where there seem to be real disjunctions in the Synoptic narratives, for example, Mark 2:1, Luke 9:51 (and par.), Luke 19:28 (and par.). It is noteworthy, however, that in the Passion Narrative John closely follows the order of Luke against that of Matthew and Mark.

Notes for the Reader

1. Section Nos. (§ §) are always shown with § or §§ prefixed, e.g. §17, §§310-314.
2. Page Nos. are always shown without any qualification.
3. Italic text or references always indicate that the passage in question is out of context in its own Gospel.
4. The curved brackets occurring from place to place around a word or words in the text of the Gospels mean that this word or these words are not found in the original Greek but are to be supplied on account of English usage in order to make the meaning clear.
5. A dotted vertical line occurring within a pericope indicates that different passages from the same Gospel are printed on either side of it.
6. The asterisk * warns the reader that there is at least some disagreement among the textual witnesses at this point. Those interested in estimating the value of the alternatives should refer to the Apparaticus Criticus of the standard editions of the Greek text.
7. The Old Testament references as a rule refer to the chapter and verse numbering of the Septuagint.
8. Wherever the main parallel or parallels are found printed in bold type, it means that each Gospel is found to be in parallel in its own order, at least according to the theory adopted for this synopsis. But if the parallels are found printed in italics it means that the passage or passages in question are not in the actual order of their own Gospel.
9. A Section No. after the title of a pericope means that either a part or the whole of that pericope will be found repeated in the order of the other Gospel at that No.
10. If a pericope (when printed in bold) happens to be isolated, either before or after (or both), from the next passage printed in bold, the next pericope of that Gospel in either direction is indicated by an arrow beside the § No.; e.g. §48, Mk 1:40-45, we note that the previous main text of Mk is to be found at (↑§46), while the next main text of Mk following is indicated on the next page by the sign (↓§51).
11. If unable to find the passage you want, turn to the Conspectus, where all the passages printed, whether in bold or in italics, are recorded.

Conspectus of Parallel Passages

VII. Jesus Teaches in Jerusalem §§288-324

Introduction
§§ 1-3

§1 Preface to Luke

§1 Preface to Luke

MT | **LK 1:1-4** | **MK** | **JN**

1 Seeing that many have taken in hand to compile a narrative about the deeds fully accomplished among us, 2 just as those who were from the beginning eye-witnesses and ministers of the word have handed on to us,
3 it seemed good also to me who have followed closely everything from the beginning, to write accurately in sequence to you, Excellent Theophilus, 4 so that you may know the certainty of the matters about which you have been instructed.

(↓ §9)

§2 Title of Mark

MT | **LK** | **MK 1:1** | **JN**

1 The beginning of the Gospel of Jesus Christ Son of God.

(↓ §17)

§3 Prologue of John

MT | **LK** | **MK** | **JN 1:1-18**

1 In the beginning was the Word, and the Word was with God, and the Word was God. 2 This (Word) was in the beginning with God.
3 All things were made through him and without him nothing that has been made was made.
4 In him was life, and the life was the light of men; 5 and the light shines in the darkness, and the darkness did not overcome it.
6 There was a man sent from God, whose name was John.
7 This (man) came for witness to bear witness about the light, so that all might believe through him.
8 This (man) was not the light, but that he might witness about the light.
9 It was the true light that enlightens every man coming into the world.
10 He was in the world and the world was made through him, and the world did not know him.
11 He came to his own, and his own (people) did not accept him.
12 But whosoever received him, to them he gave the capability to become God's sons, to the believers in his name,
13 who were begotten not of blood, nor of the will of the flesh nor of the will of man, but of God.
14 And the Word became flesh and pitched his tent among us; and we beheld his glory, the glory as of the only begotten of the

3

MT	LK	MK	JN 1:1-18

Father, full of grace and truth.

15 John witnesses about him and has cried out saying: This is he of whom I spoke. The One who comes after me came to be before me because he was before me.

16 For from his fullness we have all received, and grace upon grace.

17 For the Law was given through Moses, grace and truth came through Jesus Christ.

18 No one has seen God at any time; the only-begotten God*, the one who is in the bosom of the Father, he has explained (him).

(↓ §25)

I. The Origin and Childhood of Jesus
§§ 4-16

MT 1:1-17

1 Book of the origin of Jesus Christ, Son of David, Son of Abraham.
2 Abraham begot Isaac, and Isaac begot Jacob, and Jacob begot Judah and his brothers,
3 and Judas begot Perez and Zerah out of Tamar, and Perez begot Hezron, and Hezron begot Aram,
4 And Aram begot Amminadab, and Amminadab begot Nahshon, and Nahshon begot Salmon,
5 and Salmon begot Boaz out of Rachab, and Boaz begot Obed out of Ruth, and Obed begot Jesse,
6 and Jesse begot David the king. And David begot Solomon out of Uriah's (wife),
7 and Solomon begot Rehoboam, and Rehoboam begot Abijah, and Abijah begot Asa,
8 and Asa begot Jehoshaphat, and Jehoshaphat begot Joram, and Joram begot Uzziah,
9 and Uzziah begot Joatham, and Joatham begot Ahaz, and Ahaz begot Hezekiah,
10 and Hezekiah begot Manasseh, and Manasseh begot Amos, and Amos begot Josiah,
11 and Josiah begot Jechoniah and his brothers at the Babylonian deportation.
12 And after the Babylonian deportation Jechoniah begot Shealtiel, and Shealtiel begot Zerubbabel,
13 and Zerubbabel begot Abiud, and Abiud begot Eliakim, and Eliakim begot Azor,
14 and Azor begot Zadok, and Zadok begot Achim, and Achim begot Eliud,
15 and Eliud begot Eleazar, and Eleazar begot Maththan, and Maththan begot Jacob,
16 and Jacob begot Joseph, the husband of Mary, out of whom was begotten Jesus the one called Christ.
17 Therefore all the generations from Abraham to David are fourteen generations; and from David to the Babylonian deportation fourteen generations; and from the Babylonian deportation to the Christ fourteen generations.

LK 3:23-38

23 Now Jesus himself, (when) about to begin, was about thirty years (old), being the son, as it was thought, of Joseph, of Heli,
24 of Matthat, of Levi, of Melchi, of Jannai, of Joseph,
25 of Mattathias, of Amos, of Nahum, of Esli, of Naggai,
26 of Maath, of Mattathias, of Semein, of Josech, of Joda,
27 of Joanan, of Rhesa, of Zerubbabel, of Shealtiel, of Neri, 28 of Melchi, of Addi, of Cosam, of Elmadam, of Er,
29 of Joshua, of Eliezer, of Jorim, of Maththat, of Levi,
30 of Simeon, of Judah, of Joseph, of Jonam, of Eliakim,
31 of Melea, of Menna, of Mattatha, of Nathan, of David,
32 of Jesse, of Obed, of Boaz, of Salmon, of Nahshon,
33 of Amminadab, of Admin, of Arni, of Hezron, of Perez, of Judah,
34 of Jacob, of Isaac, of Abraam, of Terah, of Nachor,
35 of Serug, of Reu, of Peleg, of Eber, of Shelah,
36 of Cainan, of Arphaxad, of Shem, of Noah, of Lamech,
37 of Methuselah, of Enoch, of Jared, of Mahalaleel, of Kainan,
38 of Enos, of Seth, of Adam, of God.

MK   JN

§5 Origin and Birth of Jesus   (§§3, 10, 13, 14)

MT 1:18-25

18 Now the birth of Jesus Christ was thus. While his mother Mary was betrothed to Joseph, before they came together she was found to have in her womb (a child) from the Holy Spirit.
19 Now Joseph her husband, being just, and not willing to denounce her, was minded to divorce her secretly.
20 And while he was pondering these things, behold an angel of

LK 2:6-7a, 21

MK   JN

MT 1:18-25

the Lord appeared to him in a dream, saying:
Joseph, son of David, do not fear to accept Mary thy wife; for what has been begotten in her is from the Holy Spirit.
21 And she will bear a son, and thou shalt call his name Jesus; for he will save his people from their sins.
22 Now all this happened in order to fulfil what was spoken by the Lord through the prophet, saying:
23 Behold the virgin will have (a child) in the womb and will bear a son,
and they shall call his name Emmanuel,
which when translated is, God with us **(Is. 7:14; 8:8)**.
24 And Joseph arising from sleep did as the angel of the Lord had commanded, and accepted his wife;
25 and he knew her not until she bore her first-born* son,

and he called his name Jesus.

LK 2:6-7a, 21

6 And it happened while they were there the days of her pregnancy were completed, 7 and she bore her son, the first born.

21 And when the eight days were completed for circumcising him, his name was also called Jesus, which he had been called by the angel before he was conceived in the womb.

MK

JN

§6 Visit of the Wise Men

MT 2:1-12

1 Now when Jesus was born in Bethlehem of Judea in the days of Herod the king, behold wise men from the East came to Jerusalem
2 saying: Where is he who has been born king of the Jews? For we have seen his star in the East and have come to worship him.
3 And King Herod heard and was perturbed and all Jerusalem with him. 4 And assembling all the high priests and scribes of the people, he inquired of them where the Christ was to be born.
5 And they said to him:
In Bethlehem of Judea; for so it has been written by the prophet:
6 And thou Bethlehem, land of Judah,
in no wise art thou the least among the leaders of Judah.
For from thee shall come forth the leader
who will shepherd my people Israel **(Mic. 5:2)**.
7 Then Herod secretly calling the wise men inquired of them the time of the star that appeared; 8 and sending them to Bethlehem, said:
Go, investigate carefully about the child; and when you have found (him) report to me, so that I too may come and worship him.
9 And having heard the king they went; and behold the star, which they had seen in the East, went before them until it came and stood over where the child was.
10 And seeing the star they rejoiced with exceedingly great joy.

LK   MK   JN

MT 2:1-12   LK   MK   JN

11 And coming into the house they saw the child with Mary his
mother, and falling down they worshipped him; and opening their
treasures they offered him gifts, gold and frankincense and myrrh.
12 And being notified in a dream not to return to Herod, they
withdrew to their own region by another way.

§7 Massacre at Bethlehem

MT 2:13-18   LK   MK   JN

13 And when they withdrew, behold the angel of the Lord appears
in a dream to Joseph, saying:
Rise and take the child and his mother and flee into Egypt and be
there until I tell you; for Herod is about to seek the child to
destroy him.
14 And he rose and took the child and his mother by night, and
withdrew into Egypt, 15 and was there until the passing away of
Herod;
so that what had been spoken by the Lord through the prophet
was fulfilled, saying:
Out of Egypt I have called my son **(Hos. 11:1)**.
16 Then Herod seeing that he had been outwitted by the wise men
got very angry, and sent and killed all the children in Bethlehem
and in all its territories from two years old and under, according
to the time which he had learned from the wise men.
17 Then was fulfilled what had been spoken by Jeremiah the
prophet, saying:
18 A voice was heard in Ramah,
weeping and much mourning:
Rachel weeping for her children,
And she refused to be comforted, because they are no more. **(Jer.
31:15)**

§8 Return to Nazareth (§15)

MT 2:19-23   LK   MK   JN

19 And when Herod had passed away, behold, an angel of the
Lord appears in a dream to Joseph in Egypt, 20 saying,
Rise and take the child and his mother and go into the land of
Israel; for those who sought the life of the child have died.
21 And he rose and took the child and his mother and entered
into the land of Israel.
22 But having heard that Archelaus was reigning over Judea in
place of his father Herod, he was afraid to go off there.

MT 2:19-23   LK   MK   JN

And being informed in a dream he withdrew into the districts of Galilee, 23 and he came and settled in a city called Nazareth; so that there should be fulfilment of what had been spoken by the prophets that he should be called a Nazarene.

(cf. 2:39)

(↓ §17)

§9 Origin of John the Baptist

MT   LK 1:5-25   MK   JN

5 There was in the days of Herod king of Judea a certain priest, Zechariah by name, of the roster of Abijah, and he had a wife of the daughters of Aaron, and her name was Elizabeth.
6 And they were both just before God, walking in all the commandments and ordinances of the Lord without blame.
7 And they had no child because Elizabeth was barren, and they were both advanced in their days.
8 And it happened while he was serving as priest in the order of his roster before God, 9. according to the custom of the priesthood, it fell to him to enter into the sanctuary of the Lord to burn incense,
10 And the whole multitude of the people was praying without at the hour of incense.
11 And an angel of the Lord appeared to him and stood on the right of the altar of incense.
12 And Zechariah was troubled when he saw him and fear fell upon him.
13 And the angel said to him:
Do not fear, Zechariah, for your prayer has been listened to, and your wife Elizabeth will bear you a son, and you shall call his name John.
14 And you shall have joy and gladness, and many shall rejoice over his birth.
15 For he will be great before the Lord, and will not drink wine or strong drink, and he will be filled with the Holy Spirit even from his mother's womb.
16 And he will convert many of the sons of Israel to the Lord their God. 17 And he will go before him in the spirit and power of Elijah, to convert the hearts of the fathers to the children and the disobedient to the understanding of the just, to ensure for the Lord a people prepared.
18 And Zechariah said to the angel:
How shall I know this? For I am old and my wife advanced in her days.
19 And the angel answering said to him:
I am Gabriel who stands before God, and I have been sent to

10

MT	LK 1:5-25		MK	JN

speak to you and to bring you these good tidings.

20 And behold, you shall be silent and not able to speak until the day when these things come to pass, becuase you did not believe my words which will be fulfilled at their time.

21 And the people were waiting for Zechariah and marvelled at his delaying in the holy place.

22 And when he came out, he was unable to speak to them, and they understood that he had beheld a vision in the holy place; and he was making signs to them and remained dumb.

23 And it came to pass when he had fulfilled the days of his sacred service, he went away to his own house.

24 And after these days his wife Elizabeth conceived; and she hid herself for five months; saying:

25 Thus the Lord has done to me in the days on which he has looked upon (me) to take away my reproach among men.

§10 Origin of Jesus

MT	LK 1:26-38		MK	JN

26 And in the sixth month the angel Gabriel was sent from God to a city of Galilee, Nazareth by name, 27 to a virgin betrothed to a man whose name was Joseph, of the House of David, and the virgin's name was Mary.

28 And entering in unto her, he said:
Hail, full of grace, the Lord is with you.

29 But she was much disturbed at the word and deliberated what sort of greeting this was.

30 And the angel said to her: Fear not, Mary; for you have found favour with God.

31 And behold you will conceive in the womb and bear a son, and you shall call his name Jesus.

32 For he will be great, and shall be called the Son of the Most High, and the Lord God will give him the throne of David his father; 33 and he will reign over the house of Jacob for ever, and his Kingdom shall have no end.

34 And Mary said to the angel: How shall this be since I know not man?

35 And the angel answering said to her:
The Holy Spirit will come upon you, and the power of the Most High shall overshadow you; wherefore also the Holy One born will be called Son of God.

36 And behold, Elizabeth your kinswoman, she too has conceived a son in her old age, and this is the sixth month with her who is called barren. 37 For nothing at all will be impossible with God.

38 And Mary said: Behold the slave of the Lord; be it done to me according to your word.
And the angel departed from her.

11

MT	LK 1:39-56	MK	JN
	39 And Mary rising up in those days went with haste into the mountain-country to a city of Judah, 40 and entered into the house of Zechariah and greeted Elizabeth.		

39 And Mary rising up in those days went with haste into the mountain-country to a city of Judah, 40 and entered into the house of Zechariah and greeted Elizabeth.

41 And it happened that when Elizabeth heard Mary's greeting, the infant in her womb leapt, and Elizabeth was filled with the Holy Spirit, 42 and she cried out with a great cry and said: Blessed are you among women, and blessed (is) the fruit of your womb. 43 And whence (is) this to me that the mother of my Lord should come to me?

44 For behold, when the sound of your greeting came to my ears, the infant in my womb leapt for joy.

45 And blessed is she that has believed that there will be fulfilment for the things spoken to her by the Lord.

46 And Mary said:

My soul magnifies the Lord,

47 and my spirit has exulted in God my Saviour;

48 because he has regarded the humility of his slave.

For behold, from now, all generations will call be blessed.

49 Because the Mighty One has done great things to me.

And holy (is) his name,

50 and his mercy unto generations and generations,

to those who fear him.

51 He has wrought power in his arm,

he has scattered the arrogant in the thought of their heart;

52 He has deposed rulers from thrones,

and exalted the humble;

53 he has filled the hungry with good things

and the rich he has sent away empty.

54 He has taken care of Israel his servant,

remembering his mercy,

55 just as he spoke to our fathers,

to Abraham and to his seed for ever.

56 And Mary remained with her about three months, and returned to her house.

§12 Birth of John the Baptist

MT	LK 1:57-80	MK	JN

57 Now the time came to Elizabeth for her delivery, and she bore a son.

58 And her neighbors and kinsfolk heard that the Lord had magnified his mercy towards her, and they rejoiced with her.

59 And it came to pass on the eighth day they came to circumcise the child, and they called him by the name of his father Zechariah.

60 And his mother answering said: No, but he shall be called John.

MT	LK 1:57-80	MK	JN

61 And they said to her: There is nobody of your kin who is called by this name.

62 And they nodded to his father as to what he wished him to be called. 63 And having asked for a writing tablet, he wrote saying: John is his name. And all wondered.

64 And his mouth was opened immediately, and his tongue, and he spoke, blessing God.

65 And fear came upon all their neighbors, and in all the hill country of Judea all these events were discussed, 66 and all who had heard stored (them) up in their hearts, saying: What then will this child be? For indeed the hand of the Lord was with him.

67 And Zechariah his father was filled with the Holy Spirit and prophesied saying:

68 Blessed (be) the Lord the God of Israel,

for he has visited his people and wrought their redemption,

69 and raised a horn of salvation for us,

in the house of David his servant,

70 just as he spoke through (the) mouth of his holy prophets from of old,

71 salvation from our enemies

and from the hand of all who hate us;

72 to work mercy with our fathers,

and to remember his holy covenant, 73 (the) oath which he swore to Abraham our father,

to grant to us that 74 without fear, being rescued from the hand of enemies

we may worship him 75 in holiness and righteousness

before him all our days.

76 And you too, child, shall be called prophet of the Most High;

for you shall go before the Lord to prepare his ways,

77 to give knowledge of salvation to his people,

in remission of their sins,

78 through the tender mercy of our God,

by which the Orient from on High has visited us,

79 to appear to those sitting in darkness and shadow of death,

in order to guide our feet into (the) way of peace.

80 And the child grew and became strong in spirit, and he was in the deserts until (the) day of his announcement to Israel.

§13 Birth of Jesus (§5)

MT (cf. 1:25)	LK 2:1-20	MK	JN

1 And it came to pass in those days that a decree went out from Caesar Augustus that the whole world should submit to a census. 2 This first census came to pass while Quirinius was governing Syria. 3 And all went to be enrolled, each one to his own city.

| MT | LK 2:1-20 | MK | JN |

4 And Joseph went up from Galilee from the city of Nazareth into Judea to David's city, that is called Bethlehem, because of his being of the house and family of David, 5 to be enrolled with Mary his betrothed, who was with child.
6 And it came to pass while they were there, the days for her to give birth were completed, 7 and she brought forth her son, the first born, and wrapped him round and laid him in a manger, because there was no room for them in the inn.
8 And there were shepherds in that region staying in the open and keeping the watches of the night over their flock.
9 And behold an angel of the Lord stood by them, and (the) glory of the Lord shone around them, and they feared a great fear.
10 And the angel said to them:
Fear not; for behold I bring you good tidings of great joy, which shall be to all the people, 11 because there has been born to you today (the) Saviour, who is Christ the Lord, in the city of David.
12 And this (is) for you (the) sign, you will find the infant swaddled and lying in a manger.
13 And suddenly there was with the angel a multitude of the heavenly host praising God and saying:
14 Glory to God in the highest and upon earth peace to men of his good pleasure.
15 And it came to pass that when the angels went off from them into heaven the shepherds said to one another: Let us then go over to Bethlehem and let us see this thing that has happened which the Lord has made known to us.
16 And they came hasting and they found both Mary and Joseph, and the Child lying in the manger.
17 And when they saw they made known about the word spoken to them about this child.
18 And all who heard wondered about the things spoken by the shepherds to them.
19 And Mary laid up all these words, pondering (them) in her heart.
20 And the shepherds returned glorifying and praising God at all they had heard and saw just as it was spoken to them.

§14 Circumcision of Jesus

| MT | LK 2:21-38 | MK | JN |

21 And when eight days had been completed for his circumcision, his name was called Jesus, the (one) spoken by the angel before he was conceived in the womb.
22 And when the days of their cleansing were completed according to the Law of Moses, they took him up to Jerusalem to present to the Lord,-
23 just as it has been written in the Law of the Lord: Every male

MT	LK 2:21-38	MK	JN
	opening up the womb shall be called holy to the Lord **(Ex. 13:2, 12, 15)**. 24 and to give a sacrifice according to what is said in the Law of the Lord: A pair of turtle-doves or two young doves **(Lv. 12:8)**. 25 And behold there was a man in Jerusalem, Simeon by name, and this man (was) just and devout waiting for the consolation of Israel, and (the) Holy Spirit was upon him; 26 And he had been notified by the Holy Spirit that he would not see death before seeing the Christ of the Lord. 27 And he came in the Spirit into the Temple; and when the parents brought in the child Jesus for them to do for him according to the custom of the Law, 28 and he received him in his arms and blessed the Lord and said: 29 Now thou dost release thy servant, O Master, according to thy word in peace; 30 because my eyes have seen thy Salvation, 31 which thou hast prepared before the face of all the peoples, 32 (the) light for a revelation of the Gentiles, and (the) glory of thy people Israel. 33 And there was his father marvelling, and his mother, at what was said about him. 34. And Simeon blessed them and said to Mary his mother: Lo, this one is set for (the) fall and (the) rise of many in Israel, and for a sign spoken against. 35 And a sword shall also go through your own soul, so that out of many hearts thoughts may be revealed. 36 And there was Anna a prophetess, daughter of Phanuel, of the tribe of Asher; she was advanced in many days living in wedlock seven years from her virginity, 37 and she was a widow for eighty-four years, who did not depart from the Temple worshipping day and night with fasting and prayers. 38 And she being present at that hour praised God and spoke about him to all those waiting for the redemption of Jerusalem.		

§15 Residence at Nazareth (cf. §8)

MT	LK 2:39-40	MK	JN
(cf. 2:21-23)	39 And when they had accomplished everything according to the Law of the Lord they returned into Galilee to their city Nazareth. 40 And the child grew and became strong, being filled with wisdom and the favour of God was upon him.		

§16 The Twelve-Year-Old Jesus

MT	LK 2:41-52	MK	JN
	41 And his parents went year by year to Jerusalem at the feast of the Passover. 42 And when he was twelve years old, they went up according to the custom of the feast. 43 And having completed the days, when they returned the boy Jesus remained in Jerusalem and his parents did not know it. 44 And thinking that he was in the caravan they went a day's journey, and hunted for him among their kinsfolk and acquaintances. 45 And not finding him they returned to Jerusalem hunting for him. 46 And it came to pass after three days they found him in the Temple sitting in the midst of the doctors and hearing them and questioning them. 47 And all who heard him were amazed at his perception and his answers. 48 And seeing him they were overwhelmed, and his mother said to him: Son, why did you do this to us? Behold, your father and I are in great distress seeking you. 49 And he said to them: Why did you seek me? Did you not know that I had to be in my Father's House? 50 But they did not understand the word which he spoke to them. 51 And he went down with them and came to Nazareth, and was subject to them, and his mother stored up all the words in her heart. 52 And Jesus progressed in wisdom, and age and favour before God and men.		

II. The Coming of Jesus
§§ 17-35

MT 3:1-6; *11:10b*	LK 3:1-6; *7:27b*	MK *1:4, 2-6*	JN **(cf. 1:19-23)**
(↑ §8)		(↑ §2)	
1 Now in those days	1 Now in the fifteenth year of the reign of Tiberius Caesar, Pontius Pilate being ruler of Judea and Herod tetrarch of Galilee, and Philip his brother tetrarch of Iturea and the region of Trachonitis, and Lysanias tetrarch of Abilene, 2 under the high priest Annas and Caiaphas,		
there comes along John the Baptist	the word of the Lord came upon John the son of Zechariah	*4 There came John the Baptiser*	
preaching in the desert of Judea, 2 and saying:	in the desert. 3 And he came into the whole region of the Jordan preaching	*in the desert and preaching*	
Repent; for the Kingdom of the Heavens is at hand. 3 For this is he who was spoken of by Isaiah the prophet saying:	a baptism of repentance for remission of sins, 4 As it stands written in (the) book of (the) words of Isaiah the prophet:	*a baptism of repentance for remission of sins.* 2 Just as it has been written in the—Isaiah the prophet:	
11:10b Behold I send my messenger before thy face, who will prepare thy way before thee.	*7:27b Behold I send my messenger before thy face, who will prepare thy way before thee.*	Behold I send my messenger before thy face, who will prepare thy way before thee **(Mal. 3:1)**.	
A voice of one crying in the desert: prepare the way of the Lord, make straight his paths. **(Is. 40:3)** **(v. 1)**	A voice of one crying in the desert: prepare the way of the Lord make straight his paths 5 Every valley shall be filled, and every mountain and hill shall be lowered, and the crooked shall be (made) straight, and the rough into smooth ways; 6 and all flesh shall see the salvation of God **(Is. 4:3-5)**. **(v. 2)**	3 a voice of one crying in the desert: prepare the way of the Lord, make straight his paths **(Is. 40:3)**. 4 There came John the Baptiser in the desert, and preaching a baptism of repentance for remission of sins.	
4 Now John himself had his clothing of camel's hair and a leathern girdle round his waist, And his food was locusts and wild honey,		*6 And John was clothed with camel's hair, and a leathern girdle round his waist, and eating locusts and wild honey.*	
5 Then went out to him Jerusalem and all Judea and all the region of the Jordan, 6 and were baptised in the Jordan river by him confessing their sins. **(cf. v.4)**		5 And there went out to him all the Judean region and all the Jerusalemites, and were baptised by him in the Jordan river confessing their sins. 6 And John was clothed with camel's hair and a leather girdle round his waist, and eating locusts and wild honey. (↓ §20)	

§18 John's Warnings

MT 3:7-10

7 Now seeing many of the Pharisees and Sadducees coming for his baptism, he said to them:
Offspring of vipers! Who pointed out to you to flee from the wrath to come?
8 Bear fruit therefore worthy of repentance;
9 and do not think to say in yourselves:
we have Abraham (as) father;
for I say to you that God is able from these stones to raise up children to Abraham.
10 For now the axe is laid to the root of the trees;
every tree therefore not bearing good fruit is being cut down and cast into the fire.

(↓ §20)

LK 3:7-9

7 He said therefore to the crowds going out to be baptised by him:
Offspring of vipers! Who pointed out to you to flee from the wrath to come?
8 Bear fruits therefore worthy of repentance;
and do not begin to say in yourselves:
we have Abraham (as) father;
for I say to you that God is able from these stones to raise up children to Abraham.
9 For even now the axe is laid to the root of the trees;
every tree therefore not bearing good fruit is being cut down and cast into the fire.

MK

JN

§19 John's Teachings

MT

LK 3:10-14

10 And the crowds consulted him, saying:
What then should we do?
11 And answering he said to them:
He who has two tunics let him share with him who has none;
and let him who has food do likewise.
12 Now tax-collectors also came to be baptised and said to him:
Teacher, what should we do?
13 And he said to them:
Collect nothing more beside what has been authorized for you.
14 And soldiers also consulted him saying:
And what should we do?
And he said to them:
Do not menace anyone, and do not behave dishonestly, and be content with your pay.

MK

JN

§20 John the Forerunner (§25)

MT 3:11-12
(↑ §18)

11 I indeed baptise you in water unto repentance;
but he who comes after me is mightier than I,

LK 3:15-18
15 Now while the people were in expectation and all were deliberating in their hearts about John, whether perhaps he was the Christ,
16 John replied saying to all:
I indeed baptise you with water;

but he who is mightier than I is coming,

MK 1:7-8
(↑ §17)

7 And he preached saying:

He who is mightier than I is coming after me,

JN
(cf. 1: 19-28)

MT 3:11-12

whose sandals I am not fit to carry.

He will baptise you with the Holy Spirit and fire,
12 whose fan is in his hand
and he will clean out his threshing floor
and gather his corn into his barn,
but the chaff he will burn with unquenchable fire.

(↓ §22)

LK 3:15-18

the thong of whose sandals I am not fit to untie.

He will baptise you with the Holy Spirit and fire,
17 whose fan is in his hand
to clean out his threshing floor,
and gather together the corn into his barn,
but the chaff he will burn with unquenchable fire.
18 And so exhorting them many other things he evangelized the people.

MK 1:7-8

the thong of whose sandals I am not fit to stoop down and untie.
8 I baptised you with water,
but he will baptise you with the Holy Spirit.

(↓ §22)

JN

---

§21 The Imprisonment of John

MT

(cf. 14:3-4)

LK 3:19-20

19 But Herod the tetrarch, being reproved by him about Herodias the wife of his brother and about all the wicked things Herod had done, 20 added also this above all, and he shut up John in prison.

MK

(cf. 6:17-29)

JN

---

§22 The Baptism of Jesus (cf. §26)

MT 3:13-17
(↑ §20)

13 Jesus comes along from Galilee unto the Jordan to John to be baptised by him.
14 But John restrained him saying:
I have need to be baptised by you, and do you come to me?
15 But Jesus answering said to him:
Let it be now, for so it is fitting for us to fulfil all justice.
Then he let him.
16 And Jesus being baptised
rose up immediately from the water,
and behold the heavens were opened
and he saw the Spirit of God coming down

like a dove and coming upon him.
17 And behold a voice from the heavens saying:
This is my Beloved Son, in whom I am well

LK 3:21-22

21 Now it happened when all the people had been baptised,

and when Jesus was baptised and praying,

that the heaven was opened
22 and that the Holy Spirit came down in bodily form
as a dove upon him,
and that there was a voice from heaven:

Thou art my Beloved Son, in thee I am well

MK 1:9-11
(↑ §20)

9 And it happened in those days,
Jesus came from Nazareth of Galilee

and was baptised in the Jordan by John.
10 And immediately going up out of the water he saw the heavens rent
and the Spirit

as a dove coming down upon him.
11 And there was a voice from the heavens:

Thou art my Beloved Son, in thee I am well

JN

(cf. 1:29-36)

MT 3:13-17	LK 3:21-22	MK 1:9-11	JN
pleased. (↓ §24)	pleased.	pleased. (↓ §24)	

§23 The Genealogy of Jesus (cf. §4)

MT	LK 3:23-38	MK	JN
(cf. 1:1-17)	23 Now Jesus himself, (when) about to begin, was about thirty years (old), being the son, as it was thought, of Joseph, of Heli, 24 of Matthat, of Levi, of Melchi, of Jannai, of Joseph, 25 of Mattathias, of Amos, of Nahum, of Esli, of Naggai, 26 of Maath, of Mattathias, of Semein, of Josech, of Joda, 27 of Joanan, of Rhesa, of Zerubbabel, of Shealtiel, of Neri, 28. of Melchi, of Addi, of Cosam, of Elmadam, of Er, 29 of Joshua, of Eliezer, of Jorim, of Maththat, of Levi, 30 of Simeon, of Judah, of Joseph, of Jonam, of Eliakim, 31 of Melea, of Menna, of Mattatha, of Nathan, of David, 32 of Jesse, of Obed, of Boaz, of Salmon, of Nahshon, 33 of Amminadab, of Admin, of Arni, of Hezron, of Perez, of Judah, 34 of Jacob, of Isaac, of Abraam, of Terah, of Nachor, 35 of Serug, of Reu, of Peleg, of Eber, of Shelah, 36 of Kainan, of Arphaxad, of Shem, of Noah, of Lamech, 37 of Methuselah, of Enoch, of Jared, of Mahalaleel, of Cainan, 38 of Enos, of Seth, of Adam, of God.		

§24 The Temptations of Jesus

MT 4:1-11 (↑ §22)	LK 4:1-13	MK 1:12-13 (↑ §22)	JN
1 Then Jesus was led up into the desert by the Spirit to be tempted by the devil. 2 And having fasted forty days and forty nights, afterwards he was hungry. 3 And the Tempter coming up said to him: If you are the Son of God, tell these stones to become loaves of bread. 4 But he answering said:	1 Now Jesus, full of the Holy Spirit, returned from the Jordan and was being led by the Spirit in the desert 2 for forty days, being tempted by the devil. And he did not eat anything in those days, and when they were ended he was hungry. 3 And the Devil said to him: If you are the Son of God, tell this stone to become a loaf of bread. 4 And Jesus answered him:	12 And at once the Spirit drives him out into the desert. 13 And he was in the desert for forty days being tempted by Satan; and he was with the beasts,	

MT 4:1-11	LK 4:1-13	MK 1:12-13	JN

MT 4:1-11

It stands written: Not by bread alone shall
man have life, but by every word proceeding
from the mouth of God **(Dt. 8:3)**.

5 Then the devil takes him along up to the
holy city,
and set him on the pinnacle of the temple, 6
and says to him:
If you are the Son of God, throw yourself
down;
for it stands written that
command has been given to his angels about
thee,
and on (their) hands they will raise thee
lest thou strike thy foot against a stone.

(Ps. 90(91):11-12)

7 Jesus said to him:
Again it stands written:
Thou shalt not tempt the Lord thy God **(Dt.
6:16)**.
8 Again the devil takes him along to a very
high mountain
and shows him all the kingdoms of the world
and their glory.
9 And he said to him:
All these will I give you,

if you will fall down and worship me.

10 Then Jesus says to him:
Go away Satan;
for it stands written:
The Lord thy God shalt thou worship and
adore him alone **(Dt. 6:13)**.

(see vv. 5-7 above)

LK 4:1-13

It stands written that not by bread alone shall
man have life **(Dt. 8:3)**.

9 Now he led him to Jerusalem

and set him on the pinnacle of the Temple
and said to him:
If you are the Son of God, throw yourself down
from here;
10 for it stands written that
command has been given to his angels about
thee to guard thee,
11 and that on (their) hands they will raise
thee lest thou strike thy foot against a stone.

12 And answering Jesus said to him:
It has been said:
Thou shalt not tempt the Lord thy God.

5 And leading him up

he showed him all the kingdoms of the
civilized world in a moment of time.
6 And the devil said to him:
To you I will give all this authority and their
glory—because to me it has been handed over
and to whom I will I give it;
7 if you therefore will worship before me, all
will be yours.
8 And answering Jesus said to him:

It stands written:
Thou shalt worship the Lord thy God, and
adore him alone **(Dt. 6:13)**.

9 Now he led him to Jerusalem and
set him on the pinnacle of the Temple, and
said to him:
If you are the Son of God, throw yourself
down from here;
10 for it stands written that
command has been given to his angels about
thee to guard thee,
11 and that on (their) hands they will raise
thee
lest thou strike thy foot against a stone.
12 And answering Jesus said to him:
It has been said:

MT 4:1-11	LK 4:1-13	MK 1:12-13	JN
	Thou shalt not tempt the Lord your God (Dt. 6:16).		
11 Then the devil leaves him,	13 And having ended the whole temptation the devil went away from him until an opportune time.		
And behold angels came up and were ministering to him.		And the angels were **ministering to him.**	
(↓ §36)	(↓ §36)	(↓ §36)	

§25 John and the Jews' Delegation

MT	LK	MK	JN 1:19-28 (↑ §3)
			19 And this is the witness of John. When the Jews from Jerusalem sent to him priests **and Levites to** ask him, Who are you? 20 and he confessed and did not deny, and he confessed, **I am not** the Christ. 21 And they asked him; What then? Are you Elijah? And he says, I am not. Are you the Prophet? And he answered, No. 22 They said therefore to him, Who are you? That we may give an answer to those **who sent us;** what say you about yourself? 23 And he said:
(3:3)	(3:4 ff.)	(1:3)	I am the voice of one crying in the wilderness, make straight the way of the Lord, as Isaiah the prophet said. 24 And they had been sent from the Pharisees. 25 And they asked him and said to him: Why therefore do you baptise if you are neither the Christ **nor** Elijah nor the Prophet? 26 John answered them saying: I baptise in water; in your midst stands one whom **you know not,**
(3:11)	(3:16)	(1:7)	27 he who comes after me, the thong of whose sandal **I am not** worthy to loose. 28 These things happened in Bethania* beyond the **Jordan where** John was baptising.

MT	LK	MK	JN 1:29-34
			29 On the morrow he sees Jesus coming to him, and he says: See, the Lamb of God who takes away the sin of the world. 30 This is he concerning whom I said: After me comes a man who came to be before me, because he was before me. 31 And I knew him not, but in order that he should be manifested to Israel, for this I came baptising in water. 32 And John witnessed, saying, I beheld the Spirit coming down, like a dove, from heaven, and it remained upon him. 33 And I knew him not, but he who sent me to baptise in water, he said to me: The one upon whom you see the Spirit coming down and remaining upon him, this is he who baptises in the Holy Spirit. 34 And I beheld and witnessed that this is the Chosen of God.

(3:16 & par.)

§27 John Informs His Own Disciples

MT	LK	MK	JN 1:35-42
			35 On the morrow John again stood and two of his disciples, 36 and looking at Jesus as he was walking, he says, See, the Lamb of God. 37 And the two disciples heard him speaking and followed Jesus. 38 And Jesus turning and seeing them following says to them: What are you seeking? And they said to him, Rabbi—which translated means Teacher—where are you staying? 39 He says to them: Come and you will see. They came therefore and saw where he was staying, and they stayed with him that day. It was about the tenth hour. 40 Andrew the brother of Simon Peter was one of the two that heard from John and followed him. 41 He finds first his own brother Simon and says to him: We have found the Messiah—which is rendered the Christ; 42 he brought him to Jesus. Jesus looking at him said: You are Simon the son of John, you shall be called Kephas—which means Peter.

§28 Call of Philip and Nathanael

MT	LK	MK	JN 1:43-51
			43 On the morrow he purposed to go forth into Galilee, and he finds Philip.
			And Jesus says to him:
			Follow me.
			44 Now Philip was from Bethsaida, of the city of Andrew and Peter.
			45 Philip finds Nathanael and says to him:
			We have found him whom Moses wrote of in the Law and the Prophets, Jesus, son of Joseph, who (is) from Nazareth.
			46 And Nathanael said to him:
			Can anything from Nazareth be good?
			Philip says to him:
			Come and see.
			47 Jesus saw Nathanael coming towards him and says about him:
			See an Israelite indeed in whom there is no guile.
			48 Nathanael says to him:
			Whence do you know me?
			Jesus answered and said to him:
			Before Philip called you, when you were under the fig-tree, I saw you.
			49 Nathanael answered him:
			Rabbi, you are the Son of God, you are the king of Israel.
			50 Jesus answered and said to him:
			Because I said to you that I saw you underneath the fig-tree, do you believe? Greater things than these shall you see.
			51. And he says to him:
			Amen, amen, I say to you all, you will see the heaven opened and the angels of God ascending and descending upon the Son of Man.

§29 The Wedding at Cana

MT	LK	MK	JN 2:1-12
			1 And on the third day there was a wedding in Cana of Galilee, and the mother of Jesus was there,
			2 Now Jesus too was invited, and his disciples, to the wedding.
			3 And the wine failing, the mother of Jesus says to him:
			They have no wine.
			4 And Jesus says to her:
			O woman, is your concern mine (too)? My hour has not yet come.
			5 His mother says to the servants:
			Do whatever he tells you.
			6 Now there were six stone water-pots lying there, for the purification of the Jews, each holding two or three measures.
			7 Jesus says to them:
			Fill the water-pots with water.

MT	LK	MK	JN 2:1-12
			And they filled them up to the top. 8 And he says to them: Draw out now and carry to the head-steward. And they carried (them). 9 Now when the head-steward had tasted the water made wine, and did not know whence it was, but the servants knew who had drawn the water, the head-steward calls the bridegroom 10 and says to him: Every man puts the good wine out first, and after they have got drunk the inferior; you have kept the good wine till now. 11 Jesus did this beginning of the signs in Cana of Galilee, and manifested his glory and his disciples believed in him. 12 After this he went down to Capharnaum himself and his mother and his brethren and his disciples, and he stayed there not many days.

§30 The Cleansing of the Temple (§§291, 293)

MT 21:10-16	LK 19:45-46	MK 11:11, 15-17	JN 2:13-25
10 And entering into Jerusalem, the whole city was shaken, saying, Who is this? 11 But the crowds were saying: This is the prophet Jesus, who is from Nazareth of Galilee.		*11 And he entered into Jerusalem into the Temple, and looking round everything, as it was now already the evening hour, he went out to Bethany with the Twelve.*	13 And the Passover of the Jews was near and Jesus went up to Jerusalem.
12 And Jesus entered into the Temple of God,	*45 And entering into the Temple,*	*15 And they come to Jerusalem. And entering into the Temple*	14 And in the Temple he found the sellers of cattle and sheep and doves and the money-changers sitting;
and he cast out all the sellers and buyers in the Temple,	*he began to cast out the sellers and buyers in it.*	*he began to cast out the sellers and the buyers in the Temple,*	15 and making a sort of whip of little cords he cast them all out of the Temple, the sheep and the cattle; and he poured out the coins of the money-changers and overturned the tables;
and the tables of the money-changers he overturned and the chairs of the sellers of the doves;		*and the tables of the money-changers and the chairs of the sellers of the doves he overturned; 16 and he did not permit anyone to carry a burden through the Temple. 17. And he was teaching and saying to them:*	
13 and he says to them:	*46 saying to them:*		16 and to the sellers of doves he said:
It is written: My House shall be called a House of prayer,	*It is written: Indeed my House shall be a House of prayer,*	*Is it not written that my House shall be called a House of prayer for all the nations,*	Take these things away; do not turn my Father's House into a house of trade.
but you make it a den of thieves.	*but you made it a den of thieves.*	*but you have made it a den of thieves.*	17 His disciples remembered that it had been written: The zeal of thy house will eat me up **(Ps. 69[70]:9)**

MT 21:10-16	LK	MK	JN 2:13-25
			18 The Jews therefore answered and said to him: What sign do you show us, because you do these things? 19 Jesus answered and said to them: Dissolve this Temple and in three days I will raise it up. 20 The Jews therefore said: This Temple has been forty-six years under construction; and will you raise it up in three days? 21 He however was speaking about the Temple of his body. 22 When therefore he was raised from the dead, his disciples remembered that he said this, and believed the Scripture, and the word which Jesus had spoken. 23 Now when he was in Jerusalem at the Passover at the Feast, many believed in his name, beholding his signs that he did.
14 And the blind and the lame came up to him in the Temple, and he healed them. 15 And the high-priests and the Scribes seeing the wonders he did and the children crying out in the Temple and saying: Hosanna to the Son of David, were indignant; 16 and they said to him; Do you hear what these are saying? And Jesus says to them: Yes; did you never read that out of the mouths of babes and sucklings I will establish praise?			24 But Jesus himself did not trust himself to them because he knew all men, 25 and because he had no need that anyone should witness about man; for he himself knew what was in man.

§31 Jesus and Nicodemus

MT	LK	MK	JN 3:1-21
			1 Now there was a man of the Pharisees, Nicodemus by name, a ruler of the Jews. 2 This (man) came to him by night and said to him: Rabbi, we know that you have come a teacher from God; for nobody can do all the signs that you do, unless God be with him. 3 Jesus answered and said to him: Amen, amen, I say to you unless one be born again one cannot see the Kingdom of God. 4 Nicodemus says to him: How can a man be born when he is old? Can he enter a second time into his mother's womb and be born? 5 Jesus answered:

MT	LK	MK	JN 3:1-21

Amen, amen, I say to you, unless one be born of water and spirit one cannot enter into the Kingdom of God.

6 And what has been born of the flesh is flesh, and what has been born of the Spirit is Spirit.

7 Wonder not that I said to you: It is necessary for you to be born again.

8 The Spirit breathes where it wills, and you hear the sound of it, but you know not whence it comes and where it goes; such is it with everyone who has been born of the Spirit.

9 Nicodemus answered and said to him:
How can these things come to pass?

10 Jesus answered and said to him:
Are you the teacher of Israel and do not know these things?

11 Amen, amen, I say to you that we speak what we know and we witness what we have seen, and our witness you do not accept.

12 If I have spoken the things of earth to you and you do not believe, how will you believe if I spoke to you the things of heaven?

13 And no one has gone up into heaven, except the one who came down from heaven, the Son of Man who is in heaven.

14 And just as Moses lifted up the serpent in the desert, so must the Son of Man be lifted up, 15 so that everyone who believes in him may have eternal life.

16 For God so loved the world that he gave the Son, the Only-begotten, in order that everyone who believes in him may not perish but may have eternal life.

17 For God did not send his Son into the world, in order to judge the world, but that the world should be saved through him.

18 He who believes in him is not judged; but he who does not believe is already judged, because he has not believed in the name of the Only-begotten Son of God.

19 And this is the judgment, that the light has come into the world and men have loved the darkness rather than the light, for their works were evil.

20 For everyone who does worthless things hates the light and does not come to the light, lest his works be reproved

21 But he who does the truth comes to the light, so that his works may be manifested that they have been wrought in God.

§32 Jesus and the Baptist

MT	LK	MK	JN 3:22-30

22 After these things Jesus and his disciples came into the land of Judea, and there he continued with them and was baptising.

23 Now John too was baptising in Ainon near Salim, for there were many waters there, and they came along and were baptised.

29

MT	LK	MK	JN 3:22-30
			24 For not yet had John been thrown into prison.
			25 And there took place an argument between the disciples of John and the Jews* about purification.
			26 And they came to John and said to him: Rabbi, he who was with you beyond the Jordan, to whom you have witnessed, see, he is baptising and all are coming to him.
			27 John answered and said: A man cannot receive one single thing unless it has been given to him from heaven.
			28 You yourselves bear me witness that I said that I myself am not the Christ, but that I was sent before him.
			29 He that has the bride is the bridegroom; but the bridegroom's friend, the one who stands and listens to him, rejoices with joy because of the voice of the bridegroom. For this joy of mine has been fulfilled.
			30 It is for him to increase, but for me to diminish.

§33 The Witness of Jesus

MT	LK	MK	JN 3:31-36
			31 He who comes from above is over all; he who is from the earth is from the earth and from the earth he speaks. He who comes from heaven is above all.
			32 What he has beheld and heard, this he witnesses, and nobody accepts his witness.
			33 He who accepts the witness has attested that God is true.
			34 He therefore whom God has sent speaks the words of God, for God does not give the Spirit by measure.
			35 The Father loves the Son, and has placed all things in his hand.
			36 He who believes in the Son has eternal life; he who does not obey the Son shall not see life, but the wrath of God remains upon him.

§34 Jesus Sets Out for Galilee (§36)

MT	LK	MK	JN 4:1-3
			1 When therefore Jesus knew that the Pharisees had heard that Jesus was making more disciples and was baptising more than John—
			2 though Jesus himself was not baptising but his disciples—
(cf. 4:12)	(cf. 4:14)	(cf. 1:14)	3 he left Judea and went away again into Galilee.

MT	LK	MK	JN 4:4-42

4 Now he was obliged to pass through Samaria.

5 He comes therefore to a city of Samaria called Sychar, near the property which Jacob gave to his son Joseph; 6 and the well of Jacob was there.

Jesus therefore being tired out by the journey was sitting for this reason by the well; it was about the sixth hour.

7 There comes a woman of Samaria to draw water. Jesus says to her: Give me to drink.

8 For his disciples had gone away into the city, to buy food.

9 The Samaritan woman therefore says to him:

How do you being a Jew ask to drink of me who am a Samaritan woman?—for the Jews do not associate with Samaritans.

10 Jesus answered and said to her:

If you had known the gift of God, and who he is who is saying to you: Give me drink, you would surely have asked him and he would have given you living water.

11 The woman says to him:

Sir, you have not a bucket and the well is deep; how then have you the living water? 12. Are you greater than our father Jacob, who gave us the well, and he himself drank from it and his sons and his cattle?

13 Jesus answered and said to her:

Everyone who drinks of this water will thirst again; 14 but whoever drinks of the water which I shall give him, will not thirst for ever, but the water which I shall give him will become in him a fountain of water springing up into eternal life.

15 The woman says to him:

Sir, give me this water, that I may not thirst nor keep coming here to draw.

16 Jesus says to her:

Go and call your husband and come here.

17 The woman answered and said to him:

I have no husband.

Jesus says to her:

You have well said: I have no husband; 18 for you have had five husbands, and the one you now have is not your husband. What you have said is true.

19 The woman says to him:

Sir, I perceive that you are a prophet. 20 Our fathers worshipped on this mountain; and you say that in Jerusalem is the place where one must worship.

21 Jesus says to her:

Believe me, O woman, that the hour is coming when neither on this mountain nor in Jerusalem will you worship the Father. 22 You worship what you do not know, we worship what we know, because salvation is from the Jews.

23 But an hour is coming, and now is, when the true worshippers will worship the Father in spirit and in truth; for indeed the Father seeks such (people) as his worshippers. 24 God (is) Spirit,

MT	LK	MK	JN 4:4-42

and the ones worshipping him must worship in spirit and in truth.
25 The woman says to him:
I know that (the) Messiah is coming, who is called (the) Christ;
when That One comes, he will announce to us all things.
26 Jesus says to her:
I am he, who is speaking to you.
27 And thereupon his disciples came, and wondered that he was speaking with a woman; however, no one said: What do you want? Or why do you speak with her?
28 The woman therefore left her water-pot and went away into the city and says to the men:
29. Come, see a man who has told me all that I have done; is this (man) not the Christ?
30 They went out of the city and came to him.
31 In the meantime the disciples asked him, saying:
Rabbi, eat.
32 But he said to them;
I have food to eat which you do not know.
33 The disciples therefore said to one another:
Did anyone bring him to eat?
34 Jesus says to them:
My food is to do the will of him who sent me, and to accomplish his work.
35 Do you not say: 'Yet four months and the harvest comes'? Lo, I say to you, Raise up your eyes and behold the fields, that they are white for the harvest.
36 The harvester receives a wage and gathers up the produce for eternal life, so that both the sower and the harvester may rejoice together.
37 For in this is the word true that there is the one who sows and the one who harvests. 38 I have sent you to harvest what you have not laboured for; others have laboured, and you have entered into their labour.
39 Now from that city many of the Samaritans believed in him because of the word of the woman witnessing: He told me all whatever I had done.
40 When therefore the Samaritans came to him they asked him to remain with them; and he remained there two days. 41 And many more believed because of his word.
42 And to the woman they said:
No longer do we believe because of your statement; for we have heard and we know that this (man) is truly the Saviour of the World.

III. The Early Ministry in Galilee
§§ 36-89

MT 4:12	LK 4:14-15	MK 1:14a	JN 4:43-45
(↑ §24)	(↑ §24)	(↑ §24)	
12 And hearing that John was taken up, he withdrew into Galilee.	14 And Jesus returned in the power of the Spirit into Galilee.	14a And after John was taken up Jesus came into Galilee.	43 And after two days he went forth thence into Galilee **(cf. 4:3)**.
(cf. 13:57)	**(cf. 4:24)**	**(cf. 6:4)**	44 For Jesus himself witnessed that a prophet in his own homeland has no honour.
(cf. 4:23)	And a report went out through the whole region about him.	**(cf. 1:39)**	45 When therefore he came into Galilee, the Galileans received him having seen all the things that he did in Jerusalem at the feast; for they too had gone to the feast.
(↓ §39)	**(cf. 4:44)**	(↓ §39)	
	15 And he began to teach in their synagogues, being glorified by all.		
	(↓ §38)		

§37 Healing of an Official's Son (cf. §91)

MT 8:5-13	LK 7:1b-10; 13:29, 28	MK	JN 4:46-54
5 *Now when he entered into Capharnaum,*	*1b he entered into Capharnaum.*		46 So he came into Cana of Galilee where he had made the water wine. And there was a certain royal official whose son was sick in Capharnaum.
there approached him a centurion beseeching him 6 and saying: Lord, my boy is lying paralyzed in the house in terrible distress.	*2 Now a certain centurion's slave was ill, about to die, who was exceedingly dear to him. 3 And having heard about Jesus he sent to him elders of the Jews asking him to come and restore his slave. 4 And when they came along to Jesus they besought him earnestly, saying: He is worthy that you should grant this to him; 5 for he loves our nation and has himself built us the synagogue.*		47 And when he heard that Jesus had come from Judea into Galilee, he went off to him and asked (him) to come down and heal his son, for he was about to die.
7 And he says to him: I will come and heal him.	*6 And Jesus went with them. And when he was already not far away from the house*		48 Jesus therefore said to him: Unless you see signs and wonders you will not believe. 49 The royal official says to him: Lord, come down before my little boy dies. 50 Jesus says to him: Go, your son lives.
8 And the centurion answering said: Lord, I am not worthy that you should enter under my roof;	*the centurion sent friends saying to him: Lord, do not trouble, for I am not worthy that you should enter under my roof; 7 For this reason I did not consider myself worthy to come to you;*		
but only say a word and my boy will be healed. 9 For I too am a man under authority,	*but say a word and let my boy be cured. 8 For I too am a man set under authority,*		

MT 8:5-13	LK 7:1b-10; 13:29, 28	MK	JN 4:46-54
having under me soldiers, and I say to this one: Go, and he goes, *and to another: Come, and he comes,* *and to my slave: Do this, and he does it.* *10 And hearing, Jesus marvelled,* *and said to those following:* *Amen, I say to you, with no one in Israel have I found such faith.*	*having under me soldiers, and I say to this one: Go, and he goes,* *and to another: Come, and he comes,* *and to my slave: Do this, and he does it.* *9 And Jesus hearing these things marvelled at him,* *and turning to the crowd following him said:* *I say to you, not in Israel have I found such faith.*		
11 And I say to you, that many will come from east and west, *and will recline with Abraham and Isaac in the Kingdom of the Heavens,*	*13:29 And they shall come from east and west and from north and south,* *and they will recline in the Kingdom of God.*		
12 but the sons of the Kingdom will be cast out into the exterior darkness. *Weeping and gnashing of teeth shall be there.*	*28b When you see Abraham, Isaac and Jacob and all the prophets in the Kingdom of God but you yourselves cast outside.* *28a Weeping and gnashing of teeth shall be there.*		
13 And Jesus said to the centurion: Go back; be it done to you as you have believed. *And the boy was healed in that very hour.*	*10 And returning to the house, those who had been sent found the slave cured.*		The man believed the word that Jesus had spoken to him and went. 51 And while he was still going down, his slaves met him, saying: Your son lives. 52 He therefore inquired of them the hour in which he got better. They said therefore: Yesterday at the seventh hour the fever left him. 53 The father therefore knew that (it was) at that very hour at which Jesus said to him: Your son lives, and he and his whole house believed. 54 And this (is) again the second sign that Jesus did, when he went from Judea into Galilee. (↓ §49)

§38 Visit to Nazareth (Lk) (cf. §§120, 157)

MT 13:53-58	LK 4:16-30	MK 6:1-6a	JN
53 And it happened, when Jesus had ended these parables, he passed thence.	(↑ §36)	*1 And he went out from there*	

MT 13:53-58	LK 4:16-30	MK 6:1-6a	JN

MT 13:53-58

54 and coming into his own home-town,

he was teaching them in their synagogue,

so that they were amazed and said:

Whence (has) this man this wisdom,

and these mighty deeds?
55 Is he not the son of the carpenter?
Is not his mother called Mary,
and his brothers, James and Joseph and Simon and Jude?
56 And his sisters, are they not all with us? Whence therefore has this man all these things?
57 And they were scandalized over him.

But Jesus said to them:
A prophet is not without honour save in his own hometown, and in his own house.

LK 4:16-30

16 And he came into Nazareth, where he had been nurtured,
and according to his custom he entered into the synagogue on the sabbath-day, and rose up to read.
17 And there was handed to him the book of the prophet Isaiah, and opening the book he found the place where it was written:
18 The Spirit of the Lord is upon me, because he has anointed me;
to evangelize the poor he has sent me,
to preach release to the captives and restoration of sight to the blind,
to send away in release those who have been crushed,
19 to preach the acceptable year of the Lord **(Lv. 25:10-13; Is. 61:1-2).**
20 And closing the book he gave it back to the attendant and sat down. And the eyes of all in the synagogue were fixed upon him.
21 And he began to say to them:
Today this Scripture has been fulfilled in your ears.
22 And all witnessed to him and marvelled at the words of grace that came from his mouth, and they said:

Is he not the son of Joseph?

23 And he said to them: Surely you will say to me this parable: Physician, heal yourself; whatsoever we have heard done in Capharnaum, do also here in your own hometown.
24 And he said:
Amen I say to you, that no prophet is acceptable in his native place.

25 And I tell you in truth, there were many widows in the days of Elijah in Israel, when the heavens were shut for three years and six

MK 6:1-6a

and comes into his own hometown and his disciples follow him.
2 And when the Sabbath came he began to teach in the synagogue;

and many hearers were amazed, saying:

Whence (has) this man these things? And what is the wisdom given to this man?
And such mighty deeds done by his hands?
3 Is he not the carpenter,
the son of Mary,
and brother of James and Joses* and Jude and Simon?
And are not his sisters here with us?

And they were scandalized over him.

4 And Jesus said to them:
A prophet is not without honour save in his own hometown and among his own relatives, and in his own house.

MT 13:53-58	LK 4:16-30	MK 6:1-6a	JN
	months, when there came a great famine over the whole land,		
	26 and not to one of them was Elijah sent but only to Zarephath of Sidon to a widow woman.		
	27 And there were many lepers in Israel in the time of Elisha the prophet, and not one of them was healed save Naaman the Syrian.		
	28 And all in the synagogue were filled with anger when they heard these things,		
	29 and rising they threw him out of the town, and led him up to the brow of the mountain, on which the town was built, in order to hurl him down.		
	30 But he passing through their midst went on.		
58 And he did not do many mighty deeds there,	(↓ §41)	*5 And he was unable to do any mighty deeds there, save laying hands on a few sick he healed them.*	
because of their unbelief.		*6a And he marvelled because of their unbelief.*	

§39 Jesus Leaves Nazareth (§§36, 41)

MT 4:13-17	LK	MK 1:14b-15	JN
(↑ §36)		(↑ §36)	
13 And leaving Nazareth, he went and dwelt in Capharnaum-by-the- Sea in the confines of Zebulon and Naphthali;	(cf. 4:31)	(cf. 1:21)	
14 so that what had been spoken by Isaiah the prophet might be fulfilled, saying:			
15 Land of Zebulon and land of Naphthali, way of the sea, across the Jordan, Galilee of the Gentiles.			
16 The people that sat in darkness saw a great light, and for those that sat in the region and shadow of death, for them a light rose up **(Is. 9:1-2)**.			
17 From then Jesus began to preach and to say:		14b preaching the gospel of the Kingdom* of God, 15 and saying,	
Repent; for the Kingdom of the Heavens is at hand.	(10:9, ll)	The time has been fulfilled and the Kingdom of God is at hand; repent and believe in the gospel.	
(cf. 4:23)			

§40 Call of Four Fishermen (cf. §47)

MT 4:18-22

18 Now as he was walking beside the Sea of Galilee

he saw two brothers, Simon who is called Peter

and Andrew his brother,

throwing a casting-net into the sea; for they were fishermen.

19 And he says to them:

Come after me, and I will make you fishers of men.

20 And they at once leaving the nets followed him.

21 And going on from there he saw two other brothers,

James the (son) of Zebedee, and John his brother,

in the boat with Zebedee their father,

mending their nets;

and he called them.

22 And they, at once leaving the boat and their father,

followed him.

(↓ §46)

LK 5:10b

(cf. 5:1-11)

10b And Jesus said to Simon:
Fear not, from now on you will be catching living men.

MK 1:16-20

16 And as he passed along beside the Sea of Galilee

he saw Simon

and Andrew the brother of Simon,

casting a net in the sea; for they were fishermen.

17 And Jesus said to them:

Come after me, And I will make you become fishers of men.

18 And at once leaving the nets they followed him.

19 And going on a little he saw

James the (son) of Zebedee and John his brother,

and they (were) in the boat

mending the nets.

20 And at once he called them;

and leaving their father Zebedee in the boat with the hired men

they went off after him.

JN

§41 Teaching with Authority (§89)

MT 7:28b-29

(cf. 4:13)

28b The crowds were astounded at his teaching;
29 for he was teaching them as one having authority and not as the Scribes.

LK 4:31-32

(↑ §38)

31 And he went down into Capharnaum a city of Galilee.

And he was teaching them on the Sabbath;

32 And they were astounded at his teaching,

because his word was with authority.

MK 1:21-22

21 And they enter into Capharnaum

and immediately on the Sabbath entering into the synagogue he began to teach.

22 And they were astounded at his teaching,

for he was teaching them as one having authority and not as the Scribes.

JN

§42 An Unclean Spirit Expelled

MT

LK 4:33-37

33 And in the synagogue there was a man having the spirit of an unclean demon,

MK 1:23-28

23 And immediately in their synagogue there was a man in a unclean spirit,

JN

39

MT	LK 4:33-37	MK 1:23-28	JN
	and he cried out in a loud voice: 34 Ah, what have we to do with you Jesus the Nazarene? Have you come to destroy us? I know you, who you are, the Holy One of God. 35 And Jesus rebuked him, saying: Be silent and go out of him. And the demon throwing him into the midst went out of him not hurting him. 36 And amazement came on all, and they conversed with one another, saying: What is this word? For with authority and power he commands even the unclean spirits and they go out. 37 And a report about him went out to every place of the region.	24 and he cried out saying: What have we to do with you, Jesus the Nazarene? Have you come to destroy us? I know you, who you are, the Holy One of God. 25 And Jesus rebuked him, saying: Be silent and go out of him. 26 And the unclean spirit tearing him and crying in a loud voice went out of him. 27 And they were all amazed so as to question among themselves saying: What is this? What is this new teaching? For by authority* he commands the unclean spirits and they obey him. 28 And his fame went out at once everywhere into the whole region of Galilee.	

§43 Peter's Mother-in-Law Healed (§109)

MT 8:14-15	LK 4:38-39	MK 1:29-31	JN
14 And Jesus coming into the house of Peter *saw his mother-in-law prostrate and fevered.* *15 And he touched her hand* *and the fever left her.* *And she got up and served him.*	38 Now rising up from the synagogue he entered into the house of Simon. But Simon's mother-in-law was in the grip of a high fever and they asked him about her. 39 And standing by over her he rebuked the fever and it left her. And at once rising up she served them.	29 And at once going out of the synagogue he went into the house of Simon and Andrew with James and John. 30 But Simon's mother-in-law lay fevered and at once they speak to him about her. 31 And approaching he got her up grasping her hand, and the fever left her, and she served them.	

§44 Healings in the Evening (§110)

MT 8:16-17	LK 4:40-41	MK 1:32-34	JN
16 Now when evening came *they carried up to him many demon-possessed,* *and he cast out the spirits by a word and all who were ill he healed,*	40 Now as the sun was setting all those who had any sick with various ills brought them to him. And laying hands on each of them he healed them.	32 Now when evening came, when the sun set, they began to carry to him all who were ill and the demon-possessed. 33 And the whole town was gathered together at the door. 34 And he healed many who were ill with various diseases, and he cast out many demons.	

40

MT 8:16-17	LK 4:40-41	MK 1:32-34	JN
	41 And demons also went out of many shouting and saying, You are the Son of God. And rebuking (them) he would not let them speak, because they knew he was the Christ.	And he did not permit the demons to speak, because they knew him.	
17 in order that what had been spoken by Isaiah the prophet might be fulfilled saying: He bore our sicknesses and carried our ills (Is. 53:4, 11).			

§45 Jesus Leaves Capharnaum

MT (cf. 8:18)	LK 4:42-43	MK 1:35-38	JN
	42 Now when it was day going out he went to a desert place; and the crowds sought after him, and came up to him, and were for stopping him going from them. 43 But he said to them: Also to the other towns I must evangelize the Kingdom of God, because for this I have been sent.	35 And in the morning long before it was light, rising up he went out and went off to a desert place and there he prayed. 36 And Simon and those with him pursued him 37 and found him, and they say to him: All are seeking you. 38 And he says to them: Let us go elsewhere to the nearby country towns to preach there also. for I came out for this.	

§46 First Preaching Tour

MT 4:23 (↑ §40)	LK 4:44	MK 1:39	JN
23 And he went around in all Galilee teaching in their synagogues and preaching the gospel of the Kingdom and healing every sickness and every weakness in the people. (↓ §57)	44 And he was preaching to the synagogues of Judea.*	39 And he was preaching to their synagogues to all Galilee and casting out demons. (↓ §48)	

§47 The Miraculous Catch (cf. §§40, 393)

MT (cf. 4:18-22)	LK 5:1-11	MK (cf. 1:16-20)	JN 21:1-11
	1 And it came to pass while the crowd was thronging him in order to hear the word of God—for he was standing by the lake		1 After these things Jesus, Jesus manifested himself again to the disciples on the Sea of Tiberias; and he manifested himself thus.

MT | LK 5:1-11 | MK | JN 21:1-11

LK 5:1-11

of Gennesaret—

2 and he saw two boats lying by the lake; but the fishermen had gone out of them and were washing their nets.

3 And getting into one of the boats—it was Simon's—he asked him to put out a little from the land; and sitting down, he taught the crowds from the boat.
4 And when he had finished speaking, he said to Simon: Put out into the deep, and lower your nets for a catch.
5 And Simon answering said: Teacher, we toiled throughout the night and caught nothing; but at your word I will lower the nets.
6 And having done it they enclosed a great multitude of fishes; and their nets were about to break.

7 And they signalled to their partners in the other boat to come and help them. And they came and they filled both boats so that they were about to sink.

8 And when Simon Peter saw he knelt at Jesus' knees, saying: Depart from me, for I am a sinful man, O Lord.

9 For amazement gripped him and all with him at the catch of fishes they had taken,
10 and likewise both James and John the sons of Zebedee, who were partners of Simon.
And Jesus said to Simon:
Fear not, from now on you will be catching living men.
11 And bringing back the boats to land, leaving all things they followed him.

JN 21:1-11

2 There were together Simon Peter and Thomas (called Didymus) and Nathanael, the one from Cana of Galilee, and the sons of Zebedee, and two more of his disciples.
3 Simon Peter says to them: I am going off to fish. They say to him: We too are coming with you. They went out and embarked on the boat and on that night they caught nothing.
4 But when morning had already come, Jesus stood on the shore; but the disciples did not know that it was Jesus.
5 Then Jesus says to them: Children, you haven't anything to eat, have you? They answered him; No.
6 And he said to them: Cast the net on the right side of the boat and you will find. They cast therefore and they were no longer able to haul it from the multitude of the fishes.
7 Therefore that disciple, whom Jesus loved, said to Peter: It is the Lord. Simon Peter therefore, hearing that it was the Lord, fastened on (his) outer garment, for he was stripped, and threw himself into the sea.
8 But the other disciples came in the boat for they were not far from the land, but about two hundred cubits off, dragging the net with the fishes.
9 When therefore they went up onto the land, they see a charcoal fire lit and lying on it a fish and bread.
10 Jesus therefore says to them: Bring (some) of the food which you have just caught.
11 Simon Peter therefore went aboard and hauled the net to the land full of great fishes, one hundred and fifty-three; and though they were so many the net was not torn.

§48 Cleansing of a Leper (cf. §90)

MT 8:1-4

1 Now when he went down from the mountain great crowds followed him;
2 and behold a leper came up

and worshipped him saying:

Lord, if you will, you can cleanse me.
3 And extending his hand he touched him, saying:
I will; be cleansed.
And at once his leprosy was cleansed.

4 And Jesus says to him:

LK 5:12-16

12 And it happened that he was in one of the towns,

and behold a man full of leprosy, and seeing Jesus,
falling on his face he begged him saying:

Lord if you will, you can cleanse me.
13 And extending his hand he touched him, saying:
I will; be cleansed.
And at once the leprosy left him.

14 And he ordered him

MK 1:40-45
(↑ §46)

40 And a leper comes to him

beseeching him and kneeling, and saying to him:
If you will, you can cleanse me.
41. And being moved with pity, extending his hand he touched him and says to him:
I will; be cleansed.
42 And at once the leprosy left him and he was cleansed.
43 And sternly charging him, he sent him off

JN

			JN
MT 8:1-4	LK 5:12-16	MK 1:40-45	

Look, tell no one
but go off, show yourself to the priest
and offer
the gift which Moses commanded for a witness
to them.

to tell no one:
But go away, show yourself to the priest
and offer for your cleansing
just as Moses commanded, for a witness to
them.
15 But instead the word went abroad about
him,
and many crowds came together to hear and
to be healed from their sicknesses.

16 But he was withdrawn in the deserts and
praying.

(↓ §51)

at once, 44. and says to him:
Look, tell nothing to anyone,
but go off, show yourself to the priest
and offer for your cleansing
the things that Moses commanded, for a
witness to them.
45 But he went off and began to preach loudly
and to spread the word,

so that he could no longer openly go into a
town,
but he was outside in desert places,

and they came to him from everywhere.

(↓ §51)

§49 Jesus at Bethzatha

MT	LK	MK	JN 5:1-16

(↑ §37)

1 After these things there was a feast* of the Jews and Jesus went
up to Jerusalem.
2 Now there is in Jerusalem by the Probatic (Gate) a pool, that in
Hebrew is called Bethzatha* having five porches.
3 In these there lay a large number of disabled, blind, lame,
paralysed, waiting*¹ for the stirring of the waters.
4*² For the angel of the Lord at times went down in the pool and
troubled the water; the first one therefore going in after the
troubling of the water was made whole, no matter with what
infirmity he had been gripped.
5 Now there was a man there who had had his infirmity for thirty-
eight years.
6 Jesus, seeing him as he lay and knowing that he had already had
(it) a long time, says to him:
Do you wish to be made whole?
7 The infirm man answered him: Sir, I have no one when the
water is troubled, to throw me into the pool; for while I am
coming another goes down before me.
8 Jesus says to him:
Get up, take your pallet and walk.
9 And at once the man was made whole, and took up his pallet
and began to walk. Now it was the Sabbath on that day.
10 The Jews therefore said to the man who had been healed: It is

MT	LK	MK	JN 5:1-16

the Sabbath, and it is not lawful for you to take up your pallet.
11 But he answered them: The one who made me whole said to me: Take up your bed and walk.
12 They asked him: Who is the man who said to you: Take up and walk.
13 But the man who had been healed did not know who he was; for Jesus had turned away, as there was a crowd in the place.
14 After these things Jesus finds him in the Temple and says to him: See, you have been made whole: sin no more lest a worse thing befall you.
15 The man went off and told the Jews that it was Jesus who had made him whole.
16 And on this account the Jews persecuted Jesus because he did these things on the Sabbath.

§50 Discourse at Bethzatha

MT	LK	MK	JN 5:17-47

17 And Jesus answered them:
My Father is at work up to the present, and I too am at work.
18 Therefore the Jews sought all the more to kill him for the reason that he not only relaxed the Sabbath, but even said that God was his own Father, making himself equal to God.
19 Jesus therefore answered and said to them:
Amen, amen, I say to you, that the Son cannot of himself do anything except what he sees the Father doing; for whatever the latter does, the Son too does the same things likewise.
20 For the Father loves the Son, and shows him everything that he himself does, and greater works than these will he show him, that you may wonder.
21 For just as the Father raises the dead and gives life, so also the Son gives life to whom he wills.
22 Nor does the Father judge anyone, but has given all judgement to the Son, 23 so that all may honour the Son just as they honor the Father.
He who does not honour the Son, does not honour the Father who sent him.
24 Amen, amen,. I say to you, that he who hears my word and believes him who sent me, has eternal life, and does not come into judgement but has crossed over from death into life.
25 Amen, amen, I say to you, that an hour is coming, and now is, when the dead shall hear the voice of the Son of God, and those who hear will live.
26 For just as the Father has life in himself, so also he has given to the Son to have life in himself.
27 And he has given him power to perform judgement, because he

MT	LK	MK	JN 5:17-47

is the Son of Man.

28 Do not wonder at this, that an hour is coming in which all who are in the tombs will hear his voice, 29 and the ones who have done good will go forth into resurrection of life, but the ones who have done worthless things into resurrection of judgement.

30 I cannot of myself do anything; as I hear, I judge, and my own judgement is just, because I do not seek my own will, but the will of him who sent me.

31 If I bear witness about myself my witness is not true.

32 There is another who bears witness about me, and I know that the witness is true that he witnesses about me.

33 You have sent to John and he has witnessed to the truth.

34 Now I do not receive the witness from man, but I say these things so that you may be saved.

35 This (John) was the lamp that sets on fire and that shines, and you decided to rejoice for an hour in his light.

36 But I have the witness that is greater than John's; for the works which the Father gave me so that I might accomplish them, the very works which I do, witness about me that the Father has sent me.

37 And the Father who has sent me has himself witnessed about me. You have neither listened to his voice nor have you seen his appearance.

38. And you have not his word abiding in you, because the one whom he sent, in him you do not believe.

39 You search the Scriptures, for you think in them to possess eternal life: and these are they that witness about me.

40 And you do not will to come to me that you may have life.

41 I do not receive glory from men, 42 but I have known you that you have not the love of God in yourselves.

43 I have come in the name of my Father, and you do not receive me; if another comes in his own name, him you will receive.

44 How can you believe, when you receive glory from one another, but the glory belonging to the only God you do not seek?

45 Do not suppose that I shall accuse you to the Father; Moses is the one who accuses you, in whom you continue to hope.

46 For if you believed Moses, you would surely believe me; for he wrote about me.

47 For if you do not believe the writings of the latter, how will you believe my words?

(↓§161)

MT 9:1-8	LK 5:17-26	MK 2:1-12	JN
	(↑ §48)	(↑ §48)	

MT 9:1-8

1 And going up into a boat he crossed over and came to his own city.

2 And behold they began to bring to him a paralytic lying on a bed.

And Jesus seeing their faith said to the paralytic:
Take heart, child, your sins are forgiven.
3 And behold some of the Scribes said in themselves:
This man is blaspheming.

4 And Jesus knowing their thoughts said.
Why do you think evil things in your hearts?

5 For which is easier, to say: Your sins are forgiven, or to say: Get up and walk?

6 But that you may know that the Son of Man has authority upon earth to forgive sins—

then he says to the paralytic:
Get up, take away your bed

and go off into your house.
7 And he, getting up,

went back to his house,

LK 5:17-26

17 And it happened on one of the days that he was teaching, and there were seated Pharisees and law-teachers who had come from every village of Galilee and Judea and Jerusalem. And the power of the Lord was for him to heal.

18 And behold men carrying on a bed a man who had been paralysed, and they tried to bring him in and to lay him before him.
19 And not finding how to carry him in because of the crowd, going up on to the roof through the tiles

they let him down together with the stretcher

into the middle in front of Jesus.
20 And seeing their faith he said:

O man, your sins have been forgiven you.
21 And the Scribes began to argue and the Pharisees saying:
Who is this who speaks blasphemies?

Who can forgive sins but God alone?
22 And Jesus perceiving their questionings answering said to them:
Why do you question in your hearts?

23 Which is easier, to say: Your sins have been forgiven you, or to say: Get up and walk?

24 But that you may know that the Son of Man has authority upon earth to forgive sins—
he said to the paralytic:
I say to you, Get up and taking away your stretcher,
go into your house.
25 And immediately rising in front of all, taking up what he had been lying on, he went back to his house glorifying God.

MK 2:1-12

1 And again entering into Capharnaum after days it was reported that he was at home.

2 And many were gathered together so that there was no longer room not even at the door, and he was speaking to them the word.
3 And they came carrying to him a paralytic carried by four.

4 And not being able to carry him to him because of the crowd, they unroofed the roof where he was and digging through, they lower the pallet on which the paralytic was lying.

5 And Jesus seeing their faith says to the paralytic:
Child, your sins are forgiven.
6 And some of the Scribes were sitting there and arguing in their hearts:
7 Why does this (man) speak this? He is blaspheming!
Who can forgive sins but one, God?
8 And at once Jesus perceiving in his spirit that they were thus questioning in themselves, says to them:
Why do you question these things in your hearts?
9 Which is easier, to say to the paralytic: Your sins are forgiven, or to say: Get up and take away your pallet and walk?
10 But that you may know that the Son of Man has authority to forgive sins upon earth—
he says to the paralytic:
11 I say to you, Get up, take away your pallet

and go off into your house.
12 And he got up and at once, taking up the pallet, he went out in front of all,

MT 9:1-8	LK 5:17-26	MK 2:1-12	JN
8 And the crowds when they saw were afraid and glorified God who gave such authority to men.	26 And amazement seized everyone and they glorified God, and were filled with fear, saying: We have seen incredible things today.	so that all were amazed and glorified God, saying: We have never seen the like ever.	

§52 Call of Levi (§115)

MT 9:9-13	LK 5:27-32	MK 2:13-17	JN
9 And Jesus passing along from there	27 And after these things he went out, and	13 And he went out again beside the sea; and the whole crowd came to him, and he taught them. 14 And passing along	
saw a man called Matthew seated at the custom house, and he says to him: Follow me. And getting up he followed him.	he observed a tax-collector by name Levi seated at the custom house, and he said to him: Follow me. 28 And leaving all things, getting up he began to follow him.	he saw Levi the (son) of Alphaeus seated at the custom house, and he says to him: Follow me. And getting up he followed him.	
10 And it happened that while he reclined at table in the house, and behold many tax-collectors and sinners came and reclined together with Jesus and his disciples.	29 And Levi made a great feast for him in his house; and there was a great crowd of tax-collectors and others who were sitting down with him.	15 And he comes and sits down at table in his house, and many tax-collectors and sinners came and reclined together with Jesus and his disciples. For they were many and they followed him.	
11 And the Pharisees saw (it), and said to his disciples:	30 And the Pharisees and their Scribes grumbled, saying to his disciples:	16 And the Scribes of the Pharisees, seeing him eating with sinners and tax-collectors, said to his disciples:	
Why does your teacher eat with tax-collectors and sinners?	Why do you eat and drink with tax-collectors and sinners?	He eats and drinks with tax-collectors and sinners!	
12 But he hearing this said to them: The strong have no need of a healer but those who are ill.	31 And Jesus answering said to them: The healthy have no need of a healer but those who are ill.	17 And Jesus hearing says to them: The strong have no need of a healer but those who are ill.	
13 But go and learn the meaning of this: I desire mercy and not sacrifice: (Ho. 6:6) *For I did not come to call the just but sinners to repentance.**	32 For I have not come to call the just but sinners to repentance.	For I did not come to call the just but sinners to repentance.*	

§53 A Question about Fasting (§116)

MT 9:14-17	LK 5:33-39	MK 2:18-22	JN
14 Then the disciples of John came up to him, saying: Why do we and the Pharisees fast frequently,	33 And they said to him: Why do the disciples of John fast often, and	18 And the disciples of John and the Pharisees were fasting, and they come and say to him: Why do the disciples of John and the disciples	

MT 9:14-17

but your disciples do not fast?
15 And Jesus said to them:
Can the sons of the bride-chamber mourn, as long as the bridegroom is with them?

But days will come when the bridegroom will be taken away from them,
and then they will fast.

16 Now no one imposes a piece of unfulled cloth on an old garment,
for it will take away its fullness from the garment,

and a worse tear occurs.
17 Nor do they put new wine into old skins;
otherwise, the skins burst,
and the wine is spilt,
and the skins are lost.
But they put new wine into new skins,
and both are preserved.

LK 5:33-39
make prayers in the same way as those of the Pharisees also,
but yours eat and drink?
34 But Jesus said to them:
Can you make the sons of the bridechamber fast, while the bridegroom is with them?

35. But indeed days will come when the bridegroom will be taken away from them, then they will fast in those days.
36 And he spoke also a parable to them:
No one tearing a piece from a new garment imposes (it) on an old garment;
otherwise, it will both tear the new, and the piece that is from the new will not match the old.

37 And no one puts new wine into old skins; otherwise, the new wine will burst the skins, and itself will be spilt
and the skins will be lost.
38 But new wine is to be put into new skins, and both are preserved.
39 And no one drinking old immediately wants new, for he says: The old is better.

MK 2:18-22
of the Pharisees fast,

but your disciples do not fast?
19 And Jesus said to them:
Can the sons of the bridechamber fast, while the bridegroom is with them?
During whatever time they have the bridegroom with them they cannot fast.
20 But days will come when the bridegroom will be taken away from them,
and then they will fast in that day.

21 No one sews a piece of unfulled cloth on an old garment;
otherwise, it will take the fullness from it—the new from the old—

and a worse tear occurs.
22 And no one puts new wine into old skins; otherwise, the wine will burst the skins, and the wine is lost,
and the skins.
But new wine (is) to be put into new skins.

JN

§54 "Working" on the Sabbath (§135)

MT 12:1-8
1 At that time on the Sabbath Jesus went through the cornfields;
and his disciples were hungry and began to pluck the ears
and to eat.

2 And the Pharisees saw it and said to him:
Behold, your disciples are doing
what is not lawful to do on a Sabbath?
3 And he said to them:
Did you not read what David did,
when
he was hungry,
and those who were with him?
4 How he entered into the House of God

LK 6:1-5
1 And on the Second-First* Sabbath he happened to be going through the cornfields;
and his disciples were plucking

and eating the ears, rubbing them in their hands.
2 And some of the Pharisees said:
Why are you doing
what it is not lawful to do on the Sabbath?
3 And Jesus answering said to them:
Did you not read the thing that David did, when
he himself was hungry,
and those who were with him?
4. How he entered into the House of God

MK 2:23-28
23 And on the Sabbath he happened to be passing through the cornfields;
and his disciples began to make their way plucking the ears.

24 And the Pharisees said to him:
Look, why are they doing
on the Sabbath what is not lawful to do?
25. And he says to them:
Did you never read what David did,
when he was in need
and he himself was hungry,
and those who were with him?
26 How he entered into the House of God under Abiathar the high priest

JN

MT 12:1-8	LK 6:1-5	MK 2:23-28	JN
and ate the Loaves of Proposition,	and taking the Loaves of Proposition ate and gave also to those with him	and ate the Loaves of Proposition,	
which for him to eat was not lawful nor for those with him, *but for the priests alone?*	which are not lawful to eat, but (for) the priests alone?	which are not lawful to eat, but (for) the priests—and he gave also to those who were with him?	
5 Or did you not read in the Law that on the Sabbath the priests in the Temple profane the Sabbath and are blameless? *6 I say to you that a greater than the Temple is here.* *7 And if you had known the meaning of: I desire mercy and not sacrifice* (**Hos. 6:6**), *you would not have condemned the guiltless.*			
	5 And he said to them:	27 And he said to them: The Sabbath was made for man, and not man for the Sabbath.	
8 For the Son of Man is Lord of the Sabbath.	The Son of Man is also Lord of the Sabbath.	28 Thus the Son of Man is Lord of the Sabbath also.	

§55 Man with a Withered Hand (cf. §§136, 244)

MT 12:9-15a	LK 6:6-11; *14:5b*	MK 3:1-7a	JN
9 And departing thence he came into their synagogue, *10 And behold, there was a man having a withered hand,* *and they questioned him saying:*	6 And it happened on another Sabbath that he entered into the synagogue and was teaching. And there was a man there and his right hand was withered; 7 and the Scribes and the Pharisees watched him	1 And he entered again into the synagogue. And there was a man there having a withered up hand; 2 and they watched him	
Is it lawful to heal on the Sabbath? *that they might accuse him.*	if he would heal on the Sabbath, that they might find (something) to accuse him. 8 But he knew their thoughts. And he said to the man having the withered hand: Get up and stand in the middle; and rising up he stood.	if he would heal him on the Sabbath, that they might accuse him. 3 And he says to the man having the withered hand: Get up in the middle.	
11 And he said to them:	9a And Jesus said to them:	4 And he says to them:	
Will there be any man among you who will have a single sheep, *and if on the Sabbath it falls into a hole,* *will you not take hold of it and lift it out?* *12 How much more then a man than a sheep.* *Thus it is lawful to do good on the Sabbath.*	*14:5b Of which one of you will an ass* or an ox* *fall into a well,* *and he will not haul it up on the Sabbath day?*		
	9b I will question you: Is it lawful on the Sabbath to do good or to do evil, to save life or to destroy?	Is it lawful on the Sabbath to do good or to do evil, to save life, or to kill?	

49

MT 12:9-15a	LK 6:6-11; 14:5b	MK 3:1-7a	JN
		But they were silent.	
	10 And looking round on them all in anger*,	5 And looking round on them with anger, being deeply grieved at their hardness of heart,	
13 Then he says to the man: Extend your hand. And he extended (it) and it was restored sound like the other.	he said to him: Extend your hand. And he did, and his hand was restored.	he says to the man: Extend your hand. And he extended (it) and his hand was restored.	
14 But the Pharisees going out took counsel against him, how to destroy him.	11 But they were filled with madness and discussed with one another what they might do to Jesus.	6 And the Pharisees going out at once with the Herodians held counsel against him how to destroy him	
15a But Jesus knowing withdrew thence.		7a And Jesus with his disciples withdrew to the sea.	
		(↓ §57)	

§56 Choice of the Twelve (Lk) (§§58, 123, 161)

MT 5:1; 10:2-4	LK 6:12-16	MK 3:13-19	JN
5:1 Now seeing the crowds he went up onto the mountain,	12 Now it happened in these days that he went out onto the mountain to pray and he spent all night in the prayer of God.	13 And he goes up onto the mountain,	
and when he had sat down his disciples came to him.	13 And when it was day he summoned his disciples,	and he summons whom he himself wanted, and they went off to him,	
10:2 Now the names of the twelve apostles are these:	and choosing from them twelve, whom he also named Apostles,	14 and he made twelve, whom he also named Apostles, to be with him, and to send them to preach 15 and to have authority to cast out the demons. 16 And he made the Twelve, and on Simon he imposed the name of Peter,	
first Simon the one called Peter and Andrew his brother and James (son) of Zebedee and John his brother	14 Simon, whom he also named Peter, and Andrew his brother and James and John	17 and James the (son) of Zebedee and John the brother of James and he imposed on them the name of Boanerges, that is, Sons of Thunder, 18 and Andrew	
3 Philip and Bartholomew Thomas and Matthew the tax-collector James the (son) of Alphaeus and Thaddeus,* 4 Simon the Cananaean	and Philip and Bartholomew 15 and Matthew and Thomas and James of Alphaeus and Simon who is called Zealot 16 and Jude of James	and Philip and Bartholomew and Matthew and Thomas and James the (son) of Alphaeus and Thaddeus and Simon the Cananaean	
and Judas Iscariot who was also his betrayer.	and Judas Iscariot who became the traitor,	19 and Judas Iscariot who also betrayed him.	

MT 4:24-25	MT 12:15b-16	LK 6:17-19	MK 3:7b-12	JN
(↑ §46)			(↑ §55)	

LK 6:17-19

17 and coming down with them, he stood on a level place,

(cf. 4:37)   **(cf. 1:28)**

(cf. 6:18-19)   **(cf. 3:10-11)**

MT 4:24-25

24 And his fame went out into all Syria;
and they brought him all that were ill from various diseases,
and people suffering pains,
and demon-possessed
and lunatics
and paralytics
and he healed them. 25 And large crowds followed him from Galilee and Decapolis and Jerusalem and Judea

and across the Jordan.

MT 12:15b-16

15b And large crowds followed him and he healed them all.

LK

and a large crowd of his disciples and a large multitude of the people,
from all Judea and Jerusalem,

MK 3:7b-12

7b and a large multitude from Galilee followed him,

and from Judea 8 and from Jerusalem
and from Idumea and across the Jordan,
and about Tyre and Sidon,

and the coastal region of Tyre and Sidon,
18 who had come to hear him and to be cured from their diseases,
and those tormented by unclean spirits were healed.
19 And the whole crowd was trying to touch him, because power went out from him and cured all.

a large multitude, hearing what he was doing, came to him.

(cf. 13:2)

(↓ §59)

9 And he said to his disciples that a small boat should stand ready for him because of the crowd, lest they throng him.
10 For he healed many, so that whoever had afflictions fell on him in order to touch him.
11 And the unclean spirits when they observed him, fell down before him and cried out saying: You are the Son of God.
12 And he rebuked them severely that they should not make him known.

(cf. 6:19)

16 And he rebuked them that they should not make him known.

MT 5:1; 10:2-4	LK 6:12-16	MK 3:13-19	JN 6:1-4
1 And seeing the crowds he went up on to the mountain,	*12 And it happened in those days that he went out on to the mountain to pray, and he spent all night in the prayer of God.*	13 And he goes up on to the mountain,	*1 After these things Jesus went off across the Sea of Galilee, the (sea) of Tiberias. 2 And a great crowd followed him, because they had seen the signs he had done on the sick. 3 And Jesus went up onto the mountain and sat there with his disciples. 4 And it was near the Passover, the Feast of the Jews.*
and when he sat down his disciples come to him.	*13 And when it was day, he summoned his disciples*	and he summons those whom he himself wanted, and they went off to him.	
10:2 Now these are the names of the twelve apostles:	*and choosing from them Twelve, whom also he named Apostles,*	14. And he made Twelve, whom also he named Apostles*, to be with him, and that he should send them to preach, 15 and to have authority to cast out the demons. 16 And he made the Twelve,	
first Simon who is called Peter,	*14 Simon whom he also named Peter*	and he imposed on Simon the name Peter,	
and Andrew his brother, and Zebedee's James and John his brother,	*and Andrew his brother, and James and John,*	17 and Zebedee's James and John the brother of James, and he imposed on them the name Boanerges, that is, Sons of Thunder, 18 and Andrew,	
3 Philip and Bartholomew, Thomas and Matthew the tax-collector, and Alphaeus' James and Thaddeus,* 4 Simon the Cananaean and Judas the Iscariot who was also his betrayer.	*and Philip and Bartholomew 15 and Matthew and Thomas, and James of Alphaeus and Simon who is called Zealot, 16 and Jude of James, and Judas Iscariot, who became the traitor.*	and Philip and Bartholomew, and Matthew and Thomas, and Alphaeus' James and Thaddeus and Simon the Cananaean, 19 And Judas Iscariot, who also betrayed him.	
		(↓ §97)	

§59 The Beatitudes

MT 5:2-12	LK 6:20-23	MK	JN 6:5a
	(↑ §57)		
2 And opening his mouth he began to teach them, saying:	20 And he, raising his eyes to his disciples, began to say:	**(cf. 6:19)**	*5a And Jesus lifting up his eyes and observing that a great crowd was coming to him, says to Philip:*
3 Blessed are the poor in spirit for theirs is the Kingdom of the Heavens.	Blessed are the poor for yours is the Kingdom of God.		

MT 5:2-12	LK 6:20-23	MK	JN 6:5a
4 Blessed are they who mourn for they will be comforted,	(v. 21b)		
5 Blessed are the meek for they will inherit the land.			
6 Blessed are they who hunger and thirst for righteousness, for they will be filled.	21 Blessed are you who hunger now, for you will be filled. Blessed are you who now weep for you will laugh.		
(cf. v. 4)			
7 Blessed are the merciful, for they will receive mercy.			
8 Blessed are the clean of heart, for they will see God.			
9 Blessed are the peacemakers, for they will be called Sons of God.			
10 Blessed are they who suffer persecution for righteousness' sake, for theirs is the Kingdom of the Heavens.			
11 Blessed are you when they reproach and persecute you, and say every wicked thing against you, falsely, for my sake.	22 Blessed are you when men hate you, and when they exclude and reproach you, and cast out your name as wicked for the Son of Man's sake.		
12 Rejoice and be glad for your reward (is) great in the heavens, for thus they persecuted the prophets who were before you.	23 Rejoice in that day and leap for joy, for lo, your reward (is) great in heaven, for in the same way did their fathers behave to the prophets.		
(↓ §61)			

§60 The Four Woes

MT	LK 6:24-26	MK	JN
	24 But woe to you, the rich, for you possess your consolation. 25 Woe to you who are now filled up, for you will hunger. Woe to you who now laugh, for you will mourn and weep. 26 Woe when all men say well of you, for in the same way did their fathers behave to the false prophets.		
	(↓ §69)		

§61 Salt of the Earth (§§186, 250)

MT 5:13	LK 14:34-35	MK 9:49-50	JN
(↑ §59)			
13 You are the salt of the earth;		49 *Everyone shall be salted with fire, and every offering shall be salted with salt.**	
	34 *Salt therefore is good;*	50 *Salt is good;*	
but if the salt should be spoilt, how shall it be salted?	*but if even the salt should be spoilt, how shall it be restored?*	*but if the salt should become un-salty, how shall you restore it?*	
For nothing is it still of value,	35 *Neither for the ground nor for manure is it suitable;*		
except for being thrown outside to be trodden down by men.	*they throw it outside.*		
	He that has ears to hear, let him hear.	*Have salt in yourselves, and be at peace with one another.*	

§62 Light of the World (§219)

MT 5:14-16	LK 11:33	MK	JN
14 You are the light of the world.	**(cf. 8:16)**		
A city that lies on a mountain cannot be hidden.			
15 Nor do they light a lamp and put it under the measure,	33 *And no one kindling a lamp puts it in a cellar nor under the measure,*	**(4:21)**	
but upon the lampstand, and it shines for all who are in the house.	*but upon the lampstand, so that they who enter may see the light.*		
16. So let your light shine before men, that they may see your good works, and glorify your Father who is in the heavens.			

§63 Jesus and the Law (§258)

MT 5:17-20	LK 16:17	MK	JN
17 Do not think that I came to undo the Law or the Prophets; I came, not to undo, but to fulfil.			
18 For Amen I say to you,			
until the heaven and the earth pass away,	17 *But it is easier for the heaven and the earth to pass away than for one pen-stroke of the Law to fall.*		
not one iota or one pen-stroke of the Law will pass away until all things be done.			
19 Whosoever therefore undoes one of the least of these commandments, and shall so teach men,			
he will be called least in the Kingdom of the Heavens.			
And whosoever shall do and teach,			
he will be called great in the Kingdom of the Heavens.			
20 For I say to you, that if your righteousness does not abound			

MT 5:17-20
more than that of the Scribes and Pharisees, you will not enter
into the Kingdom of the Heavens.

LK 16:17

MK   JN

§64 On Murder and Anger

MT 5:21-24
21 You have heard that it was said to the Ancients: Thou shalt
not kill;
and whosoever kills shall be liable for the judgement. **(Exod.
20:13; Dt. 5:17)**
22 But I say to you that everyone who becomes angry with his
brother without reason* shall be liable for the judgement.
And whosoever should say to his brother Racha. shall be liable
for the Council.
And whosoever should say Fool, shall be liable to the Gehenna of
fire.
23 If therefore you are offering your gift upon the altar
and there you should remember that your brother has something
against you;
24 Leave your gift there before the altar and go first to be
reconciled to your brother,
and then come and offer your gift.

LK   MK   JN

§65 Defendant and Plaintiff (§235)

MT 5:25-26
25 Get on good terms with your accuser quickly,
while you are still with him on the way;
lest perhaps the opponent hand you over to the judge,
and the judge hand you over to the attendant,
and you be cast into prison.
26 Amen, I say to you, you shall not go out thence until you
have paid up the last penny.

LK 12:58-59
*58 For as you go off with your accuser before a magistrate,
on the way take pains to settle with him
unless perhaps he drag you along to the judge,
and the judge will hand you over to the constable
and the constable will cast you into prison.
59. I say to you, you shall not go out thence until you have paid
up even the last halfpenny.*

MK   JN

§66 On Controlling Evil Desires

MT 5:27-30
27 You have heard that it was said: You shall not commit adultery
(Ex. 20:14; Dt. 5:18).
28 But I say to you that everyone who looks at a woman in order

LK   MK   JN

55

MT 5:27-30
to lust after her has already committed adultery with her in his heart.
29 And if your right eye scandalize you, pluck it out and cast it from you;
for it is expedient for you that one of your members be lost and not your whole body be cast into Gehenna **(cf. 18:8-9)**.
30 And if your right hand scandalize you, cut it off and cast from you;
for it is expedient for you that one of your members be lost and not your whole body go off into Gehenna.

LK   MK   JN

§67 On Divorce (§259)

MT 5:31-32
31 Now it was said; Whosoever divorces his wife, let him give her a note of repudiation **(Dt. 24:1)**.
32 But I say to you that everyone who divorces his wife except for the reason of incest
makes her commit adultery,
and whoever shall marry the divorced woman
commits adultery.

(cf. 19:9)

LK 16:18

18 Everyone who divorces his wife

and marries another commits adultery,
and he who marries a woman divorced from her husband
commits adultery.

MK   JN

(cf. 10: 11-12)

§68 On Oaths

MT 5:33-37
33 Again, you heard that it was said to the Ancients:
Thou shalt not swear falsely, but thou shalt perform thy oaths to the Lord **(Lev. 19:12; Nu. 30:2; Dt. 23:21)**.
34 But I say to you not to swear at all,
neither by heaven, for it is the throne of God,
35 nor by the earth, for it is the footstool of his feet;
nor by Jerusalem, for it is the city of the great king;
36 nor should you swear by your head, for you cannot make one hair white or black.
37 And let your speech be "Yes, Yes," "No, No";
and what exceeds these is from the Evil One.

LK   MK   JN

MT 5:38-42

38 You have heard that it was said: An eye for an eye, and a tooth for a tooth **(Ex. 21:24; Lv. 24:20; Dt. 19:21)**.

39 Now I say to you not to resist the evil-doer;
(5:44)

but whoever strikes you on your cheek,
turn to him also the other;
40 and to him who would sue you and take your shirt,
let him have your coat too.
41 And whoever takes you forcibly one mile, go with him two.
42. Give to him who begs of you,
and him who wants to borrow from you, do not refuse.

(↓ §71)

LK 6:27-30

(↑ §60)

27 But I say to you who are listening:
Love your enemies,
do good to those who hate you,
28. bless those who speak ill of you,
pray for those who treat you spitefully.
29 To him who hits you on the cheek,
offer also the other;
and from him who takes your coat,
do not withhold your shirt.

30 Give to everyone who begs of you,
and from him who takes away your goods do not ask back.

MK   JN

§70 The Golden Rule of Conduct (§84)

MT 7:12

12 All things therefore whatever you want men to do to you, so also do you do to them.

LK 6:31

31 And just as you want men to do to you,
you also in the same way do to them.

MK   JN

§71 On Love of Enemies (§69)

MT 5:43-48

(↑ §69)

43 You have heard that it was said:
You shall love your neighbour and you shall hate your enemy
(Lev. 19:18).
44 But I say to you,
Love your enemies,
bless those who curse you, do good to those who hate you,*

and pray on behalf of those who persecute you;
45 that you may become sons of your Father in the heavens,
because he makes his sun to rise over evil and good and rains
upon just and unjust.
46 For if you love those who love you, what payment do you
deserve;
do not the tax-collectors also do the very same?
47 And if you greet only your brethren, what special thing are

LK 6:27-28, 32-36

*27 But I say to you who are hearing;
Love your enemies,
do good to those who hate you, 28 bless those who speak ill of you,
pray for those who treat you spitefully.*

32 And if you love those who love you, how much gratitude is owing to you?
For sinners also love those who love them.
33. And if therefore you do good to those who do good to you,

MK   JN

§§71-73

MT 5:43-48
you doing?
Do not the Gentiles also do the very same?

(v. 45)

48 Be you therefore perfect,
as your heavenly Father is perfect.

LK 6:27-28, 32-36
how much gratitude is owing to you?
Sinners also do the very same.

34 And if you lend (to those) from whom you hope to receive,
how much gratitude is due to you?
Sinners also lend to sinners that they may receive back an equal amount.
35. Instead, love your enemies and do them good and lend, not giving up hope;
and your reward will be great and you will be Sons of the Most High,
because he is beneficent to the unthankful and evil.
36 Become merciful,
just as your Father is merciful.

(↓ §81)

MK   JN

§72 On Almsgiving

MT 6:1-4
1 And take care not to perform your righteousness before men in order to be observed by them;
for if so, you have no reward from your Father who is in the heavens.
2 When therefore you perform an almsdeed, do not sound a trumpet before you as the hypocrites do in the synagogues and in the streets so that they may be glorified by men;
Amen, I say to you, they possess their reward.
3 But you when you do an alms let not your left hand know what your right hand is doing,
4 so that your alms may be in secret, and your Father who sees in secret will reward you.

LK   MK   JN

§73 How to Pray

MT 6:5-8
5 And when you pray, do not be like the hypocrites,
because they love to pray standing in the synagogues and at the street-corners, so that they are visible to men.
Amen, I say to you, they possess their reward.
6 But you when you pray go into your inner room and having closed the door pray to your Father, who is in secret,
and your Father who sees in secret will reward you.
7 And when you pray do not patter away like the Gentiles,

LK   MK   JN

58

MT 6:5-8   LK   MK   JN

for they think that they will be heard for their many words.
8 Do not therefore be like them;
for God your Father knows the things you need before you ask him.

§74 The Lord's Prayer (§§212, 295)

MT 6:9-13	LK 11:2b-4	MK 11:25a	JN
9 Pray you therefore thus: Our Father who (art) in the heavens hallowed be thy name; 10 thy Kingdom come; thy will be done, as in heaven, so on earth. 11 Our bread that comes down give us today. 12 And forgive us our debts, as we too have forgiven our debtors; 13 and lead us not into temptation. but deliver us from the Evil One.	2b When you pray, say: [Our]* Father [who (art) in the heavens]* hallowed be thy name; thy Kingdom come; [thy will be done, as in heaven so on earth].* 3 Our bread that comes down give us day-by-day. 4 And forgive us our sins, for we ourselves also forgive everyone in debt to us; and lead us not into temptation, [but deliver us from the Evil One].*	25a And when you stand praying,	

§75 Forgive and Be Forgiven (§295)

MT 6:14-15	LK	MK 11:25b-26	JN
14 For if you forgive men their trespasses, your heavenly Father will also forgive you. 15 But if you do not forgive men their trespasses, neither will your Father forgive you your trespasses.		25b Forgive, if you have anything against anyone, so that your Father who is in the heavens may also forgive you your trespasses. 26* But if you do not forgive, neither will your Father who is in the heavens forgive your trespasses.	

§76 On Fasting

MT 6:16-18   LK   MK   JN

16 When you fast, be not long-faced like the hypocrites;
for they make up their faces so as to appear to men to be fasting;
Amen, I say to you, they have their reward.
17 But you, when you fast, anoint your head and wash your face,
18 so as not to appear to men to be fasting, but to your Father who is in secret,
and your Father who sees in secret will reward you.

§77 On Treasures in Heaven (§229)

MT 6:19-21

19 Do not treasure for yourselves treasures upon earth where moth and rust corrode,
and where thieves dig through and steal.
20 But treasure for yourselves treasures in heaven,

where neither moth nor rust corrode, and where thieves neither dig through nor steal.
21 For where your treasure is there too will be your heart.

LK 12:33-34
33 Sell your possessions and give alms;

make for yourselves purses that do not become old, an unfailing treasure in the heavens,
and where a thief does not come nigh nor a moth corrupt.

34 For where your treasure is, there too your heart will be.

MK | JN

§78 The Sound Eye (§220)

MT 6:22-23
22 The lamp of the body is the eye.
If therefore your eye is clear your whole body will be full of light;
23 But if your eye is evil, your whole body will be full of darkness.
If therefore the light that is in you is darkness, how great the darkness.

LK 11:34-36
34 The lamp of the body is your eye.
When your eye is clear, then your whole body is full of light;

but when it is evil your body is also full of darkness.

35 Watch therefore lest the light that is in you is darkness.

36 If therefore your body is wholly bright, not having any part dark, it will be wholly bright, as when the lamp lights you with its radiance.

MK | JN

§79 On Serving Two Masters (§255)

MT 6:24
24 No one can serve two masters;
for either he will hate the one and love the other,
or he will be attached to one and despise the other.
You cannot serve God and Mammon.

LK 16:13
13 No house-slave can serve two masters;
either he will hate the one and love the other,
or he will be attached to one and despise the other.
You cannot serve God and Mammon.

MK | JN

§80 On Earthly Anxieties (§228)

MT 6:25-34

25 Wherefore I say to you:
Do not worry about your life what you eat or what you drink,
nor about your body what you wear.
Is not the life more than the food and the body than the

LK 12:22-31
22 And he said to his disciples:
Wherefore I say to you:
Do not worry about your life what you eat,
nor about your body what you wear.
23 For the life is more than the food and the body than the

MK | JN

MT 6:25-34

clothing?
26 Look at the birds of the sky:
they do not sow nor reap nor gather into barns,
yet your heavenly Father feeds them;
are not you worth more than they are?
27 And which of you by worrying can add one cubit to his
span?*

28 Why do you worry about clothing?
Learn from the lilies of the field,   .
how they grow; they neither toil nor spin.
29 And I say to you that not even Solomon in all his glory was
arrayed like one of these.
30 And if the grass of the field that exists today and tomorrow is
thrown into a furnace, God so clothes,
does he not by much more (clothe) you, O men of little faith?
31 Do not worry therefore, saying: What are we to eat? or What
are we to drink? or What are we to wear?
32 For the nations are intent on all these things;
for your heavenly Father knows that you need all these things.
33 But first seek the Kingdom of God and his justice,
and all these things will be added to you.
34 Do not worry therefore regarding the morrow; for the
morrow will worry about itself.
Sufficient for the day is the evil thereof.

LK 12:22-31

clothing.
24 Consider the ravens:
they neither sow nor reap, nor have they a store room or a barn,
yet God feeds them;
how much more are you worth than the birds!
25 And which of you by worrying can add a cubit to his span?*

26 If therefore you cannot do the littlest thing,
why do you worry about the remaining things?
27 Consider the lilies,
how they grow; they neither toil or spin.
And I say to you not even Solomon in all his glory was arrayed
like one of these.
28 And if in a field the grass that exists today and tomorrow is
thrown into a furnace, God so clothes,
by how much more you, O men of little faith!
29 And you, do not be seeking after what you eat and what you
drink, and do not be anxious.
30 For the nations of the world are intent on all these things;
but your Father knows that you need these things.
31 Seek however his Kingdom,
and all these things will be added to you.

MK

JN

§81 On Judging Others (§§104, 125, 167)

MT 7:1-5

1 Judge not that you be not
judged.
2 For with what judgement you
judge, you will be judged,
and

in the measure you measure it
will be measured to you.

MT 15:14; 10:24-25a

LK 6:37-42

(↑ §71)
37 And judge not, and be not
judged.

And condemn not, and be not
condemned,
Forgive, and you will be forgiven.
38 Give, and it will be given to
you—good measure, pressed
down, shaken together, running
over, they will give into your lap.
For with the measure you
measure it will be measured back
to you.

MK 4:24

24 And he said to them: Watch
what you hear. In the measure
you measure, it will be measured
to you, and it will be added to
you.

JN

MT 7:1-5   *MT 15:14; 10:24-25a*   LK 6:37-42   *MK 4:24*   JN

14 They are blind leaders of the blind. For if a blind man leads a blind man, both will fall into (the) ditch.

10:24 A disciple is not above his teacher nor a slave above his master.
25a It is enough for the disciple that he become like his teacher and the slave like his master.

39 And he also spoke a parable to them:
Surely a blind man cannot lead a blind man?

Will they not both fall down into (the) ditch?
40 A disciple is not above his teacher,

But everyone shall be made perfect like his teacher.

3 And why do you see the speck that is in your brother's eye, but do not notice the log that is in your eye?
4 Or how will you say to your brother:
Let me extract the speck from your eye:
and behold the log in your own eye?
5 Hypocrite, extract first the log from your eye,
and then shall you see to extract the speck from your brother's eye.

41 And why do you see the speck that is in your brother's eye, but the log that is in your own eye you do not notice?
42 Or how can you say to your brother:
Brother, let me extract the speck that is in your eye,
yourself not seeing the log that is in your own eye.
Hypocrite, extract first the log from your eye,
and then shall you see to extract the speck that is in your brother's eye.

(↓ §86)

§82 "Guard What Is Holy"

MT 7:6   LK   MK   JN
6 Do not give what is holy to the dogs,
nor cast your pearls before the swine,
lest perhaps they trample them down with their feet,
and turn and rend you.

§83 On Asking God (§214)

MT 7:7-11   *LK 11:9-13*   MK   JN
7 Ask and it shall be given to you;   *9 And I say to you: Ask, and it shall be given to you:*

MT 7:7-11	LK 11:9-13	MK	JN
seek and you will find;	*Seek and you will find;*		
knock and it will be opened to you.	*knock, and it will be opened to you.*		
8 for everyone who asks receives, and he who seeks finds, and to him who knocks it will be opened.	*10 For everyone who asks receives, and he who seeks finds, and to him who knocks it will be opened.*		
9 Or what man of you is there, whom his son will ask for bread, will give him a stone?	*11 And which one of you—the father— (if his) son shall ask for bread, will really give him a stone?*		
10 Or again will ask for a fish, will give him a snake?	*Or again* a fish, and instead of a fish will give him a snake?*		
	12 Or again will he ask for an egg, surely he will not give him a scorpion?		
11 If therefore you who are evil know how to give good gifts to your children, by how much more will your Father who is in the heavens give good things to those who ask him.	*13 If therefore you being evil know how to give good gifts to your children, by how much more will your Father who is from Heaven give the Holy Spirit to those who ask him.*		

§84 The Golden Rule (§70)

MT 7:12	LK 6:31	MK	JN
12 All things therefore whatever you want men to do to you, so also do you do to them. For this is the Law and the Prophets.	*31 And just as you want men to do to you, do you also do to them in like manner.*		

§85 The Two Ways (§241)

MT 7:13-14	LK 13:24	MK	JN
13 Enter through the narrow gate; for broad is the gate and wide-open the way that leads off to destruction, and many there are who enter through it. 14 How narrow (is) the gate and constricted the way that leads off to life, and few there are who find it.	*24 Strive hard to enter through the narrow door;* *because many, I tell you, will seek to enter* *and will not be able.*		

§86 A Tree Is Known by Its Fruits (§139)

MT 7:15-21	*MT 12:33, 35, 34b*	LK 6:43-46	MK	JN
15 Beware of false prophets who come to you in sheep's clothing, but within they		(↑ §81)		

63

MT 7:15-21	MT 12:33, 35, 34b	LK 6:43-46	MK	JN
are ravening wolves. 16 From their fruits you will know them. Surely you do not gather grapes from thorns or figs from thistles?		*44b For they do not gather figs from thorns nor do they harvest a bunch of grapes from a thorn bush.*		
17 Thus every sound tree makes good fruits, but the diseased tree makes bad fruits. 18 A sound tree cannot make bad fruits,	*33 Either make the tree good and its fruit good,* *or make the tree diseased and its fruit diseased.*	43 For a good tree does not make a diseased fruit, nor again does a diseased tree make a good fruit.		
nor the diseased tree make good fruits. 19 Every tree that does not make good fruit is cut down and is thrown into the fire **(Mt. 3:10)**. 20 So then, by their fruits you will know them.	*For from the fruit will the tree be known.*	44 For each tree is known from its own fruit. For they do not gather figs from thorns, nor do they harvest a bunch of grapes from a thorn bush.		
(cf. 7:16)	*35 The good man from his good treasure puts out good things,* *and the evil man from his evil treasure puts out evil things.*	45 The good man from the good treasure of the heart brings forth the good, and the evil from the evil brings forth the evil;		
	34b For from the overflow of the heart the mouth speaks.	for from the overflow of the heart his mouth speaks.		
21 Not everyone who says to me, Lord, Lord, will enter into the Kingdom of the Heavens, but he who does the will of my Father who is in the heavens.		46 And why do you call me Lord, Lord, and do not do what I say? (↓ §88)		

§87 On Doing the Word (§241)

MT 7:22-23	LK 13:25-27	MK	JN
22 Many will say to me in that day: Lord, Lord, **(cf. 25:10-12)** in your name did we not prophesy? and in your name did we not cast out demons? and in your name did we not work many miracles? 23 And then I shall declare to them:	*25 When the master of the house has risen and shut the door, then you will begin to stand outside and knock on the door saying: Lord, open to us;* *and answering he will say to you: I know not whence you are.* *26 Then you will begin to say:* *We ate and drank in your presence, and you taught in our streets.* *27 And saying he will say to you:*		

MT 7:22-23
I never knew you;
depart from me all you who work lawlessness.

LK 13:25-27
I know you not whence you are;
stand away from me all you workers of unrighteousness.

MK

JN

§88 The House Built on the Rock

MT 7:24-27

24 Everyone therefore, whoever hears these my words, and does them,
shall be likened to a wise man
who built his house upon the rock.

25 And the rain came down and the torrents came and the winds blew down and beat against that house,
and it did not fall.
for it was founded on the rock.
26 And everyone who hears these words of mine and does not do them
shall be likened to a foolish man who built his house upon the sand.
27 And the rain came down and the torrents came and the winds blew down and struck against that house,
and it fell, and its fall was great.

LK 6:47-49
(↑ §86)

47 Everyone who comes to me and hears my words and does them,
I will show you to whom he is like. 48 He is like a man building a house, who dug and deepened and laid the foundation upon the rock.
And when the flood arrived the torrent dashed against that house,
and it could not be shaken.
because it had been well built.
49 But he who heard and did not do

is like a man who built a house upon the earth without a foundation,
on which the torrent dashed.

and at once it collapsed, and the ruin of that house was great.

MK

JN

§89 Teaching with Authority (§41)

MT 7:28-8:1
28 And it happened that when Jesus had ended all these words,

the crowds were amazed at his teaching,
for he was teaching them as one having authority and not as their Scribes.
8:1 And when he came down from the mountain, great crowds followed him **(Ex. 32:15; 12:15)**.

LK 7:1a; *4:32*
1a When he had completed all these sayings in the ears of the people,

(↓ §91)

4:32 and they were astounded at his teaching,
because his word was with authority.

(cf. 6:17b)

MK 1:22

22 And they were astounded at his teaching,
for he was teaching them as one having
authority and not as the Scribes.

JN

IV. The Training
of the Twelve
in Galilee
§§ 90-157

§90 The Cleansing of a Leper (§48)

MT 8:2-4

2 And lo, a leper coming up

began to worship him, saying:
Lord, if you will, you can cleanse me.
3 And extending his hand he touched him,
saying:
I will; be cleansed.
And at once his leprosy was cleansed.

4 And Jesus says to him:

Look, tell no one, but go off, show yourself to
the priest
and offer
the gift which Moses commanded for a witness
to them.

LK 5:12-16

*12 And it happened that he was in one of the
towns, and lo a man full of leprosy;
and seeing Jesus,
falling on his face he begged him saying:
Lord, if you will, you can cleanse me.
13 And extending his hand he touched him,
saying:
I will; be cleansed.
And at once the leprosy left him.*

14 And he ordered him

*to tell no one: but go away, show yourself to
the priest
and offer for your cleansing
just as Moses commanded for a witness to
them.
15 But instead the word went abroad about
him,
and many crowds came together to hear him,
and to be healed from their sicknesses.*

*16 But he was withdrawn in the deserts and
praying.*

(cf. v. 15.)

MK 1:40-45

40 And a leper comes to him

*beseeching him and kneeling and saying to him:
If you will, you can cleanse me.
41 And being moved with pity extending his
hand he touched him and says to him:
I will; be cleansed.
42 And at once the leprosy left him and he
was cleansed.
43 And sternly charging him he sent him off at
once, 44 and says to him:
Look, tell nothing to anyone but go off, show
yourself to the priest
and offer for your cleansing
the things that Moses commanded for a
witness to them.
45 But he went off and began to preach loudly
and to spread the word,*

*so that he could no longer openly go into a
town,
but he was outside in desert places;*

and they came to him from everywhere.

JN

§91 A Centurion's Slave Healed (cf. §§37, 241)

MT 8:5-13

5 Now when he entered into **Capharnaum,**

there approached him a centurion beseeching
him and saying:
6 Lord, my boy is lying paralysed in the house
in terrible distress.

LK 7:1b-10; *13:29, 28*

(↑ §89)

1b he entered into **Capharnaum.**

2 Now a certain centurion's

slave was ill about to die, who was exceedingly
dear to him.
3 And having heard about Jesus he sent to
him elders of the Jews asking him to come and
restore his slave.

4 And when they came along to Jesus they
besought him earnestly, saying:
He is worthy that you should grant this to

MK

JN 4:46-54

*46 He came therefore into Cana of Galilee
where he had made the water wine.
And there was a certain royal official whose
son was sick in Capharnaum.*

*47 And when he heard that Jesus had come
from Judea into Galilee, he went off to him
and asked (him) to go down and heal his son,
for he was about to die.*

MT 8:5-13	LK 7:1b-10; *13:29, 28*	MK	JN 4:46-54

MT 8:5-13

7 And he says to him: I will come and heal him.

8. And the centurion answering said: Lord, I am not worthy that you should enter under my roof;

but only say a word and my boy will be healed.
9 For I too am a man under authority, having under me soldiers
and I say to this one: Go, and he goes,
and to another; Come, and he comes,
and to my slave: Do this and he does it.
10 And hearing, Jesus marvelled,

and said to those following:
Amen, I say to you, with no one in Israel have I found such faith.

11 And I say to you, that many will come from east and west,
and will recline with Abraham and Isaac and Jacob in the Kingdom of the Heavens.

12 But the sons of the Kingdom will be cast out into the exterior darkness;
weeping and gnashing of teeth shall be there.
13 And Jesus said to the centurion: Go back, be it done to you as you have believed.
And the boy was healed in that very hour.

(↓ §109)

LK 7:1b-10; *13:29, 28*

him; 5 for he loves our nation and has himself built us the synagogue.
6 And Jesus went with them.

And when he was already not far away from the house,
the centurion sent friends saying to him:
Lord, do not trouble, for I am not worthy that you should enter under my roof;
7 For this reason I did not consider myself worthy to come to you;
but say a word and let my boy be cured.

8 For I too am a man set under authority, having under me soldiers,
and I say to this one: Go, and he goes,
and to another: Come, and he comes,
and to my slave: Do this, and he does it.
9 And Jesus hearing these things marvelled at him,
and turning to the crowd following him said:
I say to you, not in Israel have I found such faith.

*13:29 And they shall come from east and west and from north and south,
and they will recline in the Kingdom of God.*

28b when you see Abraham, Isaac and Jacob and all the prophets in the Kingdom of God, but you (yourselves) cast outside.

28a Weeping and gnashing of teeth shall be there,

10 And returning to the house, those who had been sent found the slave cured.

JN 4:46-54

48 Jesus therefore said to him: Unless you see signs and wonders you will not believe.

49 The royal official says to him:

Lord, go down before my little boy dies.

50 Jesus says to him: Go, your son lives.

The man believed the word that Jesus had spoken to him and went. 51 And while he was still going down, his slaves met him, saying: Your son lives.
52 He therefore inquired of them the hour in which he got better; they said therefore: Yesterday at the seventh hour, the fever left him.
53 The father therefore knew that (it was) at that very hour at which Jesus said to him: Your son lives; and he and his whole house believed.
54 And this (is) again the second sign that Jesus did, when he went from Judea into Galilee.

MT	LK 7:11-17	MK	JN
	11 And it happened thereafter that he went into a city called Nain, and his disciples and a great crowd went with him. 12 And as he drew near to the gate of the city, and behold they were carrying out a dead man the only son of his mother, and she was a widow, and a large crowd of the city was with her. 13 And seeing her the Lord was filled with compassion for her, and said to her, Do not weep. 14 And coming up he touched the bier, and those who carried it stood still, and he said: Young man, I say to you, Rise up. 15 And the dead man sat up and began to speak, and he gave him to his mother. 16 And fear gripped all, and they glorified God, saying: A great prophet has risen among us; and: God has visited his people. 17 And this word went out about him in all Judea and in every district.		

§93 John's Messengers (§130)

MT 11:2-6	LK 7:18-23	MK	JN
2 Now John in the prison heard the works of the Christ, (and) sending by his disciples, he said to him: *3 Are you he who is to come or are we waiting for another?* *4 And Jesus answering said to them: Go and report to John what you hear and see;* *5 the blind see again, and the lame walk, lepers are cleansed, and the deaf hear, and the dead are raised, and the poor are evangelized;* *6 and blessed is whoever has not been scandalized over me.*	18 And his disciples reported to John about all these things, and summoning a certain two of his disciples, 19 John sent them to Jesus, saying: Are you he who is to come, or are we waiting for someone else? 20 And when the men came along they said to him: John the Baptist sent us to you, saying: Are you he who is to come, or do we wait for someone else? 21 In that very hour he healed many from diseases and afflictions and evil spirits, and he granted sight to many blind. 22 And answering he said to them: Go and report to John what you have seen and heard; the blind see again, the lame walk, lepers are cleansed, and the deaf hear, the dead are raised, the poor are evangelized; 23 and blessed is whoever has not been scandalized over me.		

§94 Jesus Praises John (§§17, 131)

MT 11:7-19	LK 7:24-35	MK 1:2	JN
7 And as they were going, *Jesus began to say to the crowds about John: Why did you go out into the desert? To behold a reed shaken by the wind?*	24 And as the messengers of John were going away, he began to say to the crowds about John: Why did you go out into the desert? To behold a reed shaken by the wind?		

MT 11:7-19	LK 7:24-35	MK 1:2	JN
8 *But why did you go out?*	25 But why did you go out?		
To see a man finely dressed?	To see a man dressed in fine clothes?		
Lo, those who dress finely (are) in the palaces of kings.	Lo, those in splendid and luxurious dress are in the rooms of royalty.		
9 *But why did you go out?*	26 But why did you go out?		
To see a prophet?	To see a prophet?		
Yes, I tell you, and more than a prophet.	Yes, I tell you, and more than a prophet.		
10 *This is he about whom it has been written:*	27 This is he about whom it has been written:	2 *Just as it has been written in the—Isaiah the prophet:*	
Behold I send my messenger before thy face who will prepare thy way before thee.	Behold, I send my messenger before thy face who will prepare thy way before thee **(Mal. 3:1)**.	*Behold I send my messenger before thy face, who will prepare thy way before thee.*	
11 *Amen, I say to you, there has not arisen among those born of women a greater than John the Baptist.*	28 I say to you, no one is a greater prophet among those born of women than John.		
But the least in the Kingdom of the Heavens is greater than he.	But the least in the Kingdom of God is greater than he.		
	29 And all the people heard, and the tax-collectors justified God, having been baptised with John's baptism.		
	30 But the Pharisees and the Lawyers rejected the plan of God with regard to themselves, not having been baptised by him.		
12 *But from the days of John the Baptist until now the Kingdom of Heaven suffers violence, and the violent snatch it away.*	**(cf. 16:16)**		
13 *For all the prophets and the Law prophesied until John;*			
14 *and if you wish to receive it, he himself is the Elijah who is to come.*			
15 *He who has ears to hear, let him hear.*			
16 *And to what shall I liken this generation?*	31 To what therefore shall I liken the men of this generation? And to whom are they like?		
It is like to boys sitting in the marketplaces,	32 They are like to boys who sit in a marketplace,		
who calling out to the others, 17 say:	and they call out to one another—who say:		
We piped to you and you did not dance;	We piped to you and you did not dance;		
we wailed to you and you did not mourn.	we wailed to you and you did not weep.		
18 *For John came neither eating nor drinking,*	33 For John the Baptist has come neither eating bread nor drinking wine,		
and they say: He has a demon.	and you say: He has a demon.		
19 *The Son of Man came eating and drinking,*	34 The Son of Man has come eating and drinking,		
and they say: Behold a man who is a glutton and a drunkard, a friend of tax-collectors and sinners.	and you say, Behold a man who is a glutton and a drunkard, a friend of tax-collectors and sinners.		
And Wisdom is justified from its deeds.*	35 And Wisdom is justified from all its children.		

MT 26:6-13	LK 7:36-50	MK 14:3-9	JN 12:1-8
6 Now Jesus happening to be in Bethany in the house of Simon the leper,	36 And someone of the Pharisees asked him to eat with him; and entering into the house of the Pharisee he reclined at table.	*3 And when he was in Bethany in the house of Simon the leper,*	*1 Jesus therefore six days before the Passover came into Bethany where was Lazarus, the one who had died,* whom Jesus had raised from the dead.*
7 there came up to him a woman	37 And behold there was a certain woman in the city, a sinner, and learning that he was at table in the house of the Pharisee,	*while he was reclining at table there came a woman*	*2 Therefore they made a supper for him there, and Martha was serving, but Lazarus was one of the ones reclining with him.*
having an alabaster phial of very expensive perfume, and poured it over his head as he was reclining at table.	bringing an alabaster phial of perfume, 38 and standing behind at his feet weeping, she began to wash his feet with her tears, and wiped them with the hair of her head, and kissed his feet and anointed (them) with the perfume.	*having an alabaster phial of very costly pure nard perfume. Breaking the alabaster phial she poured it over his head.*	*3 Mary therefore taking a pound of perfume, very expensive pure nard, anointed the feet of Jesus and wiped his feet with her hair and the house was filled with the odour of the perfume.*
8 And his disciples were irritated saying:	39 And the Pharisee who had invited him saw it and said in himself, saying: If this was the Prophet, he would surely recognize who and of what sort was the woman who is touching him, that she is a sinner.	*4 And there were some who were irritated among themselves and saying:*	*4 And Judas the Iscariot, one of his disciples, the one about to betray him, says:*
Why this waste? 9 For this could have been sold for a large sum and given to the poor.		*Why has this waste of perfume happened? 5 For this perfume could have been sold for above three hundred denarii and given to the poor; and they were angry with her.*	*5 Why was this perfume not sold for three hundred denarii and given to the poor? 6 Now he said this not because he cared about the poor, but because he was a thief, and having the begging-bag took what was dropped into it.*
	40 And Jesus answering said to him: Simon, I have something to tell you. And he says: Teacher, tell me. 41 There were two debtors of a certain creditor; the one owed five hundred denarii, and the other fifty. 42 Neither having means to pay back, he forgave both. Which of them therefore will love him more? 43 Simon answering said: I suppose the one to whom he forgave the more. And he said to him: You judged correctly.		
10 And Jesus knowing said to them:	44 And turning to the woman he said to Simon:	*6 And Jesus said:*	*7 Jesus therefore said:*
Why do you make trouble for the woman? For she has worked a good work for me;	Do you see this woman? I entered into your house, water for my feet you did not give; but she has washed my feet with tears and wiped them with her hair.	*Leave her; why do you make trouble for her? for she has worked a good work on me;*	*Leave her; that she may perform this (deed) for the day of my interment;*

MT 26:6-13	LK 7:36-50	MK 14:3-9	JN 12:1-8
11 For the poor you have with you always, but me you do not have always.	45 You gave me no kiss but she from the time I entered in has not stopped kissing my feet.	*7 For the poor you have with you always, but me you do not have always.*	*8 for the poor you have always with you, but me you do not have always.*
12 For when she poured this perfume over my body, she did it for my entombing.	46 You did not anoint my head with oil; but she has anointed my feet with perfume.	*8 She used what she had; she has anticipated anointing my body for the entombment.*	
13 Amen, I say to you: wherever this gospel shall be preached in the whole world, so too what she has done will be spoken of as a memorial of her.		*9 And Amen, I say to you; wherever this gospel shall be preached in the whole world, so also what she has done will be spoken of as a memorial of her.*	
	47 Thanks to this, I say to you, her many sins are forgiven, because she has loved much, For he loves little to whom little is forgiven.		
	48 And he said to her: Your sins are forgiven.		
	49 And the fellow-diners began to say in themselves: Who is this, who also forgives sins?		
	50 And he said to the woman: Your faith has saved you; go in peace.		

§96 The Ministering Women

MT	LK 8:1-3	MK	JN
	1 And it happened shortly after that he was journeying through city and village preaching and evangelizing the Kingdom of God, and the Twelve with him,		
	2 and some women, who had been healed of evil spirits and infirmities, Mary known as the Magdalene, from whom seven devils had gone out, 3 and Joanna wife of Chuza, Herod's steward, and Susanna, and many others, who ministered to them from their possessions.		
	(↓ §100)		

§97 Jesus' Entourage Upset

MT	LK	MK 3:20-21	JN
		(↑ §58)	
		20 And he comes into the house, and again the crowd comes	

MT	LK	MK 3:20-21		JN
		together, so that they are unable even to eat bread. 21 And when those with him heard, they went out to seize him; for they said: He is beside himself.		

§98 Blasphemy against the Spirit (§§119, 138, 215, 224)

MT 9:34	MT 12:24-26, 29, 31a, 32b	LK 11:15-18, 21-22; 12:10	MK 3:22-30	JN
34* But the Pharisees were saying:	*24 But the Pharisees heard and said:*	*15 But some of them said:*	22 And the Scribes who had come down from Jerusalem were saying:	
By the prince of the demons he casts out the demons.	*This one does not cast out the demons except by Beelzebul, prince of the demons.*	*By Beelzebul, the prince of the demons, he casts out the demons.*	He has Beelzebul, and: By the prince of the demons he casts out the demons.	
	(cf. 12:38; 16:1)			
	25 But knowing their thoughts Jesus said to them:	*16 And others tempting sought from him a sign from heaven.* *17 But knowing their intentions he said to them:*	23 And calling them up he said to them in parables: How can Satan cast out Satan?	
	(cf. 12:26)			
	Every kingdom divided over against itself comes to ruin and every city or house divided against itself will not stand.	*Every kingdom divided up against itself comes to ruin, and house against house* *falls.*	24 And if a kingdom is divided against itself, that kingdom cannot stand; 25 And if a house is divided against itself, that house will not be able to stand.	
	26 And if Satan casts out Satan he is divided against himself; how therefore shall his kingdom stand?	*18 And if Satan is divided up against himself how shall his kingdom stand?*	26 And if Satan has risen up against himself and is divided, he cannot stand, but has an end.	
	29 Or how can anyone enter into the mansion of the Mighty One and steal his property, unless he first tie up the Mighty One?	*21 When the Mighty One in full armour guards his own palace, his possessions are in peace.* *22 but when a Mightier One than he comes upon him and overcomes him, he takes away his armour on which he relied, and gives away his spoils.*	27 But no one can enter into the mansion of the Mighty One to plunder his property, unless he first tie up the Mighty One.	
	And then he will plunder his mansion.		And then he will plunder his mansion.	
	31a Wherefore I say to you, every sin and blasphemy shall be forgiven to men,	*12:10 And whoever shall say a word against the Son of Man it will be forgiven him,*	28 Amen, I say to you, that everything shall be forgiven to the sons of men, the sins and the blasphemies whatever they may	

MT 9:34

MT 12:24-26, 29, 31a, 32b

32b but whoever speaks against the Holy Spirit it will not be forgiven him, neither in this age, nor in the one to come.

LK 11:15-18, 21-22; 12:10

but to him who blasphemes against the Holy Spirit it will not be forgiven.

MK 3:22-30
blaspheme.
29 But whoever blasphemes against the Holy Spirit, has not forgiveness unto the age, but is guilty of an everlasting sin.
30 Because they said: He has an unclean spirit.

JN

§99 Jesus' Mother and Brothers (Mk) (§§108, 142)

MT 12:46-50
46 While he was yet speaking to the crowds, behold his mother and brothers stood outside seeking to speak to him.

47* And someone said to him: Behold your mother and your brothers

stand outside seeking to speak to you.
48 And he answering said to the one speaking to him:
Who is my mother and who are my brothers?
49 And stretching out his hand over his disciples he said:
Behold my mother and my brothers.
50 For whoever does the will of my Father in the heavens, he is my brother and sister and mother.

LK 8:19-21
19 Now there came along to him his mother and brothers

and they could not reach him because of the crowd.
20 And it was reported to him: Your mother and your brothers

stand outside wanting to see you.
21 And he answering said to them:

My mother and my brothers— these are those who hear and do the word of God.

MK 3:31-35
31 And his mother and his brothers came

and standing outside sent to him calling him.
32 And a crowd was sitting around him.

And they say to him:
Behold your mother and your brothers and your sisters*
outside seek you.
33 And answering he says to them:

Who is my mother, and my brothers?
34 And looking around at those sitting round him in a circle, he says:
See my mother and my brothers.
35 For whoever does the will of God,

this one is my brother and sister and mother.

JN

§100 Preaching in Parables (§143)

MT 13:1-3a

1 On that day Jesus going out of the house sat beside the sea.
2 And great crowds were assembled to him

so that he got into a boat and sat, and the whole crowd stood on the shore.

3a And he spoke many things to them in parables saying:

LK 8:4

(↑ §96)

4 And a great crowd coming together and people from every town making their way to him,

he said by a parable:

MK 4:1-2

1 And again he began to teach beside the sea;

and a very large crowd assembles to him,

so that he got into a boat and sat on the sea and the whole crowd was beside the sea upon the land.
2 And he began to teach them many things in parables, and to say to them in his teaching:

JN

MT 13:3b-9

3b Behold, the sower went out to sow,
4 and as he sowed some fell by the path

and the birds coming ate them up.
5 But others fell on the rocky patches
where they did not have much earth,
and at once they shot up because they had no
depth of earth;
6 And the sun rising, they were scorched,
and through not having a root they withered
up.
7 And others fell on the thorns
and the thorns rose up and choked them.

8 And others fell on the good soil
and yielded a crop,

the one a hundred, and another sixty, and
another thirty.
9 He that has ears to hear, let him hear.

LK 8:5-8

5 The sower went out to sow his seed,
and as he sowed it fell by the path and was
trodden down
and the birds of the sky ate it up.
6 And another fell on the rock,

and growing up

it withered up through not having moisture.

7 And another fell in the midst of thorns
and the thorns growing up choked it.

8 And another fell on the right soil
and growing up produced a crop,

a hundredfold.

Saying these things he cried: He that has ears
to hear, let him hear.

MK 4:3-9

3 Listen: Behold, the sower went out to sow.
4 And it happened as he sowed, some fell by
the path
and the birds came and ate it up.
5 And other some fell on the rocky patch,
where it did not have much earth,
and at once it shot up because it had no depth
of earth;
6 And when the sun rose it was scorched
and through not having a root it withered up.

7 And other some fell into the thorns
and the thorns rose up and suffocated it and it
did not give fruit.
8 And others fell on the good soil
and rising up and increasing, yielded a crop,
and they bore,
one thirty and one sixty and one a hundred.

9 And he said: Who has ears to hear, let him
hear.

JN

§102 Reason for Parables (§145)

MT 13:10-13

10 And the disciples came up and said to him:

Why do you speak to them in parables?
11 And he answering said to them:
To you it has been given to know the
mysteries of the Kingdom of the Heavens,
but to those it has not been given.

12 For he who has, it shall be given to him,
and he shall abound;
but he who has not, that also which he has
shall be taken away from him.
13 I speak therefore to them in parables,
because seeing they do not see,
and hearing they do not hear, nor do they take
it in.

LK 8:9-10

9 And his disciples questioned him:

What may this parable be?
10 But he said:
To you it has been given to know the
mysteries of the Kingdom of God,
but to the others in parables,

(8:18)

that seeing they may not see,
and hearing they may not take it in.

MK 4:10-12

10 And when he was alone, those around him
together with the Twelve asked him
(about) the parables.
11 And he began to say to them:
To you has been given the mystery of the
Kingdom of God,
but to those outside all things are done in
parables,

(4:25)

12 that seeing they may see and not perceive,
and hearing they may hear and not take it in,

lest they turn back and it be forgiven them.

JN

MT 13:18-23

18 Hear you therefore the parable of the sower.

19 Everyone hearing the word of the Kingdom and not taking it in,
the Evil One comes and snatches what was sown in his heart;

this is what is sown on the path.
20 And the one sown on the rocky patches,

this is the one who hears the word,
and at once with joy accepts it;
21 but he has no root in himself, but is temporary,
and when suffering or persecution happens on account of the word
he is scandalized.
22 And the one sown among the thorns,
this is the one who hears the word,
and the care of this world, and the deceitfulness of riches

choke the word, and it is rendered fruitless.

23 But the one sown upon the good soil,
this is the one who hears the word and grasps it,
who indeed brings forth fruit and makes the one a hundred, and another sixty, and another thirty.

LK 8:11-15

11 Now the parable of the sower is this.

The seed is the word of God.
12 And the ones on the path are the hearers;

then the devil comes and takes away the word from their heart, lest having come to believe they should be saved.

13 And the ones on the rock

are the ones who when they hear, with joy receive the word; and these have no root, they believe temporarily, and in time of trial

they apostatize.
14 And what fell into the thorns, these are the ones who have heard, and as they go along, by cares and riches and pleasures of life

are choked, and do not mature.

15 But that on the good soil, these are the ones who in a good and upright heart, having heard the word, hold it fast and bring forth fruit in endurance.

MK 4:13-20

13 And he says to them:
Do you not know this parable?
and how will you know all the parables?
14. The sower sows the word.
15 And the ones on the path are the ones where the word is sown and when they hear, at once Satan comes and takes away the word that was sown in them.

16 And likewise the ones sown on the rocky patches
are the ones who when they hear the word at once with joy accept it;
17 and they have no root in themselves, but they are temporary;
then when suffering or persecution happens on account of the word
they are at once scandalized.
18 And others are the ones sown among the thorns, these are the ones who have heard the word,
19 and, the cares of the world and the deceitfulness of riches and the cravings for the rest intervening,
choke the word and it is rendered fruitless.
20 And the ones sown on the really good soil are those who hear the word and embrace it,

and bring forth fruit, one thirty, and one sixty, and one a hundred.

JN

§104 Moral of the Sower (§§62, 81, 101, 144, 219)

MT 5:15; 13:9; 7:2b; 13:12

5:15 Nor do they light a lamp and put it under the measure,

but upon the lampstand,

and it shines for all who are in the house.

LK 8:16-18

16 And no one kindling a lamp hides it with a vessel

nor puts it under a bed, but puts it on the lampstand,

so that they who enter may see the light.

LK 11:33; 8:8b; 6:38b

33 No one kindling a lamp puts it into a cellar nor under the measure,

but upon the lampstand

so that they who enter may see the light.

MK 4:21-25
21 And he said to them:
Surely the lamp does not come in order to be put under the measure
or under the bed?
(is it) not that it be put on the lampstand?

JN

78

MT 5:15; 13:9; 7:2b; 13:12	LK 8:16-18	LK 11:33; 8:8b; 6:38b	MK 4:21-25	JN
(10:26; Lk. 12:2; §§126, 223)	17 For there is nothing hidden that will not become manifest, nor anything secret which will not be known, and come to be manifest.	**(12:2= Mt. 10:26; §§223, 126)**	22 For there is nothing whatever hidden that will not be manifested; nor that was secret, but will come to be manifest.	
13:9 He who has ears to hear let him hear.	18a See therefore how you hear,	*8:8b He who has ears to hear let him hear.*	23 If anyone has ears to hear let him hear. 24 And he said to them; Watch what you hear.	
7:2b in the measure you measure, it will be measured to you.		*6:38b For in the measure you measure it will be measured back to you.*	In the measure you measure, it will be measured to you and it will be added to you.	
13:12 For he who has, it shall be given to him, and he shall abound; *but he who has not, that also which he has will be taken from him.*	for whoever has, it will be given to him; and whoever does not have, that also which he thinks he has will be taken from him **(cf. 19:26= Mt. 25:29).** **(↓§108)**	**(cf. 19:26)**	25 For he who has, it will be given to him: and he who has not, that also which he has will be taken from him.	

§105 The Self-Developing Seed

MT	LK	MK 4:26-29		JN
(cf. 13: 24-30)		26 And he said: Thus is the Kingdom of God, as if a man were to cast the seed upon the earth, 27 and should sleep and get up night and day, and the seed should sprout and lengthen, how he knows not. 28 Of its own accord the earth bears a crop, first a blade, then an ear, then full corn in the ear. 29 And when the crop allows, immediately he sends the sickle because the harvest has come.		

§106 The Mustard Seed (Mk) (§§149, 239)

MT 13:31-32	LK 13:18-19	MK 4:30-32	JN
31 Another parable he put before them saying: *The Kingdom of the Heavens is like*	*18 Therefore he used to say:* *Like to what is the Kingdom of God?* *And to what shall I liken it?*	30 And he used to say: How may we liken the Kingdom of God? Or in what parable may we put it?	

MT 13:31-32	LK 13:18-19	MK 4:30-32	JN
a grain of mustard which a man took and sowed in his field, 32 which is indeed smaller than all the seeds; but when it is grown is greater than the plants and becomes a tree, so that the birds of the sky come and roost on its branches.	19 It is like a grain of mustard which a man took and sowed in his own garden, and it grew and became a great tree, and the birds of the sky roosted on its branches.	31 As a grain of mustard, which when it is sowed upon the earth— being smaller than all the seeds that are on the earth— 32 and when it is sowed, it rises up and becomes greater than all the plants and produces great branches, so that under its shade the birds of the sky are able to roost.	

§107 Jesus' Use of Parables (§151)

MT 13:34-35	LK	MK 4:33-34	JN
34 Jesus spoke all these things in parables to the crowds, and without a parable he used not to speak to them, 35 so that the word spoken through the prophet might be fulfilled, saying: I will open my mouth in parables. I will utter things that have been hidden from the foundation of the world*.		33 And with many such like parables he used to speak the word to them, according as they were able to hear; 34 but without a parable he used not to speak to them, but privately he explained everything to his own disciples. (↓ §111)	

§108 Jesus' Mother and Brothers (Lk) (§§99, 142)

MT 12:46-50	LK 8:19-21	MK 3:31-35	JN
46 While he was yet speaking to the crowds, behold his mother and brothers stood outside seeking to speak to him. 47* And someone said to him: Behold your mother and your brothers stand outside seeking to speak to you. 48 And he answering said to the one speaking to him: Who is my mother and who are my brothers? 49 And stretching out his hand over his	(↑ §104) 19 Now there came along to him his mother and brothers and they could not reach him because of the crowd. 20 And it was reported to him; Your mother and your brothers stand outside wanting to see you. 21 And he answering said to them:	31 And his mother and his brothers come and standing outside sent to him calling him. 32 And a crowd was sitting around him. And they say to him: Behold your mother and your brothers and your sisters* outside seek you. 33 And answering he says to them: Who is my mother and my brothers? 34 And looking around at those sitting round	

MT 12:46-50	LK 8:19-21	MK 3:31-35	JN
disciples he said:		*him in a circle, he says:*	
Behold my mother and my brothers.	**My mother and my brothers—**	**See my mother and my brothers.**	
50 For whoever does the will of my Father in the heavens,	*these are those who hear and do the word of God.*	*35 For whoever does the will of God,*	
he is my brother and sister and mother.	(↓§112)	*this one is my brother and sister and mother.*	

§109 Peter's Mother-in-Law Healed (§43)

MT 8:14-15	LK 4:38-39	MK 1:29-31	JN
(↑ §91)			
14 And Jesus coming into the house of Peter,	*38 Now rising up from the synagogue he entered into the house of Simon.*	*29 And at once going out of the synagogue he went into the house of Simon and Andrew with James and John.*	
saw his mother-in-law prostrate and fevered;	*But Simon's mother-in-law was in the grip of a high fever and they asked him about her.*	*30 But Simon's mother-in-law lay fevered,*	
15 And he touched her hand	*39 And standing by over her he rebuked the fever,*	*and at once they speak to him about her.* *31 And approaching he got her up grasping her hand,*	
and the fever left her. And she got up and served them.	*and it left her.* *And at once rising up she served them.*	*and the fever left her,* *and she served them.*	

§110 Healings in the Evening (§44)

MT 8:16-17	LK 4:40-41	MK 1:32-34	JN
16 Now when evening came,	*40 Now as the sun was setting,*	*32 Now when evening came, when the sun had set,*	
they carried up to him many demon-possessed,	*all those who had sick with various ills brought them to him.*	*they carried to him all who were ill and the demon-possessed.* *33 And the whole town was gathered together at the door,*	
and he cast out the spirits with a word and all who were ill he healed,	*And laying his hands upon each one of them he healed them.* *41 And demons also went out from many shouting and saying: You are the Son of God. And rebuking (them) he would not let them speak,*	*34 and he healed many who were ill with various diseases, and he cast out many demons.* *And he did not permit the demons to speak,*	
17 in order that what had been spoken by Isaiah the prophet might be fulfilled saying: He bore our infirmities, and carried our ills **(Is. 53:4, 11).**	*because they knew he was the Christ.*	*because they knew him.*	

MT 8:18-22 | LK 9:57-60 | MK 4:35 | JN

(↑ §107)

18 And Jesus seeing large crowds about him gave orders to go off to the other side.
19 And one Scribe coming up said to him:

Teacher, I will follow you wherever you go.
20 And Jesus says to him:
The foxes have holes and the birds of the sky nests,
but the Son of Man has nowhere to lay his head.

21 And another of his disciples said to him:
Lord, allow me first to go off and bury my father.
22 And Jesus says to him:
Follow me, and let the dead bury their own dead.

(cf. 8:22b below)

57 And as they were going on the way, someone said to him:
I will follow you wherever you go, Lord.
58 And Jesus said to him:
The foxes have holes and the birds of the sky nests,
but the Son of Man has nowhere to lay his head.
59 And he said to another: Follow me.
And he said:
Lord, allow me first to go off to bury my father.
60 And he said to him:
Let the dead bury their own dead. But do you go off, and announce the Kingdom of God.

35 And he says to them on that day as evening had come: Let us go across to the other side.

§112 Stilling of the Storm

MT 8:23-27 | LK 8:22-25 | MK 4:36-41 | JN

(↑ §108)

23 And when he got into the boat his disciples followed him.

(8:18)

24 And lo a great quaking occurred in the sea, so that the boat was covered by the waves.

But he continued to sleep.

25 And coming over, his disciples roused him saying:
Lord, help, we are perishing.

26 And he says to them: Why are you fearful, men of little faith?
Then rising he rebuked the winds and the sea,

and there came a great calm.

22 Now it happened on one of the days that he got into a boat and his disciples,

and he said to them: Let us go across to the other side of the lake. And they put out.
23 And while they were sailing he fell asleep. And a storm of wind came down on the lake and they were filling up and were in danger.

24 And coming over they roused him up saying:
Master, Master, we are perishing.

(cf. v. 25)

And rising up he rebuked the wind and the agitation of the water,
and they ceased and there came a calm.

36 And leaving the crowd they take him along, as he was, in the boat, and other boats were with him.

(4:35)

37 And a great storm of wind occurred and the waves struck upon the boat so that the boat was now being filled.
38 And he was in the stern sleeping on the cushion.
And they rouse him and say to him:

Teacher, does it not matter to you that we are perishing?

(cf. v. 40)

39 And rising up he rebuked the wind and said to the sea: Be silent and shut up!
And the wind stopped and there came a great calm.

MT 8:23-27	LK 8:22-25	MK 4:36-41	JN
	25 And he said to them: Where is your faith?	40 And he said to them: Why are you thus fearful? How have you not faith?	
27 And the men marvelled saying:	And fearing they marvelled saying to one another:	41 And they feared a great fear, and they said to one another:	
What sort (of man) is this for both the winds and the sea obey him?	Who then is this, for he commands the winds and the water and they obey him?	Who then is this, for both the wind and the sea obey him?	

§113 The Possessed at Gadara (Gerasa)

MT 8:28-34	LK 8:26-39	MK 5:1-20	JN
28 And when he came to the other side, to the region of the Gadarenes,*	26 And they sailed down to the region of the Gerasenes,* which is opposite to Galilee.	1 And they came to the other side of the sea, to the region of the Gerasenes.*	
there met him two men possessed by demons, coming out from the tombs,	27 And as he went out on to the land there met him a certain man from the town having demons; and for a considerable time he had not worn a tunic	2 And as he went out of the boat, there met him immediately from the tombs a man with an unclean spirit,	
	and had not stayed in a house but in the tombs.	3 who had his dwelling place in the tombs,	
		and no one any more was able to bind him with a chain. 4 Because he had many times been bound with fetters and he had burst the fetters and broken the chains,	
exceedingly fierce, so that no one could go along by that way.		and nobody was able to subdue him.	
		5 And continuously by night and day he was in the tombs crying out and cutting himself with stones.	
29 And behold they cried saying:	28 And seeing Jesus, crying out he prostrated to him and with a loud voice said:	6 And seeing Jesus from a distance he ran and worshipped him, 7 and crying out with a loud voice says:	
What have we to do with you, O Son of God?	What have we to do with you, O Jesus, Son of the Most High?	What have we to do with you, O Jesus, Son of God, the Most High?	
Have you come here before the time to torture us?	I beseech you, do not torture me.	I adjure you by God, do not torture me.	
	29 For he had commanded the unclean spirit to come out of the man. Because for long periods it had seized him, and under guard he was bound with chains and fetters, and breaking up the chains he was driven by the demon into the deserts.	8 For he had said to him: O unclean spirit, come out of the man.	
	30 And Jesus questioned him: What is your	9 And he questioned him: What (is) your	

MT 8:28-34

LK 8:26-39

MK 5:1-20

	name?	name?
	And he said: Legion, because many devils had entered into him.	And he says to him: My name is Legion because we are many.
	31 And they begged him not to command them to go off into the abyss.	10 And he begged him strongly not to send them out of the region.
30 Now some way off from them was a herd of many swine grazing.	32 Now there was in that place a considerable herd of swine grazing on the mountain;	11 Now there was in that place upon the mountain a large herd of swine grazing;
31 And the demons begged him saying: If you cast us out, send us into the herd of swine.	and they begged him to allow them to enter into them.	12 And they begged him saying: Send us into the swine, that we may enter into them.
32 And he said to them: Go. And they coming out went off into the swine;	And he allowed them. 33 And the demons coming out of the man, entered into the swine,	13 And he allowed them. And the unclean spirits coming out entered into the swine,
and lo the whole herd rushed down the precipice into the sea, and died in the waters.	and the herd rushed down the precipice into the lake and were drowned.	and the herd rushed down the precipice into the sea, about two thousand, and drowned in the sea.
33 Now the herdsmen fled;	34 Now the herdsmen seeing what had happened fled	14 And they that herded them fled
and going off into the city they reported everything and the affair of the man possessed by demons.	and reported to the city and to the farms.	and reported to the city and to the farms;
34 And lo the whole city went out	35 And they went out to see what had happened,	and they came to see what it was that had happened.
to meet Jesus, and having seen (him)	and they came to Jesus and they found sitting the man from whom the demons had gone out,	15 And they come to Jesus and behold the demon-possessed man sitting,
	fully clothed and in his right mind, at the feet of Jesus, and they were afraid.	fully clothed and in his right mind, who had had the Legion, and they were afraid.
	36 And those who saw how the demon-possessed man had been saved reported to them.	16 And those who saw how it had happened to the demon-possessed man explained to them, and about the swine.
they begged him	37 And the whole multitude of the neighbourhood of the Gerasenes begged him	17 And they began to beg him
to pass on from their territories.	to depart from them, for they were gripped with a great fear; and he, getting into the boat returned.	to depart from their territories.
	38 But the man from whom he had expelled the demons appealed to him to be with him; but he discharged him saying:	18 And as he was getting into the boat, the demon-possessed man begged him that he might be with him.
	39 Return into your house and explain the things that God did to you.	19 But he did not permit him, but says to him: Go back into your house to your own people, and report to them the things that the Lord has done to you and how he pitied you.
	And he went off through the whole town preaching what Jesus had done for him.	20 And he went off and began to preach in the Decapolis what Jesus had done for him, and all marvelled.
	(↓ §117)	(↓ §117)

MT 9:1-8

1 And going up into a boat he crossed over and came to his own city.

2 And behold they began to bring to him a paralytic lying on a bed.

And Jesus seeing their faith said to the paralytic:
Take heart, child, your sins are forgiven.
3 And behold some of the Scribes said in themselves:
This man is blaspheming.

4 And Jesus knowing
their thoughts
said:
Why do you think evil things in your hearts?

5 For which is easier,
to say: Your sins are forgiven,
or to say: Get up and walk?

6 But that you may know that the Son of Man has authority on earth to forgive sins—
then he says to the paralytic:
Get up, take away your bed

and go off into your house.
7 And getting up

he went back to his house.

LK 5:17-26

17 And it happened on one of the days,

that he was teaching, and there were seated Pharisees and law-teachers who had come from every village of Galilee and Judea and Jerusalem.
And the power of the Lord was for him to heal.

18 And behold men carrying
on a bed a man who had been paralysed,
and they tried to bring him in and put him down before him.
19 And not finding how to carry him in because of the crowd,
going up on to the roof, through the tiles

they let him down together with the stretcher

into the middle in front of Jesus.
20 And seeing their faith he said:

O man, your sins have been forgiven you.
21 And the Scribes began to argue and the Pharisees, saying:
Who is this who speaks blasphemies?

Who can forgive sins but God alone?
22 And Jesus perceiving
their questionings
answering said to them:
Why do you question in your hearts?

23 Which is easier,
to say, Your sins have been forgiven you,
or to say: Get up and walk?

24 But that you may know that the Son of Man has authority on earth to forgive sins;—
he said to the paralytic:
I say to you, Get up and taking away your stretcher,
go into your house.
25 And immediately rising in front of all,
taking up what he had been lying on,
he went back to his house glorifying God.

MK 2:1-12   JN

1 And again entering into Capharnaum after some days it was reported that he was at home.

2 And many were gathered together so that there was no longer room not even at the door, and he was speaking to them the word.
3 And they come carrying to him
a paralytic carried by four.

4 And not being able to carry him to him because of the crowd,
they unroofed the roof where he was, and digging through
they lower the pallet on which the paralytic was lying.

5 And Jesus seeing their faith says to the paralytic:
Child, your sins are forgiven.
6 And some of the Scribes were sitting there and arguing in their hearts:
7 Why does this (man) speak thus? He is blaspheming!
Who can forgive sins but one, God?
8 And at once Jesus, perceiving in his spirit that they were thus questioning in themselves, says to them:
Why do you question these things in your hearts?
9 Which is easier,
to say to the paralytic: Your sins are forgiven,
or to say: Get up and take away your pallet and walk?
10 But that you may know that the Son of Man has authority to forgive sins on earth,—
he says to the paralytic:
11 I say to you, Get up, and take away your pallet
and go off into your house.
12 And he got up
and at once taking up the pallet,
he went out in front of all,

MT 9:1-8	LK 5:17-26	MK 2:1-12	JN
8 And the crowds when they saw were afraid and glorified God who gave such authority to men.	26 And amazement seized everyone and they glorified God, and were filled with fear saying: We have seen incredible things to-day.	so that all were amazed and glorified God, saying: We have never seen the like ever.	

§115 Call of Matthew (§52)

MT 9:9-13	LK 5:27-32	MK 2:13-17	JN
9 And Jesus passing along from there saw a man called Matthew seated at the custom house, and he says to him: Follow me. And getting up he followed him. 10 And it happened that while he reclined at table in the house, and behold many tax-collectors and sinners came and reclined together with Jesus and his disciples. 11 And the Pharisees seeing (it) said to his disciples: Why does your teacher eat with tax-collectors and sinners? 12 But he hearing said to them: The strong have no need of a healer, but those who are ill. 13 But go and learn what this means: I desire mercy and not sacrifice (Ho. 6:6). For I did not come to call the just but sinners to repentance.*	27 And after these things he went out and he observed a tax-collector by name Levi, seated at the custom house, and he said to him: Follow me. 28 And leaving all things getting up he began to follow him. 29 And Levi made a great feast for him in his house; and there was a great crowd of tax-collectors and others, who were sitting with them. 30 And the Pharisees and their Scribes grumbled saying to his disciples: Why do you eat and drink with tax-collectors and sinners? 31 And Jesus answering said to them: The healthy have no need of a healer but those who are ill. 32 For I have not come to call the just but sinners to repentance.	13 And he went out again beside the sea; and the whole crowd came to him, and he began to teach them. 14 And passing by, he saw Levi the (son) of Alphaeus seated at the custom house, and he says to him: Follow me. And getting up he followed him. 15 And he comes and sits down at table in his house, and many tax-collectors and sinners came and reclined together with Jesus and his disciples. For they were many and they followed him. 16 And the Scribes of the Pharisees seeing that he was eating with the sinners and tax-collectors said to his disciples: He eats and drinks with tax-collectors and sinners! 17 And Jesus hearing says to them: The strong have no need of a healer but those who are ill. I did not come to call the just but sinners to repentance.*	

§116 A Question about Fasting (§53)

MT 9:14-17	LK 5:33-39	MK 2:18-22	JN
14 Then the disciples of John come up to him, saying: Why do we and the Pharisees fast frequently,	33 And they said to him: Why do the disciples of John fast often and make prayers, in the same way as the	18 And the disciples of John and the Pharisees were fasting and come and say to him: Why do the disciples of John and the disciples of the Pharisees fast,	

MT 9:14-17	LK 5:33-39	MK 2:18-22	JN
but your disciples do not fast?	*Pharisees also,*	*but your disciples do not fast?*	
15 And Jesus said to them:	*but yours eat and drink?*	*19 And Jesus said to them:*	
Can the sons of the bride-chamber mourn, as long as the bridegroom is with them?	*34 But Jesus said to them:* *Can you make the sons of the bride-chamber fast, while the bridegroom is with them?*	*Can the sons of the bride-chamber fast, while the bridegroom is with them? During whatever time they have the bridegroom with them they cannot fast.*	
But days will come when the bridegroom will be taken away from them, and then they will fast.	*35 But indeed days will come when the bridegroom will be taken away from them, then they will fast in those days.*	*20 But days will come when the bridegroom will be taken away from them, and then they will fast in that day.*	
	36 And he spoke also a parable to them:		
16 Now no one imposes a piece of unfulled cloth on an old garment, for it will take away its fullness from the garment,	*No one tearing a piece from a new garment imposes (it) on an old garment; otherwise, it will both tear the new and the piece that is from the new will not match the old.*	*21 No one sews a piece of unfulled cloth on an old garment; otherwise, it will take the fullness from it—the new from the old—*	
and a worse tear occurs.		*and a worse tear occurs.*	
17 Nor do they put new wine into old skins; otherwise, the skins burst, and the wine is spilt, and the skins are lost.	*37 And no one puts new wine into old skins; otherwise, the new wine will burst the skins, and itself will be spilt and the skins will be lost.*	*22 And no one puts new wine into old skins; otherwise, the wine will burst the skins, and the wine is lost, and the skins.*	
But they put new wine into new skins, and both are preserved.	*38 But new wine is to be put into new skins, and both are preserved.*	*But new wine (is) to be put into new skins.*	
	39 And no one drinking old immediately wants new, for he says: The old is better.		

§117 Raising of Jairus' Daughter

MT 9:18-26	LK 8:40-56	MK 5:21-43	JN
	(↑ §113)	(↑ §113)	
18 While he was yet speaking these things to them,	40 Now on Jesus' return	21 And when Jesus had crossed over again in the boat to the other side,	
	the crowd received him; for they were all waiting for him.	a great crowd gathered to him. and he was by the sea.	
behold a certain ruler coming up,	41 And behold, a man came, whose name was Jairus, and this (man) was a ruler of the synagogue;	22 And a certain one of the synagogue rulers comes, by name Jairus,	
	and falling at Jesus' feet he begged him to enter into his house,		
knelt to him	42 because he had an only child, a daughter, about twelve years old, and she was about to die.	and seeing him falls at his feet, 23 and begs him earnestly,	
saying: My daughter has just died.		saying: My little daughter is in extremity,	
But come and lay your hand upon her, and she will be saved.		would you come and lay hands upon her, that she may be saved and live?	
19 And rising up Jesus followed him, and his	And as he went off the crowds pressed upon	24 And he went with him. And a great crowd	

MT 9:18-26	LK 8:40-56	MK 5:21-43	JN
disciples.	him.	followed him, and thronged him.	

MT 9:18-26

disciples.
20 And behold a woman who for twelve years had had a haemorrhage

coming up behind touched the hem of his garment;
21 for she said to herself: If only I touch his garment, I shall be saved.

22 And Jesus turning

and seeing her said:
Take heart, O daughter; your faith has saved you.
And the woman was saved from that hour.

23 And Jesus coming into the house of the ruler,

LK 8:40-56

him.
43 And a woman having a flow of blood for twelve years past,
who having spent her whole fortune on doctors
could not be cured by anyone,

44 coming up behind touched the hem of his garment.

And immediately the flow of her blood stopped.

45 And Jesus said:

Who was it who touched me?
But when all denied it Peter and those with him said:
Master, the crowds surround and jostle you; and you say: Who is it who touched me?
46 But Jesus said: Someone touched me, for I know that power has gone out from me.

47 And the woman seeing that she was not hidden,
trembling came and prostrating to him

declared before all the people the reason why she touched him and how she was at once healed.
48 And he said to her:
Daughter, your faith has saved you; go in peace.

49 While he was yet speaking there comes someone from the synagogue ruler saying:
Your daughter has died; do not bother the teacher further.
50 But Jesus hearing answered him:

Fear not; only believe and she will be saved.
51 And coming to the house

he did not permit any to enter with him except Peter and John and James, and the father of

MK 5:21-43

followed him, and thronged him.
25 And a woman having a flow of blood for twelve years,
26 and having suffered much from many doctors and spent all she had,
and profited nothing, but having rather got worse,
27 hearing the things about Jesus,
coming in the crowd behind, touched his garment;
28 for she said: If I touch even his garments, I shall be saved.
29 And at once the fountain of her blood dried up, and she knew in her body that she was cured from the affliction.
30 And immediately Jesus perceiving in himself the going forth of power out of himself, turning round in the crowd he said:
Who touched my garments?
31 And his disciples said to him:

Do you see the crowd thronging you, and you say: Who touched me?

32 And he began to look around to see the one who had done it.
33 And the woman

in fear and trembling knowing what had happened to her came and prostrated to him, and told him the whole truth.

34 And he said to her:
Daughter, your faith has saved you; go back in peace,
and be whole from your affliction.
35 While he was yet speaking they come from the synagogue ruler saying: Your daughter is dead; why bother the teacher further?

36 But Jesus overhearing the message spoken, says to the synagogue ruler:
Fear not; only go on believing.
37 And

he did not permit anyone to follow along with him except Peter and James and John the

JN

MT 9:18-26	LK 8:40-56	MK 5:21-43	JN
and seeing the flute-players and the crowd in an uproar,	the girl and the mother. 52 And all were weeping and bewailing her.	brother of James. 38 And they come to the house of the synagogue-ruler, and he beholds an uproar and weeping and much lamenting. 39 And entering he says to them: Why are you in an uproar and are weeping? The child is not dead, but is asleep.	
24 said: Get out, for the little maid is not dead but is asleep. And they laughed at him.	But he said: Do not weep; she is not dead, but is asleep. 53 And they laughed at him, knowing that she was dead. 54 But he	40 And they laughed at him.	
25 And when the crowd had been excluded, going in		But having excluded them all, he brings the father of the child, and the mother and those with him, and goes into where the child was;	
he grasped her hand,	grasping her hand called, saying: Girl, get up.	41 and grasping the child's hand he says to her: Talitha koum, which means: Little maid, I say to you, Get up.	
and the little maid got up.	55 And her spirit returned, and she stood up at once. And he ordered that she be given (something) to eat. 56 And her parents were amazed.	42 And at once the little maid stood up and walked; for she was twelve years old. **(v. 43)** And at once they were amazed with a great amazement.	
	But he commanded them not to tell anyone what had happened.	43 And he strictly charged them that no one should know it, and he said she was to be given (something) to eat.	
26 And the report of this went out into all that land.	(↓ §122)	(↓ §120)	

§118 Healing of Two Blind Men (cf. §282)

MT 9:27-31	LK	MK	JN
27 And as Jesus passed along from there, two blind men followed him, crying out and saying: Have pity on us, Son of David. 28 And as he was going into the house the blind men came up to him, and Jesus says to them: Do you believe that I can do this thing? They say to him: Yes, Lord. 29 Then he touched their eyes, saying: Be it done to you, according to your faith. 30 And their eyes were opened. And Jesus charged them strongly saying: Look, let nobody know. 31 But they going out made him known in all that land.	(cf. 18: 35f)	(cf. 10: 46-52)	

§119 Healing of a Dumb Demoniac (§§98, 138, 215)

MT 9:32-34	MT 12:22-24	LK 11:14-15	MK 3:22	JN
32 And as they were going out, behold they brought him a dumb man, demon-possessed.	*22 Then there was brought to him one blind and dumb, demon-possessed,*	*14 And he was casting out a demon and it was dumb.*		
33 And the demon being cast out the dumb man spoke.	*and he healed him so that the dumb man spoke and saw.*	*And it happened, when the demon had gone out, that the dumb man spoke,*		
And the crowds marvelled saying:	*23 And all the crowds were amazed and said:*	*and the crowds marvelled.*		
Never in Israel has such a thing been seen.	*Surely this one is the Son of David.*			
34* But the Pharisees were saying:	*24 But the Pharisees heard and said:*	*15 But some of them said:*	22 And the scribes who had come down from Jerusalem were saying:	
By the prince of the demons he casts out the demons.	*This (man) does not cast out the demons except by Beelzebul prince of the demons.*	*By Beelzebul the prince of the demons he casts out the demons.*	He has Beelzebul, and: By the prince of the demons he casts out the demons.	
(↓ §121)				

§120 Visit to Nazareth (Mk) (§§38, 157)

MT 13:53-58	LK 4:16, 22-24, 28-30	MK 6:1-6a	JN
		(↑ §117)	
53 And it happened, when Jesus had ended these parables, he passed thence,		1 And he went out from there	
54 and coming into his own home-town,	*16 And he came into Nazareth, where he had been nurtured.*	and comes into his own hometown and his disciples follow him.	
he was teaching them in their synagogue,	*And according to his custom he entered into the synagogue on the Sabbath-day and rose up to read.*	2 And when the Sabbath came he began to teach in the synagogue;	
so that they were amazed and said:	*22 And all witnessed to him and marvelled at the words of grace that came from his mouth, and they said:*	and the many hearers were amazed, saying:	
Whence (has) this man this wisdom		Whence (has) this man these things? And what is the wisdom given to this man?	
and these mighty deeds?		And such mighty deeds done by his hands?	
55 Is he not the son of the carpenter?	*Is he not the son of Joseph?*	3 Is he not the carpenter,	
Is not his mother called Mary,		the son of Mary,	
and his brothers, James and Joseph* and Simon and Jude?		and brother of James and Joses* and Jude and Simon?	
56 And his sisters, are they not all with us?		And are not his sisters here with us?	
Whence therefore has this man all these things?			
57 And they were scandalized over him.		And they were scandalized over him.	
	23 And he said to them:		

MT 13:53-58	LK 4:16, 22-24, 28-30	MK 6:1-6a	JN
	Surely you will say to me this parable: Physician, heal thyself; whatever we have heard done in Capharnaum, do also here in your own hometown.		
But Jesus said to them: A prophet is not without honour save in his own hometown and in his own house.	*24 And he said: Amen I say to you that no prophet is acceptable in his native place.*	4 And Jesus said to them: A prophet is not without honour save in his own hometown, and among his own relatives and in his own house.	
	28 And all in the synagogue were filled with anger when they heard these things, 29 and rising they threw him out of the town, and led him up to the brow of the mountain, on which the town was built, in order to hurl him down. 30 But he passing through their midst went on.		
58 And he did not do there many mighty deeds,		5 And he was unable to do any mighty deed there, save lying hands on a few sick he healed them.	
because of their unbelief.		6a And he marvelled because of their unbelief.	

§121 A Summary of Jesus' Activity (§204)

MT 9:35-38	LK 10:2	MK 6:6b	JN
(↑ §119)			
35 And Jesus journeyed around all the towns and villages teaching in their synagogues and preaching the gospel of the Kingdom and healing every illness and every weakness (cf. 4:23).	(cf. 8:1)	6b And he journeyed around the villages in a circuit, teaching.	
36 And seeing the crowds he took pity on them, for they were distressed and dejected like sheep not having a shepherd.			
37 Then he says to his disciples: The harvest is great indeed, but the workers few;	*2 Then he said to them: The harvest is great indeed, but the workers few.*		
38 Beg therefore the Lord of the harvest to put forth workers into his harvest.	*Beg therefore the lord of the harvest to put forth workers into his harvest.*		

§122 Commissioning of the Twelve

MT 10:1	LK 9:1	MK 6:7	JN
	(↑ §117)		
1 And having summoned his twelve disciples,	1 And having called together the twelve apostles	7 And he summons the Twelve and began to send them two by two	
he gave them authority (over) unclean spirits, so as to cast them out, and to heal every illness and every weakness.	he gave them power and authority over all the demons, and to heal illnesses.	and gave them authority (over) the unclean spirits.	
		(cf. 6:13)	
	(↓ §124)	(↓ §124)	

§123 The Names of the Twelve (Mt) (§§56, 58)

MT 10:2-4	LK 6:13b-16	MK 3:14-19	JN	AC 1:13
2 Now the names of the twelve apostles are these:	*13b and choosing from them twelve, whom he also named Apostles,*	*14 And he made twelve, whom also he named Apostles, to be with him and to send them to preach, 15 and to have power to cast out the demons. 16 And he made the Twelve,*		*13 And when they entered they went up to the Upper Room, where there were waiting*
first Simon who is called Peter,	*14 Simon whom he also named Peter,*	*and he imposed on Simon the name Peter,*		*Peter*
and Andrew his brother, and James the (son) of Zebedee, and John his brother,	*and Andrew his brother, and James and John,*	*17 and James the (son) of Zebedee, and John the brother of James, and he imposed on them the name Boanerges, that is, Sons of Thunder, 18 and Andrew,*		*and John and James*
3 Philip and Bartholomew Thomas and Matthew the tax-collector, James the (son) of Alphaeus, and Thaddeus,* 4 Simon the Cananean, and Judas the Iscariot, who was also his betrayer.	*and Philip and Bartholomew, 15 and Matthew and Thomas, and James of Alphaeus, and Simon who is called Zealot, 16 and Jude of James, and Judas Iscarioth who became the traitor.*	*and Philip and Bartholomew and Matthew and Thomas, and James the (son) of Alphaeus, and Thaddeus and Simon the Cananean, 19 and Judas Iscarioth who also betrayed him.*		*and Andrew Philip and Thomas, Bartholomew and Matthew, James of Alphaeus, and Simon the Zealot and Jude of James.*

§124 Missionary Discourse (§§132, 204)

MT 10:5-15	LK 9:2-5	LK 10:9, 4, 7c, 5-6, 10-12	MK 6:8-11	JN
	(↑ §122)		(↑ §122)	
5 These twelve Jesus sent,	2 And he sent them		8 And he commanded them	

MT 10:5-15	LK 9:2-5	LK 10:9, 4, 7c, 5-6, 10-12	MK 6:8-11	JN
commanding them, saying: Into a way of the Gentiles do not go, and into a city of Samaritans do not enter; 6 but go rather to the lost sheep of the House of Israel.				
7 And as you go preach, saying: The Kingdom of the Heavens has come.	to preach the Kingdom of God	9 And heal the sick in it and say to them: The Kingdom of God has come upon you.		
8 Heal the sick, raise the dead, cleanse the lepers, cast out demons; freely you received, freely give.	and cure the sick.			
	3 And he said to them: Take nothing for the way,			
9 Do not acquire gold nor silver nor copper for your belts,		4 Do not carry a purse	to take nothing for the way,	
10 nor a bag for the way, nor two coats nor sandals,		nor a bag nor sandals		
nor a staff.	neither a staff nor a bag nor bread, nor money,		except a staff only, neither bread, nor bag, nor copper in the belt. 9 But be shod with sandals, and do not put on two coats.	
	nor have two coats each.			
		and greet no one on the way.		
For the workman is worthy of his food.		7c For the workman is worthy of his wage.		
11 But into whichever town or village you enter, find out who in it is worthy, and there remain until you go away.	4 And into whichever house you enter, there remain and from there go away.	5 But into whichever house you enter,	10 And he said to them: Wherever you enter into a house, remain there until you go away from there.	
12 And as you go into the house, greet it.		first say: Peace to this house.		
13 And if indeed the house be worthy, let your peace come upon it. But if it be not worthy, let your peace turn back to you.		6 And if there be there a son of peace, your peace shall rest upon him. But if not, it shall come back upon you.		
14 And whoever does not receive you, and does not hearken to your words, going forth outside that house or city shake out the dust of your feet.	5 And whoever do not receive you, going forth from that city even shake off the dust from your feet	10 But into whichever city you enter, and they do not receive you, going forth into its streets, say, 11 Even the dust from your city that adheres to our feet, we wipe off against you.	11 And whichever place does not receive you, and they do not hearken to you, going out thence, shake out the earth that is under your feet	

MT 10:5-15	LK 9:2-5	LK 10:9, 4, 7c, 5-6, 10-12	MK 6:8-11	JN
	as a witness upon them.	*But know this, that the Kingdom of God has come.* *12 I say to you that for the Sodomites it will be more tolerable on that day than for that city.*	as a witness to them.	
15 Amen I say to you, it will be more tolerable for the land of Sodom and Gomorrah in the day of judgement than for that city **(cf. Mt. 11:24)**.				
	(↓ §129)		(↓ §129)	

§125 Persecutions Will Come (§§204, 225, 309)

MT 10:16-25	MT 24:9, 13	LK 10:3; 21:12-19; 6:40	LK 12:11-12	MK 13:9-13	JN
16 Lo, I send you like sheep in the midst of wolves; be you therefore as wise as serpents and as simple as doves. 17 But beware of men;		*10:3 Go forth; lo, I send you like lambs in the midst of wolves.*			
				9 But you yourselves look out!	
for they will betray you to councils and in their synagogues they will scourge you;	*9a Then they will betray you into tribulation,*	*21:12 But before all these things they will lay their hands on you and persecute, betraying you to synagogues and prisons,*	*11 But when they bring you before the synagogues and the authorities and the magistrates,*	*They will betray you to councils, and in synagogues you will be beaten.*	
18 and before governors and kings too you will be led for my sake, for a witness to them		*to be led off before kings and governors for the sake of my name;* *13 It will turn out for you as a witness.*		*And you will stand before governors and kings for my sake* *for a witness to them.*	
and to the nations.	**(cf. 24:14)**			*10 And to all the nations must the Gospel first be preached.*	
19 And when they betray you, do not worry how or what you should speak;				*11 And when they lead you, betraying you,* *do not worry beforehand what you should speak;*	
		14 Fix therefore in your hearts not to premeditate your defence; *15 for I will give you a mouth and wisdom*	*do not worry how or what defence you should make, or what you should say;* *12 For the Holy Spirit will teach you in the very hour the things you are to say.*		
for it will be given to you in that hour what you shall speak.				*but whatever is given to you in that hour, speak that.*	
20 For you are not the ones speaking but (it is) the Spirit of your Father				*For you are not the ones speaking, but the Holy Spirit.*	

94

MT 10:16-25	MT 24:9, 13	LK 10:3; 21:12-19; 6:40	LK 12:11-12	MK 13:9-13	JN
who is speaking in you.		which all they who oppose you will not be able to withstand or contradict.			
21 And brother will betray brother to death and (the) father (his) son,		16 And you will be betrayed even by parents and brothers and relatives and friends,		12 And brother will betray brother to death and (the) father (his) son,	
and children will rise up against (their) parents, and will put them to death.	9b and they will kill some of you.	and they will put to death some of you.		and children will rise up against parents and will put them to death.	
22 And you will be hated by all because of my name.	And you will be hated by all the nations because of my name.	17 And you will be hated by all because of my name. 18 And not by any means will a hair of your head perish.		13 And you will be hated by all because of my name.	
But he who perseveres to the end, he will be saved.	13 But he who perseveres to the end, he will be saved.	19 In your perseverance you will gain your souls.		But he who perseveres to the end, he will be saved.	
23 And when they persecute you in this city, fly to the other; Amen I say to you, you will not finish the cities of Israel until the Son of Man comes. 24 A disciple is not above (his) teacher nor a slave above his master. 25 Sufficient for the disciple that he become like his teacher, and the slave like his master. If they named the master of the house Beelzebul, by how much more his house-slaves.		6:40 A disciple is not above (his) teacher; but everyone shall be made perfect like his teacher. (cf. 11:15)		(cf. 3:22)	

§126 Call to Fearless Confession (§223)

MT 10:26-33	LK 12:2-9	MK	JN
26 Therefore do not be afraid of them; for there is nothing covered which will not be uncovered, and hidden which will not be made known.	2 And there is nothing covered up which will not be uncovered, and hidden which will not be made known (cf. 8:17).	(4:22)	

MT 10:26-33	LK 12:2-9	MK	JN
27 What I say to you in the dark, do you say in the light; and what you hear in the ear, preach on the house-tops. 28 And do not be afraid of those who kill the body but are not able to kill the soul; but rather fear the one able to destroy both body and soul in Gehenna. 29 Are not two sparrows sold for a penny? And not one of them falls to the ground without your Father. 30 And even the hairs of your head have all been numbered. 31 Therefore do not be afraid: you surpass many sparrows. 32 Therefore everyone who will confess me before men, I too will confess him before my Father who is in the heavens; 33 But whoever denies me before men, I too will deny him before my Father who is in the heavens **(cf. 16:27).**	*3 Wherefore, whatever you said in the dark,* *shall be heard in the light;* *and what you spoke into the ear in the inner rooms,* *shall be preached on the house-tops.* *4 And I say to you, my friends, do not be afraid of those who kill the body,* *and after that have no more they may do.* *5 But I will show you whom you should fear; you should fear the one who after the killing has power to cast down into Gehenna. Yes, I say to you, fear this one.* *6 Are not five sparrows sold for two pence?* *And not one of them is forgotten before God.* *7 But even the hairs of your head have all been numbered* **(cf. 21-18).** *Do not be afraid; you surpass many sparrows.* *8 I say to you, everyone whoever confesses me before men,* *the Son of Man too will confess him before the angels of God.* *9 But the one who denies me in front of men* *will be denied in front of the angels of God* **(cf. 9:26).**		**(cf. 8:38)**

§127 Discipleship and Sacrifice (§§233, 248, 267)

MT 10:34-39	LK 12:51-53; 14:26-27; 17:33	MK	JN
34 Do not suppose that I came to cast peace upon the earth; I came to cast not peace but a sword. 35 For I came to set at variance a man against his father **(Mic. 7:6).** and a daughter against her mother, and a daughter-in-law against her mother-in-law, 36 and a man's enemies (will be) his own household. 37 He who loves father or mother above me, is not worthy of me. And he who loves son or daughter above me is not worthy of me. 38 And he who does not take up his cross and follow after me, is not worthy of me **(Mt. 16:24f).** 39 He who has found his life, will lose it, and he who has lost his life for my sake will find it.	*51 Do you imagine that I arrived to give peace on the earth; not at all, I tell you, but rather division.* *52 For from now on there will be five divided in one house, three against two, and two against three;* *53 they shall be divided father against son, and son against father,* *mother against daughter, and daughter against her mother,* *mother-in-law against her daughter-in-law, and daughter-in-law against her mother-in-law.* *14:26 If anyone comes to me and does not hate his father and mother, and wife* *and children and brothers and sisters, and besides also his own life, he cannot be my disciple.* *27 Whoever does not carry his own cross and come after me, cannot be my disciple* **(9:23f.).** *17:33 Whoever would seek to preserve his life will lose (it), and whoever will lose (it), will cause it to come alive.*		**(8:34f.)**

§128 Receiving an Apostle (§§183, 184)

MT 10:40-42
40 He who receives you receives me and he who receives me receives him who sent me **(cf. 18:5)**.
41 He who receives a prophet in the name of a prophet, will receive the reward of a prophet.
42 And whoever gives one of these little ones only a cup of cold water to drink in the name of a disciple,
Amen I say to you, he will not lose his reward.

LK 9:48b
48b And whoever receives me, receives him who sent me (cf. 10:16).

MK 9:37b, 41
37b And whoever receives me, does not receive me, but him who sent me.

41 For whoever will give you a cup of water to drink in (my) name, because you are Christ's,

Amen I say to you, that he will not lose his reward.

JN

§129 The Twelve Go Off Alone (§160)

MT 11:1
1 And it happened, when Jesus had ended instructing his twelve disciples, he passed thence to teach and preach in their towns.

LK 9:6
(↑ §124)
6 And setting out they went about, village by village, evangelizing and healing everywhere.
(↓ §158)

MK 6:12-13
(↑ §124)
12 And having set out they preached that they should repent 13 and they cast out many demons and anointed with oil many sick and healed (them).
(↓ §158)

JN

§130 John Sends Messengers (§93)

MT 11:2-6
2 And when John in prison had heard the works of Christ, he sent through his disciples and said to him:

3 Are you he who is to come, or do we wait for another?

4 And Jesus answering said to them:
Go and report to John what you hear and see **(cf. Mt. 10:8)**;
5 the blind see again and the lame walk, lepers are cleansed, and the deaf hear, and the dead are raised and the poor are evangelized;
6 And blessed is he who has not been scandalized over me.

LK 7:18-23
18 And his disciples reported to John about all these things. And John summoning a certain two of his disciples 19 sent them to Jesus saying:
Are you he who is to come, or do we wait for someone else?
20 And the men coming along to him said: John the Baptist sent us to you saying: Are you he who is to come, or do we wait for someone else?
21 In that very hour he healed many from diseases and afflictions and unclean spirits, and he granted sight to many blind.
22 And answering he said to them:
Go and report to John what you have seen and heard;
the blind see again, the lame walk,
lepers are cleansed and the deaf hear,
the dead are raised, the poor are evangelized;
23 And blessed is he who has not been scandalized over me.

MK **JN**

MT 11:7-19	LK 7:24-30; 16:16; 7:31-35	MK 1:2	JN
7 And as they were going Jesus began to say to the crowds about John: Why did you go out into the desert? To behold a reed shaken by the wind? 8 But why did you go out? To see a man finely dressed? Lo, those who dress finely, (are) in the palaces of kings. 9 But why did you go out? To see a prophet? Yes, I tell you, and more than a prophet. 10 This is he about whom it has been written: Lo, I send my messenger before thy face, who will prepare thy way before thee (**Mal. 3:1; Ex. 23:20**). 11 Amen I say to you, there has not arisen among those born of women a greater than John the Baptist; But the least in the **Kingdom of the Heavens** is greater than he.	24 And as John's messengers were going away he began to say to the crowds about John: Why did you go out into the desert? To behold a reed shaken by the wind? 25 But why did you go out? To see a man dressed in fine clothes? Lo, those in splendid and luxurious dress are in the rooms of royalty? 26 But why did you go out? To see a prophet? Yes, I tell you, and more than a prophet. 27 This is he about whom it has been written: Lo, I send my messenger before thy face, who will prepare thy way before thee. 28 I say to you, no one is a greater prophet among those born of women than John; But the least in the Kingdom of God is greater than he. 29 And all the people heard and the tax-collectors justified God, having been baptised with John's baptism. 30 But the Pharisees and the lawyers rejected the plan of God with regard to themselves not having been baptised by him.	2 Just as it has been written in the—Isaiah the prophet: Behold I send my messenger before thy face, who will prepare thy way before thee.	
12 But from the days of John the Baptist until now the Kingdom of the Heavens suffers violence and the violent snatch it away. 13 For all the Prophets and the Law prophesied until John. 14 And if you wish to receive it, he himself is the Elijah who is to come. 15 He who has ears to hear let him hear. 16 And to what shall I liken this generation? It is like to boys sitting in the market-places, who, calling out to the others, say: 17 We piped to you, and you did not dance; we wailed to you and you did not mourn. 18 For John came neither eating nor drinking, and they say: He has a demon. 19 The Son of Man came eating and drinking,	16:16 The Law and the Prophets were till John; from then the Kingdom of God is evangelized, and everyone uses violence against it. 31 To what therefore shall I liken the men of this generation, and to whom are they like? 32 They are like to boys who are sitting in a market-place and they call out to one another—who say: We piped to you, and you did not dance; we wailed to you and you did not weep. 33 For John the Baptist has come neither eating bread nor drinking wine; and you say: He has a demon. 34 The Son of Man has come eating and drinking,		

MT 11:7-19	LK 7:24-30; 16:16; 7:31-35	MK 1:2	JN
and they say: Lo, a man who is a glutton and a drunkard, a friend of tax-collectors and sinners. And Wisdom is justified from its deeds.*	*and you say: Lo, a man who is a glutton and a drunkard, a friend of tax-collectors and sinners.* *35 And Wisdom is justified from all its children.*		

§132 Woes to Unrepentant Cities (cf. §§124, 204, 205)

MT 11:20-24	LK 10:13-15, 12	MK	JN
20 Then he began to reproach the towns in which his numerous mighty deeds had been done for not having repented: 21 Woe to you Chorazin, Woe to you Bethsaida; for if in Tyre and Sidon were done the mighty deeds done in you, long ago they would have repented in sack-cloth and ashes. 22 Indeed I tell you, it will be more tolerable for Tyre and Sidon on judgement day than for you, 23 And you, Capharnaum, will you be exalted up to heaven? You shall go down to Hades. For if in Sodom had been done the mighty deeds done in you, it would have remained until today. 24 Indeed I tell you that in the day of judgement it will be more tolerable for the land of Sodom than for thee **(cf. 10:15)**.	*13 Woe to you, Chorazin, Woe to you Bethsaida; for if Tyre and Sidom had been done the mighty deeds done in you, long ago they would have repented, sitting in sackcloth and ashes.* *14 Indeed it will be more tolerable for Tyre and Sidon in the judgement than for you.* *15 And you Capharnaum, will you be exalted up to heaven? You shall go down to Hades.* ___ *12 I say to you that it will be more tolerable in that day for Sodom than for that city.*		

§133 Jesus Thanks His Father (§207)

MT 11:25-27	LK 10:21-22	MK	JN
25 In that time Jesus answering said: I praise thee Father, Lord of heaven and earth, because thou hast hidden these things from the wise and understanding, and revealed them to babes; 26 Yes, O Father, because thus it was pleasing before thee. 27 All things have been entrusted to me by my Father, and no one recognizes the Son but the Father, nor does anyone know the Father except the Son, and he to whom the Son wills to reveal (him).	*21 In that hour he rejoiced in the Holy Spirit, and said: I praise thee, Father, Lord of heaven and earth, because thou hast hidden away these things from the wise and understanding, and revealed them to babes: Yes O Father, because thus it was pleasing before thee.* *22* And turning to the disciples he said: All things have been entrusted to me by my Father, and no one knows who the Son is but the Father, and who the Father is except the Son, and he to whom the Son wills to reveal (him).*		

MT 11:28-30   LK   MK   JN
28 Come unto me, all who are toiling and burdened, and I will
give you rest.
29 Take my yoke upon you and learn of me, for I am meek and
humble of heart,
and you will find rest for your souls;
30 for my yoke is pleasant and my burden is light.

§135 "Working" on the Sabbath (§54)

MT 12:1-8	LK 6:1-5	MK 2:23-28	JN
1 At that time on the Sabbath Jesus went through the cornfields;	*1 And on the Second-First* Sabbath he happened to be travelling through the cornfields;*	*23 And on the Sabbath he happened to be passing through the cornfields;*	
and his disciples were hungry and began to pluck the ears and to eat.	*and his disciples were plucking* *and eating the ears, rubbing them in their hands.*	*and his disciples began to make their way plucking the ears.*	
2 And the Pharisees saw it and said to him: Behold, your disciples are doing what it is not lawful to do on a Sabbath?	*2 And some of the Pharisees said: Why are you doing what it is not lawful to do on the Sabbath?*	*24 And the Pharisees were saying to him: Look, why are they doing on the Sabbath what is not lawful to do?*	
3 And he said to them: Did you not read what David did, when he was hungry, and those who were with him?	*3 And Jesus answering said to them: Did you not read the thing that David did, when he himself was hungry, and those who were with him?*	*25 And he says to them: Did you never read what David did, when he was in need and he himself was hungry, and those who were with him?*	
4 How he entered into the House of God	*4 How he entered into the House of God*	*26 How he entered into the House of God under Abiathar the high-priest,*	
and ate the Loaves of Proposition,	*and taking the Loaves of Proposition, ate and gave also to those with him,*	*and ate the Loaves of Proposition*	
which for him to eat was not lawful, nor for those with him, but for the priests alone?	*which are not lawful to eat,* *but (for) the priests alone?*	*which are not lawful to eat,* *but (for) the priests, and he gave (them) also to those who were with him?*	
5 Or did you not read in the Law that on the Sabbath the priests in the Temple profane the Sabbath and are blameless? 6 I say to you that a Greater than the Temple is here (cf. 12:41). 7 And if you had known the meaning of this: I desire mercy and not sacrifice (Hos. 6:6), you would not have condemned the guiltless.			
8 For the Son of Man is Lord of the Sabbath.	*5 And he said to them:* *The Son of Man is also Lord of the Sabbath.*	*27 And he said to them: The Sabbath was made for man, and not man for the Sabbath. 28 Thus the Son of Man is Lord of the Sabbath also.*	

MT 12:9-15a	LK 6:6-11	MK 3:1-7a	JN
9 And departing thence he came into their synagogue.	6 And it happened on another Sabbath that he entered into the synagogue and was teaching.	1 And he entered again into the synagogue.	
10 And behold there was a man having a withered hand, and they questioned him saying:	And there was a man there, and his right hand was withered; 7 and the Scribes and the Pharisees watched him	And there was a man there having a withered up hand; 2 and they watched him	
Is it lawful to heal on the Sabbath? that they might accuse him.	if he would heal on the Sabbath, that they might find (something) to accuse him. 8 But he knew their thoughts. And he said to the man having the withered hand: Get up and stand in the middle. And rising up he stood.	if he would heal him on the Sabbath, that they might accuse him. 3 And he says to the man having the withered hand; Get up in the middle.	
11 And he said to them: Will there be any man among you who will have a single sheep, and if on the Sabbath it falls into a hole, will he not take hold of it and lift it out? 12 How much more then a man than a sheep. Thus it is lawful on the Sabbath to do good.	9 And Jesus said to them: (cf. 14:5, 3b, 6) I will question you: Is it lawful on the Sabbath to do good or to do evil, to save life or to destroy?	4 And he says to them: Is it lawful on the Sabbath to do good or to do evil, to save life or to kill? But they were silent.	
13 Then he says to the man:	10 And looking round on them all in anger* he said to him:	5 And looking round on them with anger, being deeply grieved at their hardness of heart, he says to the man:	
Extend your hand. And he extended (it), and it was restored sound like the other. 14 But the Pharisees going out took counsel against him, how to destroy him.	Extend your hand. And he did, and his hand was restored. 11 But they were filled with madness, and they discussed with one another what they might do to Jesus.	Extend your hand. And he extended (it), and his hand was restored. 6 And the Pharisees going out held counsel against him at once with the Herodians how to destroy him. 7a And Jesus with his disciples withdrew to the sea.	
15a But Jesus knowing withdrew thence.			

§137 Great Crowds Follow Jesus (§57)

MT 12:15b-21	MT 4:25, 24	LK 6:17-19	MK 3:7b-12	JN
15b And large crowds followed him	25 And large crowds followed him from Galilee and the Decapolis	17 And coming down with them he stood on a level place, and a large crowd of his disciples and a large multitude of people	7b and a large multitude followed him from Galilee,	

MT 12:15b-21	MT 4:25, 24	LK 6:17-19	MK 3:7b-12	JN
	and Jerusalem and Judea	from all Judea and Jerusalem	and from all Judea 8 and from Jerusalem	
	and across the Jordan.		and from Idumea and across the Jordan	
	24 And his fame went off into all Syria;	and the surroundings of Tyre and Sidon,	and about Tyre and Sidon,	
		18 who had come to hear him,	a great multitude, hearing the things he was doing had come to him.	
and he healed them all.	and they brought him all that were ill from diverse diseases and (people) suffering pains and demon-possessed and lunatics, and he healed them.	and to be cured from their diseases, and those tormented by unclean spirits were healed.		
		19 And the whole crowd was trying to touch him, because power went out from him, and he cured all.	9 And he told his disciples that a small boat should stay by him because of the crowd, lest they should throng him. 10 For he healed many, so that whoever had afflictions fell on him in order to touch him, 11 and the unclean spirits, when they beheld him, fell down in front of him, and they cried out saying: You are the Son of God. 12 And he charged them severely not to make him known.	
16 And he charged them not to make him known, 17 to fulfil what was said by Isaiah the prophet, saying: 18 Behold my servant whom I have chosen, My Beloved in whom my soul is well pleased; I will put my Spirit upon him, and he will announce judgement to the nations, 19 He will not quarrel nor shout, nor will anyone hear his voice in the streets; 20 a bruised reed he will not break nor quench a smouldering wick, until he put forth judgement unto victory. 21 And in his name the nations will hope (Is. 42:1-4).				

MT 12:22-32	MT 9:32-34	LK 11:14-23; 12:10	MK 3:22-30	JN
22 Then there was brought to him one demon-possessed, blind and dumb. And he healed him, so that the dumb man spoke and saw.	*32 And as they were going out, behold they brought him a dumb man, demon-possessed. 33 And the demon being cast out the dumb man spoke.*	*14 And he was casting out a demon, and it was dumb.* *And it happened, when the demon had gone out that the dumb man spoke.*		
23 And all the crowds were amazed and said: Surely this one is the Son of David?	*And the crowds marvelled saying:* *Never in Israel has such a thing been seen.*	*And the crowds marvelled.*		
24 But the Pharisees heard and said: This (one) does not cast out the demons except by Beelzebul prince of the demons.	*34* But the Pharisees were saying:* *By the prince of the demons he casts out the demons.*	*15 But some of them said:* *By Beelzebul the prince of the demons he casts out the demons.*	*22 And the Scribes who had come down from Jerusalem were saying: He has Beelzebul, and: By the Prince of the demons he casts out the demons.*	
25 But knowing their thoughts Jesus said to them:		*16 But others tempting were seeking for a sign from him. 17 But knowing their intentions he said to them:*	*23 And calling them up he said to them in parables:*	
Every kingdom divided over against itself comes to ruin,		*Every kingdom divided up against itself comes to ruin,*	*How can Satan cast out Satan? 24 And if a kingdom is divided against itself, that kingdom cannot stand.*	
and every city or house divided against itself will not stand.		*and house against house* *falls.*	*25 And if a house is divided against itself, that house will not be able to stand.*	
26 And if Satan casts out Satan he is divided against himself; how therefore shall his kingdom stand?		*18 And if Satan too is divided up against himself, how shall his kingdom stand?*	*26 And if Satan has risen up against himself, and is divided, he cannot stand, but has an end.*	
27 And if I by Beelzebul cast out the demons, by whom do your sons cast them out? Wherefore they themselves shall be your judges. 28 But if by the Spirit of God I cast out the demons, then upon you has come the Kingdom of God.		*For you say that I cast out the demons by Beelzebul. 19 But if I by Beelzebul cast out the demons, by whom do your sons cast them out? Wherefore they themselves shall be your judges. 20 But if by the finger of God I cast out the demons, then upon you has come the Kingdom of God.*		
29 Or how can anyone enter into the mansion of the Mighty One		*21 When the Mighty One in full armour guards his own palace his possessions are in peace;*	*27 But no one can enter into the mansion of the Mighty One*	
and steal his property, unless he first tie up the Mighty One?		*22 But when a Mightier One than he comes up and overcomes him,*	*to plunder his property, unless he first tie up the Mighty One.*	

MT 12:22-32   MT 9:32-34   LK 11:14-23; 12:10   MK 3:22-30   JN

		he takes away his armour on which he had relied, and gives away his spoils.	
And then he will plunder his mansion. 30 He who is not with me is against me, and he who gathers not with me, scatters.		*23 He who is not with me is against me, and he who gathers not with me, scatters* **(cf. 9:50).**	*And then he will plunder his mansion.*
31 Wherefore I say to you, every sin and blasphemy shall be forgiven to the sons of men,			*28 Amen, I say to you, that everything shall be forgiven to the sons of men,—the sins and the blasphemies—whatever they may blaspheme;*
but the blasphemy of the Spirit will not be forgiven. 32 And whoever should say a word against the Son of Man, it shall be forgiven him; but whoever shall speak against the Holy Spirit, it shall not be forgiven him, neither in this age nor in the one to come.		*12:10 And everyone who shall say a word against the Son of Man it shall be forgiven him; but to the one who blasphemes at the Holy Spirit it shall not be forgiven.*	*29 but whoever should blaspheme at the Holy Spirit does not have forgiveness unto the age, but is guilty of an ageless sin. 30 For they said: He has an unclean spirit.*

§139 A Tree and Its Fruits (§86)

MT 12:33-37   MT 7:18, 20   LK 6:43-44a, 45   MK   JN

33 Either make the tree good and its fruit good, or make the tree diseased and its fruit diseased. For from the fruit is the tree known.	*18 A sound tree cannot make bad fruits,* *nor can a diseased tree make good fruits.* *20 For by their fruits you will know them.*	*43 For a good tree does not make a diseased fruit, nor again does a diseased tree make a good fruit. 44a For each tree is known from its own fruit.*	
34 Offspring of vipers, how can you, being evil, speak good things? for from the abundance of the heart the mouth speaks. 35 The good man out of the good store utters good things, and the evil man from the evil store utters evil things.		*45 The good man out of the good store of the heart brings forth what is good, and the evil from the evil brings forth what is evil; for from the abundance of the heart the mouth speaks.*	
36 And I say to you that every idle word			

MT 12:33-37
which men will speak, they will render
account for it in the day of judgement.
37 For by your words you will be
justified, and by your words you will be
condemned.

MT 7:18, 20

LK 6:43-44a, 45

MK

JN

§140 The Sign of Jonah (§§171, 218)

MT 12:38-42
38 Then some of the Scribes and
Pharisees answered him, saying:
Teacher, we want to see a sign
from you.
39 And answering he said to
them:

An evil and adulterous generation
inquires for a sign,
and a sign shall not be given to it,
except the sign of Jonah.

40 For just as Jonah was in the
belly of the whale for three days
and three nights,
so will the Son of Man be in the
heart of the earth for three days
and three nights.
41 The men of Nineveh will stand
up in the judgement with this
generation and condemn it
because they repented at the
preaching of Jonah, and lo,
something greater than Jonah
here.

42 The queen of the south will
rise in the judgement with this
generation and will condemn it;

for she came from the ends of the
earth to hear the wisdom of
Solomon, and lo, something
greater than Solomon here.

MT 16:1-2a, 4
*1 And the Pharisees and the
Sadducees coming up tempting
asked him to show them a sign
from heaven.
2a And answering he said to
them:*

*4 An evil and adulterous
generation inquires for a sign,
and a sign shall not be given to it,
except the sign of Jonah.*

LK 11:29-30, 32, 31
*29 And while the crowds were
thronging him, he began to say:*

*This generation is an evil
generation; it seeks a sign,
and a sign shall not be given to it,
except the sign of Jonah.*

*30 For even as Jonah became a
sign to the Ninevites,*

*so also will the Son of Man be to
this generation.*

*32 The men of Nineveh will rise
up in the judgement with this
generation and will condemn it;
because they repented at the
preaching of Jonah, and lo,
something greater than Jonah
here.*

*31 The queen of the south will
rise in the judgement with the
men of this generation and will
condemn them;
for she came from the ends of the
earth to hear the wisdom of
Solomon, and lo, something
greater than Solomon here.*

MK 8:11-12
*11 And the Pharisees went out
and began to debate with him,
asking from him a sign from
heaven, tempting him.
12 And sighing deeply in his
spirit, he says:*

*Why does this generation seek a
sign?
Amen I say to you, on no
account shall a sign be given to
this generation!*

JN

§141 Return of the Unclean Spirit (§216)

MT 12:43-45   **LK 11:24-26**   **MK**   **JN**

MT 12:43-45	LK 11:24-26
43 Now when the unclean spirit has gone out from the man, he goes through waterless places seeking rest, and does not find it.	24 Now when the unclean spirit has gone out from the man, he goes through waterless places seeking rest; and not finding it,
44 Then he says: I will return into my house whence I came out; and coming he finds it vacant and swept and in order.	then he says: I will go back into my house whence I came out; 25 and coming he finds it vacant, swept and in order.
45 Then he goes and takes with him seven other spirits worse than himself, and entering in dwells there, and the last things of that man become worse than the first. Thus shall it also be with this evil generation.	26 Then he goes and takes seven other spirits worse than himself, and entering in dwells there, and the last things of that man become worse than the first.

§142 Jesus' Mother and Brothers (Mt) (§§99, 108)

MT 12:46-50   **LK 8:19-21**   **MK 3:31-35**   **JN**

MT 12:46-50	LK 8:19-21	MK 3:31-35
46 While he was yet speaking to the crowds, behold his mother and brothers stood outside seeking to speak to him.	19 Now there came along to him his mother and brothers	31 And his mother and his brothers come and standing outside sent to him calling him. 32 And a crowd was sitting around him.
47* And someone said to him: Lo your mother and your brothers stand outside seeking to speak to you.	and they could not reach him because of the crowd. 20 And it was reported to him: Your mother and your brothers stand outside wanting to see you.	And they say to him: Lo your mother and your brothers and your sisters* outside seek you.
48 And he answering said to the one speaking to him: Who is my mother and who are my brothers? 49 And stretching out his hand over his disciples he said: Behold my mother and my brothers.	21 And he answering said to them:	33 And answering he says to them: Who is my mother and my brothers? 34 And looking around at those sitting round him in a circle, he says: See my mother and my brothers.
50 For whoever does the will of my Father in the heavens he is my brother and sister and mother.	My mother and my brothers— these are those who hear and do the word of God.	35 For whoever does the will of God, this one is my brother and sister and mother.

§143 Preaching in Parables (§100)

MT 13:1-3a   **LK 8:4**   **MK 4:1-2**   **JN**

MT 13:1-3a	LK 8:4	MK 4:1-2
1 On that day Jesus, going out of the house, sat beside the sea; 2 and great crowds assembled to him,	4 And a great crowd coming together and people from every town making their way to him,	1 And again he began to teach beside the sea; and a very large crowd assembles to him
so that he got into a boat and sat,		so that he got into a boat and sat on the sea,

MT 13:1-3a	LK 8:4	MK 4:1-2	JN
and the whole crowd stood on the shore.		*and the whole crowd were on the land at the sea.*	
3a And he spoke to them at length in parables saying:	*he said by a parable:*	*2 And he began to teach them at length in parables, and to say to them in his teaching:*	

§144 Parable of the Sower (§101)

MT 13:3b-9	LK 8:5-8	MK 4:3-9	JN
3b Lo, the sower went out to sow,	*5 The sower went out to sow his seed,*	*3 Listen; Lo, the sower went out to sow.*	
4 and as he sowed, some fell by the path	*and as he sowed, it fell by the path and was trodden down,*	*4 And it happened as he sowed some fell by the path*	
and the birds coming ate them up.	*and the birds of the sky ate it up.*	*and the birds came and ate it up.*	
5 But others fell on the rocky patches where they did not have much earth,	*6 And another fell on the rock*	*5 And other some fell on the rocky patch where it did not have much earth,*	
and at once they shot up, because they had no depth of earth.	*and growing up*	*and at once it shot up, because it had no depth of earth;*	
6 And the sun rising, they were scorched, and through not having a root they withered up.	*it withered up through not having moisture.*	*6 and when the sun rose it was scorched, and through not having a root it withered up.*	
7 And others fell on the thorns and the thorns rose up and choked them.	*7 And another fell in the midst of the thorns and the thorns growing up choked it.*	*7 And other some fell into the thorns and the thorns rose up and suffocated it.*	
8 And others fell on the good soil and yielded a crop,	*8 And another fell on the right soil and growing produced a crop*	*8 And others fell on the good soil and yielded a crop rising up and increasing, and they bore*	
the one a hundred, and another sixty, and another thirty.	*a hundredfold.*	*one thirty, and one sixty, and one a hundred.*	
9 He that has ears to hear, let him hear.	*Saying these things he cried: He that has ears to hear, let him hear.*	*9 And he said: He that has ears to hear, let him hear.*	

§145 Reason for Using Parables (§§102, 104)

MT 13:10-15	LK 8:9-10, 18b	MK 4:10-11, 25, 12	JN
10 And the disciples coming up said to him:	*9 And his disciples questioned him:*	*10 And when he was alone, those around him together with the Twelve asked him (about) the parables.*	
Why do you speak to them in parables?	*What may this parable be?*	*11 And he began to say to them:*	
11 And he answering said to them:	*10 And he said:*	*To you has been given the mystery of the Kingdom of God,*	
To you it has been given to know the mysteries of the Kingdom of the Heavens, but to those it has not been given.	*To you it has been given to know the mysteries of the Kingdom of God, but to the others in parables,*	*but to those outside all things are done in parables,*	
12 For he who has, it shall be given to him,	*18b For whoever has, it will be given to him;*	*25 For he who has, it will be given to him,*	

MT 13:10-15
and he shall abound;
but he who has not, that too which he has will
be taken from him.
'13 I speak therefore to them in parables,
because seeing they do not see,
and hearing they do not hear, nor do they take
it in.
14 And the prophecy of Isaiah is fulfilled in
them that says (Is. 6:9-10):
With hearing you will hear and not
understand;
And seeing you will see and not perceive.
15 For the heart of this people has become
thick,
and with their ears they heard hardly,
and they shut their eyes;
lest perhaps they see with their eyes
and hear with their ears,
and understand with their heart,
and turn back, and I heal them.

LK 8:9-10, 18b

*and whoever does not have, that which he
thinks he has, will be taken from him.*

*that seeing they may not see,
and hearing they may not take it in.*

MK 4:10-11, 25, 12

*and he who has not, that also which he has
will be taken from him.*

*12 that seeing they may see and not perceive,
and hearing they may hear and not take it in,*

lest they turn back and it be forgiven them.

JN

§146 "Blessed Your Eyes . . . " (§208)

MT 13:16-17

16 Blessed are your eyes because they see, and your ears because
they hear.
17 For Amen I say to you, Many prophets and just men desired
to see the things that you see and did not see (them),
and to hear the things that you hear and did not hear them.

LK 10:23-24
*23 And turning to the disciples in private he said:
Blessed are the eyes that see the things that you see,*

*24 For I say to you, Many prophets and kings wanted to see the
things that you yourselves see and did not see (them),
and to hear the things that you hear and did not hear them.*

MK   JN

§147 Meaning of the Sower (§103)

MT 13:18-23
18 Hear you therefore the parable of the
sower.
19 Everyone hearing the word of the Kingdom
and not taking it in,

the Evil One comes and snatches what was
sown in his heart;

LK 8:11-15
11 Now the parable is this:

*The seed is the word of God.
12 And the ones on the path are the hearers;*

*then the devil comes and takes away the word
from their heart lest having come to believe*

MK 4:13-20
*13 And he says to them: Do you not know this
parable, and how will you know all the parables?
14 The sower sows the word. 15 And these are
the ones on the path, where the word is sown
and when they hear,
at once Satan comes and takes away the word
that was sown in them.*

JN

MT 13:18-23

This is what is sown on the path.
20 And the one sown on the rocky patches,

this is the one who hears the word,
and who at once with joy accepts it,
21 but he has no root in himself
but is temporary,
and when suffering or persecution happens on account of the word he is at once scandalized.

22 And the one sown among the thorns,

this is the one who hears the word
and the care of this age and the deceitfulness of riches

chokes the word, and it is rendered fruitless.
23 But the one sown upon the good soil,

this is the one who hears the word and takes it in,
who indeed brings forth fruit and produces the one a hundred, and another sixty, and another thirty.

LK 8:11-15
they should be saved.

13 And the ones on the rock

are the ones who when they hear
with joy receive the word;
and these have no root,
they believe for a time,
and in time of trial they apostatize.

14 And what fell into the thorns,

these are the ones who have heard
and as they go along, by cares and riches and pleasures of life

are choked, and do not mature.
15 But that on the good soil,

these are the ones who in a good and sound heart, having heard the word, hold it fast and bring forth fruit in patience.

MK 4:13-20

16 And likewise the ones sown on the rocky patches
are the ones who when they hear the word at once with joy accept it,
17 and they have no root in themselves but they are temporary,
then when suffering or persecution happens on account of the word they are at once scandalized.
18 And others are the ones sown among the thorns,
these are the ones who have heard the word,
19 and the cares of the age and the deceitfulness of riches and the cravings for the rest intervening,
choke the word, and it is rendered fruitless.
20 And the ones that are sown on the really good soil
are those who hear the word and embrace it

and bring forth fruit, one thirty and one sixty and one a hundred.

JN

§148 The Wheat and the Weeds (§105)

MT 13:24-30

24 Another parable he set before them, saying:
The Kingdom of the Heavens is to be likened to a man sowing good seed in his field.
25 And while the men were sleeping his enemy came and oversowed weeds in the midst of the wheat, and went away.
26 And when the plant sprouted and bore fruit, then the weeds too were noticed.
27 And the slaves of the master of the house coming up said to him:
Sir, did you not sow good seed in your field; whence therefore has it weeds?
28 And he said to them: Some enemy has done this.
And the slaves say to him: Do you want us to go out and gather them up?
29 But he says:
No; lest perhaps when gathering up the weeds, you uproot together with them the wheat.
30 Leave both to grow up together until the harvest; and in the

LK

MK 4:26-29
26 And he said:
Thus is the Kingdom of God, as if a man were to cast the seed upon the earth,
27 and should sleep and get up night and day and the seed should sprout and lengthen, how he knows not.
28 Of its own accord the earth bears a crop, first a blade, then an ear, then full corn in the ear.
29 And when the crop allows, immediately he sends the sickle because the harvest has come.

JN

MT 13:24-30 | LK | MK 4:26-29 | JN

time of the harvest I will say to the harvesters: Gather up first
the weeds and bind them into bundles in order to burn them; but
gather up the wheat into my barn.

§149 The Mustard Seed Parable (§§106, 239)

MT 13:31-32
31 Another parable he put before them saying:
The Kingdom of the Heavens is like

a grain of mustard which a man took and
sowed in his field,
32 which is indeed smaller than all the seeds,

but when it is grown
is greater than the plants
and becomes a tree,
so that the birds of the sky come and roost on
its branches.

LK 13:18-19
18 Therefore he used to say:
Like to what is the Kingdom of God?
And to what shall I liken it?
19 It is like a grain of mustard which a man
took and sowed in his own garden,

and it grew

and became a great tree,
and the birds of the sky roosted on its
branches.

MK 4:30-32
30 And he used to say:
How may we liken the Kingdom of God?
Or in what parable may we put it?
31 As a grain of mustard which when it is
sowed upon the earth—
being smaller than all the seeds that are on the
earth—
32 and when it is sowed, it rises up
and becomes greater than all the plants
and produces great branches,
so that under its shade the birds of the sky are
able to roost.

JN

§150 The Leaven (§240)

MT 13:33
33 Another parable he spoke to them:
The Kingdom of the Heavens is like leaven,
which a woman took and covered up in three measures of flour
until all was leavened.

LK 13:20-21
20 And again he said:
To what shall I liken the Kingdom of God? 21 It is like leaven,
which a woman took and covered in three measures of flour
until all was leavened.

MK | JN

§151 Jesus' Use of Parables (§107)

MT 13:34-35
34 All these things Jesus spoke in parables to the crowds,

and he used to speak nothing to them without a parable,

35 so that what was said by the prophet might be fulfilled,
saying:
I will open my mouth in parables,
I will utter things hidden from the foundation of the world*
(Ps. 77[78]:2).

LK

MK 4:33-34
33 And with many such like parables he used to speak the word
to them, according as they were able to hear;
34 But without a parable he did not speak to them, but privately
to his own disciples he explained everything.

JN

MT 13:36-43	LK	MK	JN
36 Then leaving the crowds he came into the house. And his disciples came up to him, saying: Clarify for us the parable of the weeds of the field. 37 And he answering said: He who sows the good seed is the Son of Man, 38 and the field is the world; and the good seed, these are the sons of the Kingdom; and the weeds are the sons of the Evil One; 39 and the enemy who sowed them is the Devil; and the harvest is the conclusion of the age, and the harvesters are the angels. 40 Therefore, just as the weeds are gathered up and burnt by fire, so shall it be at the conclusion of the age. 41 The Son of Man will send his angels, and will gather up all the scandals out of the Kingdom and those who do the law-breaking, 42 and will cast them into the furnace of the fire; weeping and gnashing of teeth shall be there (cf. 8:12; 13:50). 43 Then will the righteous shine out like the sun in the Kingdom of their Father. He that has ears to hear let him hear.			

§153 The Treasure

MT 13:44	LK	MK	JN
44 The Kingdom of the Heavens is like to a treasure hidden in the field, which when a man found he hid, and in his joy goes off and sells everything whatever he has and purchases that field.			

§154 The Pearl of Great Price

MT 13:45-46	LK	MK	JN
45 Again the Kingdom of the Heavens is like to a man, a merchant seeking good pearls; 46 and having found one exceedingly valuable pearl, he went off and sold everything whatever he had and purchased it.			

§155 The Net

MT 13:47-50   LK   MK   JN

47 Again the Kingdom of the Heavens is like to a net cast into the
sea and gathering up every kind;
48 which when it was filled, they drew it up on the shore
and sitting down gathered up the good into containers, and threw
out the useless.
49 Thus shall it be at the conclusion of the age;
the angels will go forth and will separate the evil from the midst
of the righteous,
50 and cast them into the furnace of the fire;
weeping and gnashing of teeth shall be there **(cf. Mt. 13:42)**.

§156 Scribe of the New Kingdom

MT 13:51-52   LK   MK   JN

51 Have you understood all these things?
They say to him: Yes.
52 And he said to them:
Therefore every scribe who has become a disciple of the Kingdom
of the Heavens, is like to a man, a master of the house, who
brings out of his treasure new things and old.

§157 Visit to Nazareth (Mt) (§§38, 120)

MT 13:53-58	LK 4:16, 22-24, 28-30	MK 6:1-6a	JN
53 And it happened, when Jesus had ended these parables, he passed thence, 54 and coming into his own home-town		1 And he went out from there and comes into his own home-town and his disciples follow him.	
	16 And he came into Nazareth, where he had been nurtured,		
he was teaching them in their synagogue,	and according to his custom he entered into the synagogue on the Sabbath-day, and rose up to read.	2 And when the Sabbath came he began to teach in the synagogue;	
so that they were amazed and said:	22 And all witnessed to him and marvelled at the words of grace that came from his mouth, and they said:	and the many hearers were amazed, saying:	
Whence (has) this man this wisdom		Whence (has) this man these things? And what is the wisdom given to this man? And such mighty deeds done by his hands?	
and these mighty deeds? 55 Is he not the son of the carpenter? Is not his mother called Mary, and his brothers James and Joseph* and Simon and Jude?	Is he not the son of Joseph?	3 Is he not the carpenter, the son of Mary, and brother of James and Joses* and Jude and Simon?	

MT 13:53-58	LK 4:16, 22-24, 28-30	MK 6:1-6a	JN
56 And his sisters are they not all with us? Whence therefore has this man all these things? 57 And they were scandalized over him.		*And are not his sisters here with us?* *And they were scandalized over him.*	
	23 And he said to them: *Surely you will say to me this parable:* *Physician, heal yourself; whatsoever we have heard done in Capharnaum, do also here in your own home-town.* *24 And he said:*		
But Jesus said to them: A prophet is not without honour save in his own home-town, and in his own house.	*Amen, I say to you that no prophet is accepted in his own home-town.*	*4 And Jesus said to them:* *A prophet is not without honour save in his own home-town and among his own relatives; and in his own house.*	
	28 And all in the synagogue were filled with anger when they heard these things, *29 And rising they threw him out of the town, and led him up to the brow of the mountain, on which the town was built, in order to hurl him down.* *30 But he passing through their midst went on.*		
58 And he did not do there many mighty deeds, because of their unbelief.		*5 And he was unable to do any mighty deed there, save laying hands on a few sick he healed them.* *6a And he marvelled because of their unbelief.*	

V. The Later Ministry in Galilee
§§ 158-192

§158 Herod's Interest in Jesus (§174)

MT 14:1-2

1 At that time Herod the tetrarch heard the fame of Jesus.

(cf. 16:13-14)

2 And he said to his courtiers:
This (man) is John the Baptist;
he himself has been raised from the dead,
and because of this the mighty deeds are at work in him.

LK 9:7-9

(↑ §129)

7 Now Herod the tetrarch heard all that was happening,
and he was puzzled because it was said
by some that John was raised from the dead,

(cf. 9:19f)

8 and by others that Elijah had appeared,
and by others that some prophet of the Ancients had arisen.
9 But Herod said:
John I beheaded;

But who is this one about whom I hear such things?
and he sought to see him.

(↓ §160)

MK 6:14-16

(↑ §129)

14 And Herod the king heard, for his name had become public,
and they were saying
that John the Baptiser had been raised from the dead,
and because of this the mighty deeds are at work in him **(cf. 8:28 f.).**

15 Others were saying that he is Elijah;
others were saying that (he is) a prophet like one of the prophets.
16 But Herod heard and was saying:
Whom I beheaded, John;
this (man) has been raised.

JN

§159 Martyrdom of the Baptist (cf. §21)

MT 14:3-12

3 For Herod having seized John bound him and put (him) away in prison
on account of Herodias the wife of Philip his brother;

4 For John said to him: It is not lawful for you to have her.

5 And wanting to kill him,

he feared the crowd, because it held him as a prophet.

6 Now when Herod's birthday came,

the daughter of Herodias danced in the midst
and she pleased Herod,

7 so that he promised with an oath to give her whatever she asked for.
8 And she, instructed by her mother:

LK
(cf. 3: 19-20)

MK 6:17-29

17 For Herod himself had sent and seized John and bound him in prison
on account of Herodias the wife of Philip his brother, because he had married her.
18 For John said to Herod: It is not lawful for you to have your brother's wife.
19 And Herodias held it against him, and wanted to kill him, but was not able to.
20 For Herod was afraid of John, knowing him to be a just and holy man,
and he guarded him, and having heard him, he was very much in two minds, and he heard him gladly.
21 And a suitable day came, when Herod on his birthday held a feast for his magnates and chiliarchs and the first men of Galilee,
22 and the daughter of Herodias herself came in and danced,
she pleased Herod, and his guests.
And the king said to the young lady:
Ask me for whatever you want and I will give it you.
23 And he swore to her strongly: I will give you whatever you ask me, up to half my kingdom.
24 And going out she said to her mother: What may I ask?

JN

MT 14:3-12	LK	MK 6:17-29	JN
		And she said: The head of John the Baptist.	
		25 And coming in at once with haste before the king, she asked, saying:	
Give me, she says, here upon a dish the head of John the Baptist.		I want you to give me now upon a dish the head of John the Baptist.	
9 And the king was sad, but because of the oaths and the guests,		26 And the king, becoming very sad, because of the oaths and the guests, did not want to deny her.	
10 commanded (it) to be given		27 And at once the king sending a bodyguard ordered his head to be brought.	
and sending he beheaded John in the prison.		And going off he beheaded him in the prison.	
11 And the head was brought on a dish and was given to the young lady, and she brought it to her mother.		28 and he brought his head on a dish and gave it to the young lady and the young lady, gave it to her mother.	
12 And his disciples came up and took his corpse and buried it,		29 And his disciples hearing came and took his corpse, and laid it in a tomb.	
and coming they informed Jesus.	**(cf. 9:10a)**	**(cf. 6:30)**	
(↓ §161)			

§160 Return of the Apostles (cf. §129)

MT	LK 9:10a	MK 6:30-31	JN
	(↑ §158)		
(cf. 14: 12-13)	10a And the apostles having returned related to him whatsoever they had done.	30 And the apostles are assembled to Jesus, and informed him of all whatsoever they had done and taught.	
		31 And he says to them: Come you yourselves apart to a deserted place and rest a little.	
		For there were many coming and going, and they had no proper time to eat.	

§161 Feeding of the Five Thousand (§58)

MT 14:13-21	LK 9:10b-17	MK 6:32-44	JN 6:1-15
(↑ §159)			(↑ §50)
13 And when Jesus heard, he withdrew from there in a boat to a deserted place apart; and the crowds hearing followed him on foot from the towns.	10b And taking them, he withdrew apart to a town called Bethsaida.	32 And they went off in the boat to a desert place apart **(cf. 6:45)**;	1 After these things Jesus went off across the Sea of Galilee, the (sea) of Tiberias.
	11 But the crowds learning followed him,	33 And they saw them going off and many knew, and ran together there on foot from all the towns and came before them.	2 And a great crowd followed him, because they had seen the signs he had done on the sick.
(cf. 5:1-2)	**(cf. 6:20)**		3 And Jesus went up on to the

MT 14:13-21	LK 9:10b-17	MK 6:32-44	JN 6:1-15
			mountain and sat there with his disciples. 4 And it was near the Passover, the Feast of the Jews.
14 And coming out he saw a great crowd,		34 And coming out he saw a great crowd,	5 And Jesus lifting up his eyes and observing that a great crowd was coming to him,
and he was moved with pity for them (cf. 9:36),	and welcoming them	and he was moved with pity for them, because they were like sheep without a shepherd, and he began to teach them many things.	
and he healed their sick.	he began to speak to them about the Kingdom of God, and he cured those who had need of healing.		
15 And when evening came, his disciples came up to him, saying: The place is uninhabited and the hour is now past; dismiss therefore the crowds so that going off into the villages they may buy food for themselves.	12 And the day began to decline; and the Twelve coming up said to him: Dismiss the crowd so that going into the villages and farms around they may lodge and find provisions, because we are here in an uninhabited place.	35 And the hour now being late, his disciples coming up to him, said: 36 The place is uninhabited and the hour is now late; dismiss them, so that going off into the farms and villages around they may buy something to eat for themselves.	
			says to Philip: Whence may we buy loaves that these may eat? 6 He said this to test him, for he himself knew what he would do. 7 Philip answered him: Two hundred denarii worth of loaves do not suffice for them that each one should take a little.
16. But Jesus said to them: They have no need to go; you give them to eat.	13 And he said to them: You give them to eat.	37 And he answering said to them: You give them to eat. And they say to him: Should we go off and buy two hundred denarii worth of loaves, and give them to eat? 38 But he says to them: How many loaves have you? Go and see.	
17 And they say to him: We have nothing here but five loaves and two fishes.	And they said: We have not more than five loaves and two fishes; unless we are to go and buy food for all this people?	And having found out they say to him: Five, and two fishes.	8 One of his disciples, Andrew the brother of Simon Peter, says to him: 9 There is a young lad here who has five barley loaves and two fishes; but what are these among so many?
(v. 21)	14 For there were about five thousand men.	**(v. 44)**	**(v. 10)**
18 And he said: Bring them here to me.			

MT 14:13-21	LK 9:10b-17	MK 6:32-44	JN 6:1-15
19 And commanding the crowds to recline on the grass,	And he said to his disciples: Sit them down in groups of about fifty each.	39 And he ordered them all to recline, company by company, upon the green grass.	10 Then Jesus said: Make the men sit down. And there was much grass in the place.
	15 And they did so and they all sat.	40 And they sat down section by section by hundreds and by fifties.	The men therefore sat down, in number about five thousand.
taking the five loaves and the two fishes, looking up to heaven, he blessed and breaking gave the loaves to the disciples, and the disciples to the crowds.	16 Now taking the five loaves and the two fishes, looking up to heaven, he blessed them and broke (them) up and gave to the disciples to be set before the crowd.	41 And taking the five loaves and the two fishes looking up to heaven, he blessed and broke up the loaves and gave to his disciples to set before them; and he divided the two fishes to all.	11 Jesus therefore took the loaves and giving thanks, gave out to those sitting and likewise of the fishes whatever they wanted.
20 And all ate and were satisfied;	17 And they ate, and all were satisfied;	42 And they all ate, and were satisfied,	12 And when they were full up, he says to his disciples: Gather together the fragments remaining over, so that nothing be lost.
and they took up the surplus of the fragments, twelve full baskets.	and their surplus of fragments was taken up, twelve baskets. (↓ §174)	43 And they took up the fragments, the contents of twelve full baskets, and from the fishes.	13 Therefore they gathered together, and filled twelve baskets of fragments of the five barley loaves which were surplus to those who had eaten.
21 And those who had eaten were about five thousand men, apart from women and children.	(cf. v. 14)	44 And those who ate the loaves were five thousand men.	(v. 10)
			14 The men therefore seeing the sign that he had done said: This one is truly the prophet who is to come into the world.
(14:23)		(6:46)	15 Jesus therefore knowing that they were about to come and seize him to make him king, withdrew again to the mountain himself alone.

§162 Jesus Walks on the Water

MT 14:22-33	LK	MK 6:45-52	JN 6:16-21
22 And at once he compelled his disciples to get on to the boat and to go before him to the other side while he dismissed the crowds.		45 And at once he compelled his disciples to get on to the boat and to go before him to the other side to Bethsaida while he himself dismisses the crowd,	16 And when it was evening, his disciples went down to the sea 17 and going on to a boat, they came across the sea to Capharnaum.
23 And having dismissed the crowds he ascended the mountain by himself to pray. And when evening came he was there alone.	(cf. 9:10)	46 And having said farewell to them he went away up the mountain to pray. 47 And when evening came, the boat was in the midst of the sea, and he alone upon the land.	And darkness had now come, and Jesus had not yet come to them,
24 But the boat was already many furlongs from the land, buffeted by the waves, for the wind was		48 And seeing them being buffeted as they	18 and, a great wind blowing, the sea was

MT 14:22-33	LK	MK 6:45-52	JN 6:16-21
contrary.		rowed, for the wind was contrary to them,	roused up.
25 And in the fourth watch of the night he came to them walking on the sea.		about the fourth watch of the night he comes to them walking on the sea; and he intended to go by them.	19 When therefore they had rowed about twenty-five or thirty furlongs,
26 And the disciples seeing him walking on the sea were troubled saying: It is a phantom, and they shouted from fear.		49 And seeing him walking on the sea they thought it was a phantom, and they shouted out. 50 For all saw him and were troubled.	they beheld Jesus walking on the sea and coming near the boat. and they were frightened.
27 But Jesus at once spoke to them saying:		But he at once spoke with them, and says to them:	20 But he says to them:
Take heart, I am I, fear not. 28 And Peter answering him said: Lord, if it is you, command me to come to you on the waters. And he said: Come. 29 And getting down from the boat, Peter began to walk on the waters, and came towards Jesus. 30 But seeing the strong wind he got frightened, and beginning to sink he shouted saying: Lord, save me. 31 And at once stretching out his hand, Jesus grasped him and says to him: O one of little faith why did you waver?		Take heart, I am I; fear not.	I am I; fear not.
32 And when they went up onto the boat, the wind ceased. 33 And those who were in the boat worshipped him, saying: Truly, you are the Son of God.		51 And he went up to them onto the boat, and the wind ceased,	21 And they assented therefore to take him into the boat, and at once the boat came to the land to which they were going. (↓ §164)
		and they were exceedingly above measure amazed in themselves and wondered; 52 for they did not understand about the loaves, but their heart had been hardened.	

§163 Healings at Gennesaret

MT 14:34-36	LK	MK 6:53-56	JN
34 And crossing over they came to land at Gennesaret.		53 And crossing over, they came to land at Gennesaret, and they anchored.	
35 And the men of that place recognized him and sent into all that region around, and carried to him all who were ill.		54 And when they came out of the boat they recognized him at once 55 and ran round all that region, and began to carry around on beds (those) who were ill, wherever they heard that he was. 56 And wherever he entered into villages or into towns, or into farms, they put the sick in the market-places.	
36 And they begged him that they might touch only the hem of		And they begged him that they might touch but the hem of his	

MT 14:34-36
his garment,
and those who touched were completely saved.

(↓ §167)

LK

MK 6:53-56
garment,
and whoever touched were saved.

(↓ §167)

JN

§164 The "Work of God"

MT   LK   MK   JN 6:22-34

(↑ §162)

22 On the morrow, the crowd that had stood on the far side of the sea had seen that there was no other boat there but one and that Jesus had not got into the boat with his disciples, but his disciples alone had gone away—

23 Other boats came* from Tiberias near to the place where they had eaten the bread after the Lord had given thanks.

24 When therefore the crowd had seen that Jesus was not there nor his disciples, they embarked on the boats and came to Capharnaum looking for Jesus.

25 And having found him on the far side of the sea they said to him: Rabbi, when did you get here?

26 Jesus answered and said to them: Amen, amen I say to you, you are seeking me not because you saw signs, but because you ate of the loaves and were satisfied.

27 Work not for the food that perishes, but for the food that remains unto eternal life, which the Son of Man will give you. For on him has God the Father set his seal.

28 They said therefore to him: What should we do to work the works of God?

29 Jesus answered and said to them:
This is the work of God, that you believe in the one whom He has sent.

30 They said therefore to him: What sign then do you do that we may see and believe you? What do you work?

31 Our fathers ate the manna in the desert, just as it has been written: He gave them bread from heaven to eat (Ps. 77[78]:24; Ex. 16:4).

32. Jesus therefore said to them:
Amen, amen I say to you, Moses did not give you the bread from heaven, but my Father gives you the true bread from heaven;

33 for the bread of God is that which comes down from heaven and gives life to the world.

34 They said therefore to him: Lord, give us always this bread.

MT	LK	MK	JN 6:35-59
			35 Jesus said to them:
			I am the bread of life; he that comes to me will not be hungry, and he that believes in me will never thirst.
			36 But I said to you that you have both seen me and do not believe.
			37 Everything that the Father gives me will come to me, and he that comes to me I will certainly not cast out,
			38 because I have come down from heaven not that I may do my own will but the will of him who sent me.
			39 And this is the will of him who sent me, that everything that he has given to me I shall not lose (any) of it, but I shall raise it up on the last day.
			40 For this is the will of my Father, that everyone who beholds the Son and believes in him may have eternal life, and I will raise him up on the last day.
			41 The Jews therefore murmured about him because he said: I am the bread that came down from heaven,
			42 and they said: Is not this (man) Jesus the son of Joseph, whose father and mother we know? How says he now: I have come down from heaven?
			43 Jesus answered and said to them: Stop murmuring with one another.
			44 Nobody can come to me unless the Father who sent me draw him, and I will raise him up on the last day.
			45 It has been written in the Prophets: And they shall all be taught of God (Is. 54:13). Everyone who has heard and learned from the Father comes to me.
			46 Not that anyone has beheld the Father, except the one who is from God; he has beheld the Father.
			47 Amen, amen I say to you, he who believes in me has eternal life.
			48 I am the bread of life.
			49 Your fathers ate the manna in the desert and died;
			50 this is the bread that comes down from heaven, so that (if) anyone eats of it, indeed he will not die.
			51 I am the living bread that comes down from heaven; if anyone eats of this bread he will live forever; and indeed the bread which I will give is my flesh for the life of the world.
			52 The Jews therefore began to quarrel among themselves, saying: How can this man give us his flesh to eat?
			53 Jesus therefore said to them: Amen, amen I say to you, unless you eat the flesh of the Son of Man and drink his blood, you will not have life in yourselves.
			54 He who consumes my body and drinks my blood has eternal life, and I will raise him up on the last day.
			55 For my flesh is veritable food and my blood is veritable drink.
			56 He who consumes my flesh and drinks my blood remains in me and I in him.

MT   LK   MK   JN 6:35-59

57 Just as the living Father has sent me and I live because of the Father, so also he who consumes me he also will live because of me.

58 This is the bread that comes down from heaven—not just as your fathers ate the manna and died—he who consumes this bread will live forever.

59 These things he said teaching in the synagogue at Capharnaum.

§166 "This Word Is Hard"

MT   LK   MK   JN 6:60-71

60 Many therefore of his disciples who had heard said: This word is hard; who can listen to it?

61 And Jesus knowing in himself that his disciples were murmuring about this, said to them: Does this scandalize you?

62 If then you should behold the Son of Man ascending where he was before?

63 The Spirit is the life-giving (thing), the flesh does not profit anything; the words that I have spoken to you are Spirit and are life.

64 But there are among you some who do not believe. For Jesus knew from the beginning who they were who did not believe and who the one to betray him was.

65 And he said: This is why I have said to you: Nobody can come to me unless it has been given to him from the Father.

66 From this (time) many of his disciples turned back and no longer walked with him.

67 Jesus therefore said to the Twelve: Do you too wish to go away?

68 Simon Peter answered him: Lord, to whom shall we go? You have the words of eternal life; 69 and we have believed and have realized that you are the Holy One of God.*

70 Jesus answered them: Did not I choose you the Twelve, and of you one is a devil?

71 Now he was speaking of Judas (son) of Simon Iscariot; for he was the one about to betray him, one of the Twelve.

(↓ §193)

MT 15:1-20   LK 6:39   MK 7:1-23   JN

(↑§163)

1 Then Pharisees and Scribes from Jerusalem
come up to Jesus,

saying:

2 Why do your disciples transgress the
tradition of the elders?
for they do not wash hands when they eat
bread.
3 And he answering said to them:

Why do you also transgress the commandment
of God for the sake of your tradition?

4 For God said:
Honour your father and your mother,
and: He who curses father or mother shall die
the death **(Ex. 20:12; Dt. 5:16)**.
5 But you say:
Whoever says to father or mother:
Anything of mine (through) which you might
be benefited is a sacred gift,
6 will certainly not be honouring his father
or his mother;
and you have annulled the word of God for
the sake of your tradition.

7 Hypocrites, Isaiah well prophesied about you
saying:
8 This people honours me with the lips,
but their heart is far distant from me;
9 In vain do they worship me,
teaching as doctrines the commandments of
men **(Is. 29:13, LXX)**.

3 And he answering said to them:

(↑§163)

1 And the Pharisees and some of the Scribes
coming from Jerusalem gather together to
him.
2 And seeing some of his disciples eating bread
with defiled, that is, unwashed hands,—
3 For the Pharisees and all the Jews do not
eat without washing hands properly,*
observing the tradition of the elders,
4 and (returning) from the market-place they
do not eat unless they have washed; and
many other things there are which they have
taken over to observe, the washings of cups
and utensils and copper pots and beds*—
5 And the Pharisees and the Scribes
questioned him:
Why do your disciples not walk according to
the tradition of the elders?
but eat bread with defiled hands?

6a And he said to them:

(see v. 8 below)

10 For Moses said:
Honour your father and your mother,
and he who curses father or mother shall die
the death.
11 But you say:
If a man says to father or mother:
Anything of mine (through) which you might
be benefited is Korban, that is, a sacred gift,
12 you no longer allow him to do anything for
father or for mother,
13a annulling the word of God by your
tradition, which you have handed on.

6b Well did Isaiah prophesy about you
hypocrites, as it has been written:
This people honours me with the lips,
but their heart is far distant from me;
7 In vain do they worship me,
teaching as doctrines the commandments of
men **(Is. 29:13, LXX)**.
8 Leaving the commandment of God, you hold
the tradition of men.
9 And he used to say to them:

MT 15:1-20   LK 6:39   MK 7:1-23   JN

Why do you also transgress the commandment   Truly you negate the commandment of God in
of God for the sake of your tradition?   order to observe your tradition.
4 For God said: 10 For Moses said:
Honour your father and your mother,   Honour your father and your mother,
and: He who curses father or mother shall die   and: He who curses father or mother shall die
the death.   the death.
5 But you say: 11 But you say:
Whoever says to father or mother,   If a man says to father or mother:
Anything of mine (through) which you might   Anything of mine (through) which you might
be benefited is a sacred gift,   be benefited is Korban, that is, a sacred gift,
6 will certainly not be honouring his father or   12 you no longer allow him to do anything for
his mother;   father or mother,
and you have annulled the word of God for   13 annulling the word of God by your
the sake of your tradition.   tradition, which you have handed on.
                                                                                           And many similar things you are frequently
                                                                                           doing.
10 And summoning the crowd, he said to   14 And summoning again the crowd, he began
them: to say to them:
Hear and take it in.   Hear me, all, and take it in.
11 Nothing that enters into the mouth defiles   15 There is nothing from without the man that
the man;   enters into him that can defile him;
but what comes out of the mouth, this defiles   but the things that come out of the man are
the man.   the things that defile the man.
                                                                                           16 If anyone has ears to hear, let him hear.
12 Then his disciples coming up say to him: 17 And when he entered into the house away
                                                                                           from the crowd, his disciples questioned him
Do you know that the Pharisees hearing the
word were scandalized?
13 And he answering said: *39 And he also spoke a parable to them:*
Every plant which my heavenly Father did not
plant shall be uprooted.
14 Leave them; they are blind leaders of the
blind;
and if a blind man leads a blind man,   *Surely a blind man cannot lead a blind man?*
both will fall into (the) ditch.   *Will not both fall down into (the) ditch?*
15 And Peter answering said to him:
Explain to us this parable.   (about) the parable.
16 And he said: 18 And he says to them:
Really, are you also without understanding?   So, are you also without understanding?
17 Do you not know that everything that   Do you not know that everything from
enters into the mouth removes into the   without that enters into the man is unable to
stomach   defile him, 19 because it does not enter into
                                                                                           his heart but into the stomach,
and is cast out into a drain?   and goes out into the drain?—
                                                                                           making all foods "clean."
                                                                                           20 And he used to say: What comes out of the
18 But the things that come out of the mouth   man,
come out of the heart,   this defiles the man.
and these things defile the man.

MT 15:1-20	LK 6:39	MK 7:1-23	JN
19 For from the heart come forth evil schemings, murders, adulteries, sexual sins, thefts, perjuries, blasphemies. 20 These are the things that defile the man; but to eat with unwashed hands does not defile the man.		21 For from within from the heart of men go out schemings that are evil, sexual sins, thefts, murders, 22 adulteries, excesses, iniquities, deceit, lewdness, the evil eye, blasphemy, arrogance, folly. 23 All these, the evil things from within, go out and defile the man.	

§168 The Syrophoenician Woman

MT 15:21-28	LK	MK 7:24-30	JN
21 And coming forth thence Jesus withdrew into the parts of Tyre and Sidon. 22 And lo a Canaanite woman from those districts coming out shouted, saying: Have pity on me, Lord, Son of David; my daughter is evilly possessed by a demon. 23 But he did not answer her a word. And his disciples coming up to him asked him saying: Dismiss her, because she is shouting behind us. 24 And he answering said: I have not been sent, except to the lost sheep of the House of Israel **(cf. Mt. 10:5)**. 25 But she coming knelt to him, saying: Lord, help me. 26 And he answering said: It is not good to take the bread of the children and throw it to the puppies. 27 But she said: Yes, Lord, for the puppies also eat of the crumbs that fall from the table of their masters. 28 Then Jesus answering said to her: O woman, great is your faith; be it done to you as you wish. And her daughter was cured from that hour.		24 And rising up thence he went away into the districts of Tyre and Sidon. And entering into a house he wanted no one to know and he could not be hidden. 25 But at once a woman hearing about him, whose daughter had an unclean spirit, coming fell down at his feet. 26 Now the woman was a Greek, a Syrophoenician by race; and she asked him to cast the demon out of her daughter. 27 And he said to her: Let the children first be fed; for it is not good to take the bread of the children and throw it to the puppies. 28 But she answered and says to him: Yes, Lord, the puppies under the table also eat of the crumbs of the children. 29 And he said to her: For this saying, Go away; the demon has gone forth out of your daughter. 30 And coming back into her house, she found the child laid on the bed and the devil gone forth.	

§169 Healing of a Deaf Mute and Many Others

MT 15:29-31   LK   MK 7:31-37   JN

29 And passing thence Jesus came beside the sea of Galilee.

And going up on to the mountain, he sat there (cf. Mt. 5:1).
30 And many crowds came up to him, having with them the lame, the maimed, the blind, the dumb, and many others, and they dropped them at his feet, and he healed them;

31 And again going forth from the districts of Tyre he came through Sidon to the sea of Galilee up through the districts of the Decapolis.

(cf. 6:3)

32 And they bring him one dumb and impeded in speech, and they beg him to lay his hand on him.
33 And taking him away from the crowd apart he thrust his fingers into his ears, and spitting he touched his tongue,
34 and looking up to heaven he sighed and says to him: Ephphatha, which means, Be opened.
35 And at once his hearing was restored, and at once the binding of his tongue was set free, and he began to speak properly.
36 And he charged them not to tell anyone; but the more he charged them, the more effusively they proclaimed (it).

31 so that the crowd marvelled that they were seeing the dumb speaking, the maimed whole, and the lame walking, and the blind seeing; and they glorified the God of Israel.

37 And they were exceedingly amazed, saying: He has done all things well; he causes both the deaf to hear and the dumb to speak.

§170 Feeding of the Four Thousand

MT 15:32-39   LK   MK 8:1-10   JN

32 And Jesus summoning his disciples, said:

I am taking pity on the crowd, for already they remain with me for three days and have nothing to eat;
and I do not intend to dismiss them fasting,
lest perhaps they faint on the way.

1 In those days again, when there was a great crowd, and they had nothing to eat, summoning his disciples, he says to them:
2 I am taking pity on the crowd, for already they remain with me for three days and have nothing to eat,
3 and if I were to dismiss them fasting to their homes, they will faint on the way; and some of them are from a long way off.

33 And his disciples say to him:
Whence do we in this barren place get as many loaves as to satisfy such a crowd?
34 And Jesus says to them:
How many loaves do you have?
And they said: Seven, and a few small fish.
35 And having told the crowd to sit down on the ground,
36 he took the seven loaves and the fishes, and giving thanks he broke
and gave to his disciples, and the disciples to the crowds.

4 And his disciples answered him:
Whence will anyone be able here at this barren place to satisfy these with loaves?
5 And he asked them:
How many loaves do you have?
And they said: Seven.
6 And he tells the crowd to sit down on the ground;
and taking the seven loaves, giving thanks he broke

and gave to the disciples to set before them, and they set before the crowd.
7 And they had a few little fishes; and having blessed them, he said they also should be set before them.

37 And all ate and were satisfied. And the surplus of the fragments they took up, seven full hampers.

8 And they ate and were satisfied. And they took up the surpluses of the fragments, seven hampers.

MT 15:32-39	LK	MK 8:1-10	JN
38 And the eaters were four thousand men, apart from women and children. 39 And having dismissed the crowds, he got into the boat and came to the borders of Magadan.		9 And there were about four thousand, and he dismissed them. 10 And at once having got into the boat with his disciples, he came to the parts of Dalmanutha.	

§171 "No Sign but That of Jonah" (§§140, 218, 234)

MT 16:1-4	MT 12:38-39	LK 11:29	LK 12:54-56	MK 8:11-13	JN
1 And the Pharisees and Sadducees coming up (and) tempting (him), asked him to show them a sign from heaven.	*38 Then some of the Scribes and Pharisees answered him saying: Teacher, we want to see a sign from you.*	*29 And while the crowds were thronging he began to say:*		11 And the Pharisees went out and began to debate with him, asking him for a sign from heaven, tempting him:	
2 And answering he said to them: When evening comes* you say: Good weather, for the sky is fiery; 3 and in the early morning: Stormy today, for the sky is overcast and red.	*39 And answering he said to them:*		*54 And he said also to the crowds: When you see a cloud rising over the west, at once you say that a shower is coming, and it so happens. 55 And when (you see) a south wind blowing you say that it will be scorching, and it happens.*	12 And sighing deeply in his spirit, he says:	
While you know how to descry the face of the sky, yet the signs of the times you cannot.			*56 Hypocrites, you know how to discern the face of the earth and of the sky, but how do you not discern this time?*		
4 An evil and adulterous generation is looking for a sign, and a sign shall not be given to it, except the sign of Jonah. And leaving them he went away.	*An evil and adulterous generation is looking for a sign, and a sign shall not be given to it, except the sign of Jonah the prophet.*	*This generation is an evil generation; it is seeking a sign, and a sign shall not be given to it, except the sign of Jonah.*		Why does this generation seek a sign? Amen I say to you, on no account shall a sign be given to this generation! 13 And leaving them, again embarking he went away to the other side.	

§172 Leaven of the Pharisees (§222)

MT 16:5-12	LK 12:1	MK 8:14-21	JN
5 And the disciples coming to the other side forgot to take loaves.	*1 Meanwhile as the myriads of the crowd were gathering together so as to trample on one another,*	14 And his disciples forgot to take loaves, and they had not even one loaf with them in the boat.	
6 And Jesus said to them: See and beware of the leaven of the Pharisees and Sadducees.	*he began to say to his disciples first:* *You yourselves beware of the leaven, that is, the hypocrisy of the Pharisees.*	15 And he charged them saying: See and watch out for the leaven of the Pharisees and the leaven of Herod.	
7 But they argued among themselves saying: We have not brought loaves.		16 And they argued with one another saying: We do not have loaves.	
8 But Jesus knowing said: Why do you argue among yourselves, men of little faith, because you have no loaves?		17 And Jesus knowing says to them: Why do you argue, because you have no loaves?	
9 Do you not perceive		Do you not perceive nor understand? Have you your heart hardened?	
		18 Having eyes, do you not see, and having ears do you not hear.	
nor remember the five loaves of the five thousand and how many baskets you took?		And do you not remember 19 when I broke the five loaves among the five thousand, how many full baskets of fragments you gathered? They say to him: Twelve.	
10 Nor the seven loaves of the four thousand and how many hampers did you gather?		20 When the seven to the four thousand, the contents of how many hampers of fragments did you gather? And they say: Seven.	
		21 And he said to them: Do you not yet understand?	
11 How do you not perceive that I spoke to you not about loaves? But beware of the leaven of the Pharisees and Sadducees.			
12 Then they perceived that he did not tell them to beware of the leaven of the loaves, but of the teaching of the Pharisees and Sadducees.			
(↓ §174)			

§173 Blind Man of Bethsaida

MT	LK	MK 8:22-26	JN
		22 And they come into Bethsaida. And they bring him a blind man and beg him to touch him.	
		23 And grasping the hand of the blind man he led him out of the village; and spitting into his eyes, laying hands on him, he questioned him: Do you see anything?	
		24 And looking he said: I see men, because I behold as it were trees walking.	
		25 Then again he laid hands on his eyes, and he looked steadily	

MT	LK	MK 8:22-26	JN
		and was restored, and he saw everything clearly. 26 And he sent him to his house saying: Do not enter into the village.	

§174 Peter's Confession

MT 16:13-20	LK 9:18-21	MK 8:27-30	JN
(↑ §172)	(↑ §161)		

MT 16:13-20

(↑ §172)

13 And when Jesus came into the parts of Caesarea Philippi,

he asked his disciples saying:
Who do men say that the Son of Man is?
14 And they said:
Some indeed John the Baptist, but others Elijah,
and still others Jeremiah, or one of the prophets.
15 He says to them:
And you, who do you say that I am?
16. And Simon Peter answering said:
You are the Christ, the Son of the Living God.
17 And Jesus answering said to him:
Blessed are you Simon Bar-Jona, because flesh and blood has not revealed (it) to you, but my Father, who is in the heavens.
18 And I say to you, that you are Peter, and upon this rock I will build my church, and the gates of Hades will not prevail against it.
19 And I will give to you the keys of the Kingdom of the Heavens,
and whatever you bind upon earth shall be bound in the heavens,
and whatever you loose upon the earth shall be loosed in the heavens.
20 Then he warned the disciples not to tell anyone that he was the Christ.

LK 9:18-21

(↑ §161)

18 And it happened that when he was praying alone, his disciples were with him, and
he questioned them saying:
Who do the crowds say that I am?
19 And they answering said:
John the Baptist, but others Elijah,

and others that some prophet of the Ancients has arisen **(9:8)**.
20 And he said to them:
And you, who do you say that I am?
And Peter answering said:
The Christ of God.

21 And warning them he instructed them not to tell this to anyone.

MK 8:27-30

27 And Jesus and his disciples went out into the villages of Caesarea Philippi,
and on the way

he questioned his disciples saying to them:
Who do men say that I am?
28 And they said to him saying:
John the Baptist, and others: Elijah,

and others: One of the prophets **(6:15)**.

29 And he questioned them:
And you, who do you say that I am?
Then Peter answering says to him:
You are the Christ.

30 And he warned them not to tell anyone about him.

§175 The First Passion Prediction

MT 16:21	LK 9:22	MK 8:31-32a	JN
21 From then Jesus began to show his disciples that he was to go up to Jerusalem and to suffer much from the elders and high priests and scribes and to be killed, and on the third day to be raised.	22 saying: The Son of Man is to suffer much, and to be rejected, from the elders and high priests and scribes and to be killed, and on the third day to be raised. (↓ §177)	31 And he began to teach them that the Son of Man was to suffer much and to be rejected by the elders and the high priests and the scribes and to be killed, and after three days to be raised up. 32a And he spoke of the matter without constraint.	

§176 Peter Rebuked by Jesus

MT 16:22-23	LK	MK 8:32b-33	JN
22 And Peter taking him aside, began to warn him saying: (God be) merciful to you, Lord; by no means shall this be to you. 23 But he turning said to Peter: Go behind me, Satan; you are a scandal to me, because you do not perceive the things of God but the things of men.		32b And the Peter taking him aside began to warn him. 33 But he turning and seeing his disciples warned Peter and says: Go behind me, Satan; because you do not perceive the things of God, but the things of men.	

§177 The Cross and Self-Denial

MT 16:24-28	LK 9:23-27	MK 8:34-9:1	JN
	(↑ §175)		
24 Then Jesus said to his disciples: If anyone wants to come after me, let him deny himself and take up his cross and follow me. 25 For whoever wishes to save his soul will lose it; and he who would lose his soul for my sake, will find it. 26 Therefore, what will a man be benefited, if he should gain the whole world, but forfeit his soul? Or what will a man give as an exchange for his soul?	23 And he used to say to all: If anyone wants to come after me, let him deny himself and take up his cross daily and follow me. 24 For whoever wishes to save his soul will lose it; and he who would lose his soul for my sake, he will save it. 25 Therefore, what is a man benefited, gaining the whole world, but losing or forfeiting himself? 26 For whoever is ashamed of me and of my words,	34 And summoning the crowd with his disciples, he said to them: If anyone wants to come after me, let him deny himself and take up his cross and follow me. 35 For whoever wishes to save his soul will lose it; and he who would lose his soul for my sake and the gospel will save it. 36 Therefore, what benefit is it for a man to gain the whole world, but forfeit his soul? 37 What therefore may a man give as an exchange for his soul? 38 For whoever is ashamed of me and of my words, in this adulterous and sinful generation,	(cf. 12:25)

MT 16:24-28

27 For the Son of Man is going
to come in the glory of his Father with his
angels,
and then he will reward each one according to
his deeds.

28 Amen I say to you, that there are some
standing here who will not taste death,
until they see the Son of Man coming in his
Kingdom.

LK 9:23-27

of him will the Son of Man be ashamed
when he comes in the glory also of the Father
and the holy angels.

27 And I say to you truly, there are some
standing here who will not taste death,
until they see the Kingdom of God.

MK 8:34-9:1

the Son of Man too will be ashamed of him,
when he comes in the glory of his Father with
the holy angels.

9:1 And he said to them:
Amen I say to you, that there are some
standing here who will not taste death,
until they see the Kingdom of God having
come in power.

JN

§178 The Transfiguration

MT 17:1-9

1 And after six days

Jesus takes Peter and James and John his
brother
and brings them up onto a high mountain by
themselves.
2 And he was transformed in front of them,
and his face shone like the sun,

and his garments became white as the light.

3 And lo, they saw Moses and Elijah
conversing with him.

4 But Peter answering said to Jesus:

Lord, for us to be here is good;
if you wish, I will make three tents here, one
for you, and one for Moses and one for Elijah.

5 While he was yet apeaking lo, a bright cloud
overshadowed them,

and lo, a voice from the cloud, saying:

LK 9:28-36

28 And it came to pass about eight days after
these events
and taking Peter and John and James,

he went up onto the mountain to pray.

29 And while he was praying the appearance
of his face became different,
and his vesture gleaming white.

30 And lo, two men were conversing with him,
who were Moses and Elijah,
31 who appearing in glory were speaking of
his departure, which he was about to
accomplish in Jerusalem.
32 Now Peter and those with him were heavy
with sleep; but being wakened up they saw his
glory and the two men who stood by him.
33 And it came to pass when they were
departing from him, Peter said to Jesus:
Master, for us to be here is good;
and let us make three tents, one for you, and
one for Moses, and one for Elijah,
not knowing what he was saying.

34 And while he was saying these things, a
cloud came and overshadowed them; and they
were frightened as they entered into the cloud.
35 And a voice came from the cloud, saying:

MK 9:2-10

2 And after six days

Jesus takes Peter and James and John,

and brings them up onto a high mountain by
themselves alone.
And he was transformed in front of them,

3 and his garments became shining exceedingly
white, such as no fuller upon the earth can
make so white.
4 And they saw Elijah with Moses, and they
were conversing with Jesus.

5 And Peter answering says to Jesus:

Rabbi, for us to be here is good;
and let us make three tents, one for you, and
one for Moses, and one for Elijah;
6 for he did not know what he was answering,
for they were afraid.
7 And a cloud came overshadowing them,

and a voice came from the cloud saying:

JN

MT 17:1-9	LK 9:28-36	MK 9:2-10	JN
This is my Son, the Beloved, in whom I am well pleased; hear him. 6 And when the disciples heard, they fell on their faces and were very afraid. 7 And Jesus came up and touching them said: Rise up and fear not. 8 And lifting up their eyes, they saw no one save Jesus himself alone. 9 And as they were coming down from the mountain, Jesus enjoined them saying: Tell the vision to no one, until the Son of Man be raised up from the dead.	This is my Son, The Chosen; hear him. 36 And when the voice came, Jesus was found alone. And they kept silence, and in those days reported to no one any of the things they had beheld. (↓ §180)	This is my Son, The Beloved; hear him. 8 And looking about instantly they no longer saw anyone save Jesus alone with them. 9 And as they were coming down from the mountain, he ordered them that they should not relate to anyone what they had seen, except when the Son of Man has risen from the dead. 10 And they retained the matter among themselves, debating the meaning of 'to rise from the dead.'	

§179 The Coming of Elijah

MT 17:10-13	LK	MK 9:11-13	JN
10 And his disciples questioned him, saying: Why then do the Scribes say that Elijah must come first **(Mal. 4:5)**? 11 And he answering, said: Elijah indeed is coming and will restore all things. 12 But I say to you, that Elijah has already come, and they did not recognize him, yet did with him whatever they willed; so also the Son of Man is about to suffer by them. 13 Then the disciples understood that he was speaking to them about John the Baptist.		11 And they questioned him, saying: The Scribes say that Elijah must come first. 12 And he said to them: Elijah indeed coming first restores all things; and how has it been written about the Son of Man that he will suffer greatly and be brought to nought? 13 Yet I say to you, that Elijah has indeed come, and they did to him whatever they willed as is written about him.	

MT 17:14-21   LK 9:37-43a; *17:5-6*   MK 9:14-29   JN

                              (↑ §178)

14 And when they came to the crowd,   37 And it came to pass on the following day   14 And coming to the disciples they saw a
                              when they came down from the mountain a   large crowd around them and scribes debating
                              large crowd met him.   with them.
                                                                       15 And at once the whole crowd seeing him
                                                                       were astonished and running forward to him
                                                                       greeted him.
                                                                       16 And he questioned them:
                                                                       What are you debating with them?
a man came up to him kneeling to him 15 and   38 And lo a man from the crowd cried out,   17 And one out of the crowd answered him:
saying: saying:
Lord have pity on my son   Teacher, I beg you to look upon my son,   Teacher, I have brought my son to you,
                              because he is my only child;

because he is a lunatic and suffers greatly; for   39 and lo a spirit takes him and suddenly cries   having a dumb spirit. 18 And wherever it
he often falls into the fire and often into the   out and convulses him foaming, and scarcely   seizes him, it tears him, and he foams and
water.   departs from him bruising him;   grinds his teeth, and is wasting away;
16 And I brought him to your disciples, and   40 and I begged your disciples to cast him out,   and I told your disciples to cast him out, and
they could not heal him.   and they could not.   they were not able.
17 And Jesus answering said: 41 And Jesus answering said: 19 And Jesus answering says to them:
O unbelieving and perverted generation, how   O unbelieving and perverted generation, how   O unbelieving and perverted* generation, how
long shall I be with you?   long shall I be with you   long shall I be with you;
how long shall I put up with you?   and put up with you?   how long shall I put up with you?
Bring him to me here.   Lead your son here.   Bring him to me.
                              42 And while he was still coming, the demon   20 And they carried him to him. And seeing
                              tore him and convulsed him;   him the spirit at once convulsed him, and
                                                                       falling to the ground, he rolled about foaming.
                                                                       21 And he questioned his father:
                                                                       How long has he been like this?
(cf. v. 15)   And he replied: From infancy. 22 And often it
                                                                       threw him now into the fire, and now into
                                                                       water in order to destroy him; but if you can,
                                                                       help us, taking pity on us.
                                                                       23 And Jesus said to him:
                                                                       If you can believe, all things are possible to
                                                                       him who believes.
                                                                       24 Crying out at once the father of the child
                                                                       said with tears:* I believe; help you my
                                                                       unbelief.
18 And Jesus rebuked him   and Jesus rebuked the unclean spirit   25 And Jesus seeing that a crowd was
                                                                       gathering, rebuked the unclean spirit, saying to
                                                                       it:
                                                                       Dumb and deaf spirit, I command you, go out
                                                                       of him, and no more enter into him.
                                                                       26 And crying out and convulsing (him)
and the demon went out of him.   violently, it went out. And he became as it
                                                                       were dead so that many said that he was dead.
And the youth was healed from that hour.   and he healed the youth, and gave him back to   27 But Jesus grasped his hand and raised him
                              his father.   up, and he stood up.

MT 17:14-21

LK 9:37-43a; *17:5-6*

MK 9:14-29

JN

43a And all were amazed at the majesty of God.

19 Then the disciples coming up privately said to Jesus:
Why were we not able to cast him out?
20 And he says to them:
Because of your little faith.

28 And when he entered the house, his disciples questioned him privately:
Wherefore were we not able to cast him out?
29 And he said to them:

17:5 And the apostles said to the Lord:
Increase our faith.
6 And the Lord said:
If you have faith like a grain of mustard seed,

Amen I say to you, that if you have faith like a grain of mustard seed,
you shall say to this mountain: Remove hence there, and it shall be removed; and nothing will be impossible to you.
21* But this kind does not go forth except by prayer and fasting.

you would say to this mulberry tree: Be you uprooted and planted in the sea; and it would obey you.

This kind cannot go out by anything except by prayer and fasting.*

§181 The Second Passion Prediction

MT 17:22-23

LK 9:43b-45
43b And while all were marvelling at all the things he was doing,

MK 9:30-32

JN

22 And while they were together in Galilee,

30 And going out from there he was travelling through Galilee, and did not wish anyone to know it, 31 because he was teaching his disciples;
and he was saying to them:

Jesus said to them:

he said to his disciples:
44 Do you put into your ears these words:
For the Son of Man is about to be betrayed into the hands of men.

The Son of Man is about to be betrayed into the hands of men, 23 and they will kill him, and on the third day, he will be raised.

The Son of Man is being betrayed into the hands of men, and they will kill him, and being killed after three days he will be raised up.
32 But they understood not the saying, and they were afraid to question him.

And they were exceedingly grieved.

45 But they understood not this saying, and it had been veiled from them so that they should not perceive it, and they were afraid to ask him about this saying.

(↓§183)

(↓§183)

136

MT 17:24-27   LK   MK   JN

24 And when they entered Capharnaum those who collected the
didrachmas came up to Peter and said: Does not your teacher pay
the didrachmas?
25. He says: Yes.
And when he entered the house, Jesus forestalled him saying:
Simon, what do you think? Do the kings of the earth levy tax or
tribute from their sons or from the others?
26 And he replying: From the others, Jesus said to him:
Surely then the sons are free. 27 But lest we should scandalize
them, go to the sea, cast a hook, and take the first fish coming up,
and opening its mouth you will find a stater. Taking that, give it
to them for me and you.

§183 Discourse on True Greatness (§§128, 205)

MT 18:1-5   MT 10:40   LK 9:46-48   MK 9:33-37   JN
                                                     (↑ §181)   (↑ §181)

1 In that hour   33 And they entered
                                                                                Capharnaum, and coming into
                                                                                the house he questioned them:
                                                                                What were you debating on the
                                                                                way?
                                                                                34 But they were silent,
the disciples came up to Jesus,   46 And a debate started among   for among themselves they were
saying: Who then is greatest in   them, about who was greatest   disputing on the way, who is
the Kingdom of the Heavens?   among them.   greatest.
                                                     47 But Jesus knowing the debate 35 And sitting down he called the
                                                     of their heart,   Twelve and says to them:
(cf. 19:30)   If anyone wants to be first, he
                                                                                shall be last of all and servant of
                                                                                all.
2 And calling up a little child, he   and taking up a little child, he   36 And taking a little child, he
stood him in their midst,   stood him beside himself.   stood him in their midst,
3 and he said: 48 And he said to them: and hugging him he said to them:
Amen I say to you, unless you
turn and become as little children,   **(cf. 18:17)**   **(cf. 10:15)**
you may by no means enter into
the Kingdom of the Heavens.
4 Whoever therefore humbles
himself like this little child, he is
the greatest in the Kingdom of
the Heavens.
5 And whoever receives one such   Whoever receives this little child   37 Whoever receives one of such
little child in my name, receives   in my name receives me;   little children in my name,
me **(19:13ff.).**   receives me;

137

MT 18:1-5	MT 10:40	LK 9:46-48	MK 9:33-37	JN
(↓§185)	*40 He who receives you receives me and he who receives me receives him who sent me.*	and whoever receives me receives him who sent me (**cf. Lk. 10:16**). For the one who is the least among you all, he is the great one.	and whoever receives me, receives not me, but him who sent me.	

§184 The Unauthorized Exorcist (§128)

MT 10:42	LK 9:49-50	MK 9:38-41	JN
	49 And John answering said: Master, we saw someone casting out demons by your name. and we prevented him, because he does not follow with us. 50 But Jesus said to him: Do not prevent (him);	38 John answered him: Teacher, we saw someone casting out demons your name, who does not follow us, and we prevented him, because he was not following us. 39 But Jesus said: Do not prevent him; for there is no one who will work a mighty deed in my name, and will be able quickly to speak evil of me. 40 For he who is not against us is for us.	
(cf. Mt. 12:30=Lk 11:23) *42 For whoever will give one of these little ones a cup of cold water only in the name of a disciple, Amen I say to you, he will not lose his reward.*	for he who is not against you is for you. (↓§192)	41 For whoever will give you to drink a cup of water in my name, because you are Christ's, Amen I say to you, that he will not lose his reward.	

§185 Warnings about Temptations (§261)

MT 18:6-9	LK 17:2, 1	MK 9:42-48	JN
(↑§183)			
6 And whoever should scandalize one of these little ones who believe in me; it is advantageous for him for an ass's mill-stone to be suspended about his neck, and to be submerged in the depth of the sea.	*2 It were better for him if a mill-stone were hung round about his neck and he had been thrown into the sea, (rather) than that he should scandalize one of these little ones.*	42 And whoever should scandalize one of these little ones who believe in me: it is good for him rather if an ass's mill-stone were hung round about his neck, and he had been cast into the sea.	
7 Woe to the world from scandals; for it is necessary for scandals to come, but woe to that man through whom the scandal comes.	*1 And he said to his disciples: It is impossible for scandals not to come, but woe (to him) through whom they come.*		

MT 18:6-9	LK 17:2, 1	MK 9:42-48	JN
8 If your right hand or your foot scandalizes you,		43 If your right hand should scandalize you,	

8 If your right hand or your foot scandalizes you,
cut it off and cast it from you;
for it is good for you to enter into life maimed or lame
than having two hands or two feet to be cast into the everlasting fire.

(cf. 18:8)

9 And if your eye scandalizes you, take it out, and cast it from you;
for it is good for you with one eye to enter into life,
than having two eyes to be cast into the Gehenna of Fire.

(↓ §187)

43 If your right hand should scandalize you,
cut it away;
for it is good for you to enter into life maimed
than having both hands to go away into Gehenna, into the unquenchable fire,
44* where their worm does not die, and the fire is not quenched **(Is. 66:24)**.
45 And if your foot scandalize you, cut it away; for it is good for you to enter into life lame,
than having both feet to be cast into the Gehenna of unquenchable fire.*
46* where their worm does not die, and the fire is not quenched.
47 And if your eye scandalize you, cast it out;
for it is good for you with one eye to enter into the Kingdom of God,
than having two eyes to be cast into the Gehenna of Fire, 48 where their worm does not die, and the fire is not quenched.

§186 About Salt (§§61, 250)

MT 5:13	LK 14:34-35	MK 9:49-50	JN

13 You are the salt of the earth.
but if the salt should be spoiled, how shall it be salted?
For nothing is it still of value,

except for being thrown outside to be trodden down by men.

(cf. 13:9)

34 Salt therefore is good;
but if even the salt should be spoiled, how shall it be restored?
35 Neither for the ground nor for manure is it suitable;
they throw it outside.

He that has ears to hear, let him hear.

49 For everyone shall be salted with fire, and every offering shall be salted with salt.*
50 Salt is good;
but if the salt should become un-salty, how shall you restore it?

Have salt in yourselves and be at peace with one another.

(↓ §192)

§187 The Lost Sheep (§§251, 283)

MT 18:10-14	LK 19:10; 15:3-7	MK	JN
(↑§185)			
10 Look, do not despise one of these little ones;	**(cf. 17:1b, 2)**	**(cf. 9:42)**	
for I say to you that their angels in heaven continually see the face of my Father who is in the heavens.		**(cf. 10:15)**	
11* For the Son of Man came to save what has been lost.	10 For the Son of Man came to seek and to save what has been lost.		
12 What think you?	15:3 And he told them this parable, saying:		
If some man should own a hundred sheep and one of them should stray,	4 Some man among you having a hundred sheep and losing one of them,		
will he not leave the ninety-nine on the mountains, and go and seek the one gone astray?	does he not forsake the ninety-nine in the desert and go after the lost one until he find it?		
13 And should he happen to find it,	5 And having found (it) he sets (it) upon his shoulders rejoicing,		
	6 and coming into the house he invites his friends and neighbours saying to them:		
	Rejoice with me, because I have found my sheep that was lost.		
Amen I say to you, that he rejoices over it	7 I say to you that so there will be joy in heaven over one sinner repenting,		
more than over the ninety-nine who have not strayed.	(more) than over the ninety-nine just who have no need of repentance.		
14 Thus, it is not the will of your Father who is in the heavens that one of these little ones be lost.			

§188 On Reproving a Brother (§262)

MT 18:15-18	LK 17:3b	MK	JN
15 And if your brother should sin against you, go off, reprove him between you and him alone; if he should hear you, you have gained your brother.	3b If your brother should sin, rebuke him; and if he should repent, forgive him.		
16 But if he should not hear you, take with you again one or two, so that by the mouth of two or three witnesses every word shall stand.			
17 And if he refuses to listen to them, tell the church; and if he also refuses to listen to the church, let him be to you as the Gentile and the tax-collector.			
18 Amen I say to you, whatever you bind upon earth shall be bound in heaven, and whatever you loose upon earth shall be loosed in heaven **(cf. 16:19)**.			

§189 Christ in His Church

MT 18:19-20 LK MK JN

19 Again, Amen I say to you, that if two of you on earth agree together about any matter whatever they ask for, it will be done for them by my Father who is in the heavens.
20 For where there are two or three gathered together in my name, there am I in their midst.

§190 On Forgiveness (§262)

MT 18:21-22

21 Then Peter came up and said to him:
Lord, how many times shall my brother sin against me, and I shall forgive him? Up to seven times?
22 Jesus says to him:
I do not say to you up to seven times,
but up to seventy-seven times.

LK 17:4 MK JN

4 And if he should sin against you seven times a day, and seven times turn back to you, saying, I repent,

you shall forgive him.

§191 The Unforgiving Servant

MT 18:23-35 LK MK JN

23 Therefore the Kingdom of the Heavens has been likened to a man, a king, who decided to hold an audit with his servants.
24 And when he began to hold (it), there was brought to him one owing ten thousand talents.
25 And as he had not (the means) to pay back, his master ordered him to be sold together with his wife and children and all his possessions in order to repay.
26 The servant, therefore, fell on his knees to him, saying: Master, be patient with me, and I will pay back everything to you.
27 And the Lord of that servant taking pity on him released him and forgave him the debt.
28 Now that servant going out found one of his fellow-servants, who owed him a hundred denarii; and seizing him, began to throttle (him) saying: Pay back whatever you owe.
29 His fellow-servant therefore fell down and begged him: Be patient with me and I will repay you.
30 But he refused and going off cast him into prison until he repaid the debt.
31 His fellow-servants therefore seeing what had happened were exceedingly upset, and came and explained to their lord all that had happened.
32 Then his master summoning him says to him: Evil servant, I forgave you the whole debt, because you begged me to. 33 Ought not

MT 18:23-35   LK   MK   JN
you then to have been merciful to your fellow-servant, just as I was
merciful to you?
34 And his lord being angered handed him over to the torturers until
he repaid him the whole debt.
35 Thus indeed will your heavenly Father do to you, if you do not,
each one, forgive his brother from your hearts.

§192 Jesus Leaves Galilee

MT 19:1-2   LK 9:51   MK 10:1   JN

                                   (↑§184)   (↑§186)

1 And it happened that when Jesus had ended   51 Now it happened that when the days of his
these words,   Assumption were coming to an end,
he passed over from Galilee and came into the   he then set his face to go to Jerusalem.   1 And rising up from there he comes into the
territory of Judea across the Jordan.   territory of Judea and across the Jordan,
2 And many crowds followed him, and he healed   and again crowds go together to him, and, as he
them there.   had been accustomed, he again continued to
                                                                                               teach them.

        (↓§274)   (↓§202)   (↓§274)

VI. The Journey towards Jerusalem
§§ 193-287

MT	LK	MK	JN 7:1-13

(↑§166)

1 And after these things Jesus continued to walk in Galilee; for he was not willing to walk in Judea, because the Jews were seeking to kill him.
2 And it was near the Feast of the Jews, the Festival of Tabernacles.
3 His brethren therefore said to him: Leave from here and go into Judea, so that your disciples will also behold your works which you do.
4 For nobody does something secretly, yet seeks to be in public. If you do these things show yourself to the world.
5 For neither did his brethren believe in him.
6 Jesus therefore says to them:
My time is not yet come, but your time is always ready.
7 The world cannot hate you, but it hates me, because I bear witness about it that its works are evil.
8 Go you up to the festival; I do not go up to this festival, because my time is not yet fulfilled.
9 And having said these things to them he himself remained in Galilee.
10 But when his brethren had gone up to the festival, then he also went up, not openly, but as it were in secret.
11 The Jews therefore were seeking him at the festival, and were saying: Where is that man?
12 And there was a great murmuring about him among the crowds; for some were saying, He is good; but others were saying: No, but he is deceiving the crowd. 13 Nobody however spoke openly about him for fear of the Jews.

§194 Jesus' Authority to Teach

MT	LK	MK	JN 7:14-36

14 And now in the middle of the festival Jesus went up to the Temple, and began to teach.
15 The Jews therefore marvelled, saying: How does this man know letters, never having had instruction?
16 Jesus answered them therefore and said:
My teaching is not mine but his who sent me; 17 if anyone wishes to do his will, he shall know about the teaching whether it is from God or whether I speak by myself.
18 He who speaks by himself seeks his own glory; but he who seeks the glory of him who sent me, this (man) is true and there is no unrighteousness in him.
19 Has not Moses given you the Law? And none of you keeps the Law. Why do you seek to kill me?
20 The crowd answered:

MT	LK	MK	JN 7:14-36

You have a demon; who is seeking to kill you?
21 Jesus answered and said to them:
I did one work and you all marvelled **(Jn. 5:1-17)**.
22 For this reason Moses gave you circumcision,—not that it is from Moses but from the fathers—and on the Sabbath you circumcise a man. 23 If the man receives circumcision on the Sabbath, in order that the Law of Moses should not be broken, are you angry with me because I made the whole man well on the Sabbath?
24 Do not judge according to appearance, but judge the just judgement.
25 Some therefore of the Jerusalemites said:
Is not this (man the one) whom they are seeking to kill? 26 And see, he is speaking publicly and they say nothing to him. Have the rulers perhaps really concluded that this (man) is the Christ? 27 But we know whence this (man) is; but when the Christ comes nobody knows whence he is.
28 Jesus therefore cried out while teaching in the Temple and saying:
You both know me and you know whence I am; and I have not come of myself, but he who has sent me is true, whom you do not know;
29 I know him, because I am from him, and he himself has sent me.
30 They sought therefore to arrest him, and nobody laid hands upon him, because his hour had not yet come. 31 Now many of the crowd believed in him, and said: When the Christ shall come, surely he will not do more signs that this (man) has done?
32 The Pharisees heard the crowd murmuring these things about him, and the high priests and the Pharisees sent attendants to arrest him.
33 Jesus therefore said:
Yet a little time I am with you, and I go away to him who sent me. 34 You will seek me and you will not find me, and where I myself am you cannot come.
35 The Jews therefore said to one another: Where will this (man) go that we shall not find him? Will he really go to the dispersion of the Greeks and teach the Greeks? 36 What is this word that he has said: You will seek me and you will not find me, and where I myself am you cannot come?

§195 The Jews Powerless to Arrest Jesus

MT	LK	MK	JN 7:37-52

37 And on the last day, the great (day) of the festival Jesus stood and cried, saying:
If any one is thirsty, let him come to me and drink. 38 He who believes in me, just as the Scripture has said, Rivers of living water will flow forth from his belly **(Prov. 18:4; Is. 58:11)**.
39 Now this he said about the Spirit which those who believed in him

MT	LK	MK	JN 7:37-52

were about to receive; for not yet had the Spirit been given because Jesus was not yet glorified.

40 (Some) of the crowd that heard these words said: This (man) is surely the Prophet.

41 Others said: This (man) is the Christ; but others said: Surely not, for does the Christ come from Galilee? 42 Did not the Scripture say that the Christ comes of the seed of David, and from Bethlehem the village where David was **(Mic. 5:2)**?

43 There was therefore a division in the crowd because of him.

44 And some of them wanted to arrest him, but nobody laid their hands upon him.

45 The attendants therefore came to the high priests and Pharisees, and the latter said to them: Why did you not bring him?

46 The attendants answered: Never did a man speak thus like this man.

47 The Pharisees therefore answered them: Surely you too have not been deceived? 48 Has any of the rulers believed in him, or any of the Pharisees? 49 But this crowd, that does not know the Law is accursed.

50 Nicodemus says to them, he who came earlier to him, being one of them:

51 Surely our Law does not judge the man unless it has first heard him and knows what he is doing?

52 They answered and said to him: Are you too from Galilee? Search and see that a prophet does not arise from Galilee.

§196 The Woman Taken in Adultery

MT	LK	MK	JN 7:53-8:11*

53 And each one went to his house,

1 but Jesus went to the Mount of Olives.

2 In the morning he again came along to the Temple, and the whole people came to him, and sitting down he taught them.

3 And the Scribes and the Pharisees bring a woman taken in adultery, and standing here in the midst 4. they say to him:

Teacher, this woman was taken in the act of committing adultery; 5 now in our Law Moses commanded such (women) to be stoned. What therefore do you say?

6 Now they said this tempting him, so that they should have (matter for) accusing him.

But Jesus bending down wrote with his finger on the ground.

7 But as they persisted questioning him, he straightened up and said to them:

Let him who is without sin among you be the first to cast a stone upon her.

8 And again bending down he continued to write on the ground.

MT	LK	MK	JN 7:53-8:11*

9 And those who had heard went out one by one, beginning with the Elders and Jesus alone was left behind and the woman who was in the middle.
10 And straightening up Jesus said to her:
Woman, where are those accusers of yours? Has nobody condemned you?
11 And she said: Nobody, Lord.
Jesus said:
Neither do I condemn you; Go, and from now no longer sin.

§197 Jesus Defends His Authority

MT	LK	MK	JN 8:12-20

12 Again therefore Jesus spoke to them, saying:
I myself am the light of the world; he who follows me will not be walking in darkness, but will have the light of life.
13 The Pharisees therefore said to him: You bear witness regarding yourself; your witness is not true.
14 Jesus answered and said to them:
Even if I bear witness about myself, my witness is true, because I know whence I came and where I am going; you indeed neither know whence I come nor where I am going.
15 You judge according to the flesh, I myself do not judge anyone.
16 Yet even if I myself do the judging, my own judgement is true, because I am not alone, but I and the Father who sent me.
17 But indeed in the Law that is yours it is written that the witness of two men is true.
18 It is I who bear witness regarding myself, and the Father who sent me bears witness.
19 They said therefore to him: Where is your Father?
Jesus answered:
You do not know either me or my Father; if you knew me, you would also know my Father.
20 These utterances he spoke in the Treasury, while teaching in the Temple; and nobody arrested him, because his hour had not yet come.

§198 Jesus Is from the Father

MT	LK	MK	JN 8:21-30

21 He said therefore to them again:
I go away and you will seek me, and you will die in your sin; where I

MT	LK	MK	JN 8:21-30

am going away to, you cannot come.
22 Therefore the Jews said: Surely he will not kill himself, because he says: Where I am going away to, you cannot come?
23 And he said to them:
You are of what is below, I am of what is above; you are of this world, I am not of this world. 24 Therefore I said to you that you will die in your sins. For if you will not believe that I myself am, you will die in your sins.
25 Therefore they said to him:
Who are you?
Jesus said to them:
Entirely that which I am also telling you.* 26 I have much to speak and to judge in your regard; but he who has sent me is true, and what I have heard from him these things I speak to the world—
27 they did not understand that he spoke to them of the Father.
28 Jesus therefore said to them:
When you shall lift up the Son of Man, then you will know that I myself am, and that of myself I do nothing, but just as the Father has taught me, these things I speak. 29 And he who sent me is with me; he has not left me alone, because I always do the things that please him.
30 When he was saying these things many believed in him.

§199 Jesus and Abraham

MT	LK	MK	JN 8:31-59

31 Jesus therefore said to the Jews who had come to believe in him:
If you remain in the word that is mine, you are truly my disciples, 32 and you will know the truth, and the truth will make you free.
33 They answered him:
We are seed of Abraham, and we have never been enslaved to anyone; how say you that we shall become free?
34 Jesus answered them:
Amen, amen I say to you, that everyone who commits sin is a slave of sin. 35 But the slave does not remain in the house for ever; the son remains for ever. 36 So if the Son shall make you free, truly you will be free.
37 I know that you are seed of Abraham; yet you seek to kill me, because the word that is mine has no place in you.
38 What I myself have beheld with the Father I speak; and you therefore what you have heard from your father, you do.
39 They answered and said to him:
Abraham is our father.
Jesus says to them:

MT	LK	MK	JN 8:31-59

If you were children of Abraham, you would do the works of Abraham.

40 But now you seek to kill me, a man who has spoken to you the truth which I heard from God; this Abraham did not do.

41 You are doing the works of your father. They said therefore to him: We have not been begotten of fornication; we have one father,—God.

42 Jesus said to them:

If God were your father, you would love me. For I myself have proceeded forth and have come from God; for I have not come of myself, but he has sent me.

43 Why do you not know the speech that is mine? Because you cannot hear the word that is mine.

44 You are from (your) father the devil and you want to do the desires of your father. That one was a murderer from the beginning, and did not stand in the truth, because truth is not in him. When he utters falsehood he speaks of what is his, because he is a liar and its father.

45 But I, because I tell the truth, you do not believe me.

46 Which of you shall convict me of sin?

If I tell the truth, why do you not believe me?

47 He who is of God hears the utterances of God; for this (reason) you do not hear, because you are not of God.

48 The Jews therefore answered and said to him:

Do we not say rightly that you are a Samaritan and have a demon?

49 Jesus answered:

I do not have a demon but I honour my Father, and you are dishonouring me. 50 And I do not seek my own glory; there is One who seeks and judges.

51 Amen, amen I say to you, if anyone will keep my word, he will not behold death for ever.

52 The Jews therefore said to him:

Now we have understood that you have a demon. Abraham died, and the prophets, and you say: If anyone will keep my word, he will not taste death for ever. 53 Are you greater than our father Abraham, who died, and the prophets died? Whom do you make yourself?

54 Jesus answered:

If I shall glorify myself, my glory is nothing; it is my Father who glorifies me, whom you say that he is your God, 55 And you have not known him, but I know him. And if I say that I do not know him, I shall be like you a liar. But I know him and I keep his word.

56 Abraham your Father rejoiced to see my own day, and he saw (it) and rejoiced.

57 the Jews therefore said to him: You are not yet fifty years old and you have beheld Abraham?

58 Jesus said to them:

Amen, amen I say to you, before Abraham came to be, I myself am.

MT	LK	MK	JN 8:31-59
			59 They took up stones therefore to cast upon him; but Jesus hid (himself), and went out of the Temple.

§200 Jesus Heals a Man Born Blind

MT	LK	MK	JN 9:1-41
			1 And as he passed by, he saw a man blind from birth.
			2 And his disciples asked him saying:
			Rabbi, who has sinned, this (man) or his parents, that he should be born blind?
			3 Jesus answered:
			Neither has this (man) sinned, nor his parents—but that the works of God should be manifested in him.
			4 It is necessary for me to work the works of him who sent me while it is day; for the night comes when nobody can work. 5 When I am in the world, I am the light of the world.
			6 Saying these things he spat on the ground, and made mud of the spittle, and smeared the mud on his eyes, 7 and said to him:
			Go over and wash in the pool of Siloam—which means "One sent." He went away therefore and washed, and he came seeing.
			8 Then the neighbours and those who had seen him before, when he was a beggar, said: Is this (man) not the one who used to sit and beg?
			9 Some said: He is; others said: No, but he is like him.
			But he himself said: I am he.
			10 They said therefore to him:
			How then were your eyes opened?
			11 The man answered:
			The man who is called Jesus made mud and spread (it) on my eyes and said to me, Go over to Siloam and wash; I went away therefore and having washed I saw.
			12 And they said to him:
			Where is that (man)?
			He says: I do not know.
			13 They bring him to the Pharisees, the man formerly blind.
			14 Now the day on which Jesus made mud and opened his eyes was the Sabbath.
			15 Again therefore the Pharisees too asked him how he saw.
			And he said to them:
			He laid mud on my eyes, and I washed and I see.
			16 Some of the Pharisees then said: This man therefore is not from God, because he does not keep the Sabbath.
			But others said: How can a man perform such signs (if he is) a sinner? And there was a division among them.
			17 Again therefore they say to the blind man:
			What say you about him, because he has opened your eyes?
			And he said: He is a prophet.

151

MT	LK	MK	JN 9:1-41

JN 9:1-41

18 The Jews therefore did not believe about him that he had been blind and saw, until they had called the parents of the one now seeing, 19 and had asked them saying: Is this (man) your son, whom you say that he was born blind? How therefore does he now see?
20 His parents therefore answered and said:
We know that this is our son, and that he was born blind; 21 but how he now sees we do not know, nor do we know who has opened his eyes. Ask him, he is of age, he will speak about himself.
22 His parents said these things because they feared the Jews; for the Jews had already agreed that if anyone should confess him to be Christ, he should be put out of the synagogue. 23 That is why his parents said: He is of age, question him.
24 A second time therefore they called the man, who was blind, and said to him:
Give glory to God; we know that this man is a sinner.
25 He therefore answered:
I do not know if he is a sinner; one thing I do know, that being blind now I see.
26 They said therefore to him:
What did he do to you? How did he open your eyes?
27 He answered them:
I have told you already and you did not listen; why do you want to hear again? Do you really want to become his disciples?
28 And they reviled him and said:
You are a disciple of that (man), but we are disciples of Moses. 29 We know that God has spoken to Moses, but whence this man is we do not know.
30 The man answered and said to them:
In this then is the marvellous thing, that you do not know whence he is, and he has opened my eyes. 31 We know that God does not hear sinners, but that if anyone be God-fearing and does his will, he hears him. 32 From before time it has never been heard that anyone opened the eyes of one born blind. 33 If this (man) was not from God, he could not do this thing.
34 They answered and said to him:
You were totally born in sins, and do you teach us?
And they put him away outside.
35 Jesus heard that they had put him away outside, and having found him said:
Do you believe in the Son of Man?
36 The (man) answered and said:
And who is he, Lord, that I may believe in him?
37 Jesus said to him:
Indeed you have both seen him and it is the one who is speaking to you.
38* And he said: I believe, Lord; and he worshipped him.
39 And Jesus said:
For judgement did I myself come into this world, in order that those who see not may see and those who see become blind.

MT	LK	MK	JN 9:1-41

40 (Some) of the Pharisees, the ones that were with him,
heard and said to him:
Surely we are not also blind?
41 Jesus said to them: If you were blind, you would not have sin;
but now you say: We see. Your sin remains.

§201 Jesus—Shepherd and Sheepfold

MT	LK	MK	JN 10:1-21

1 Amen, amen I say to you, he who enters not through the gate into
the fold of the sheep, but goes up another way, that (man) is a thief
and a robber;
2 But he who enters through the gate is the shepherd of the sheep.
3 To him the gate-keeper opens, and the sheep hear his voice, and he
calls his own sheep by name, and he leads them out.
4 When he has got out all his own, he goes before them, and the
sheep follow him, because they know his voice.
5 But they will not follow a stranger, but will flee from him, because
they do not know the voice of the strangers.
6 This simile Jesus spoke to them; but those (men) did not
understand the things that he spoke to them. 7 Therefore Jesus again
said:
Amen, amen I say to you, that I myself am the gate of the sheep.
8 All those who came before me are thieves and robbers; but the
sheep did not listen to them.
9 I myself am the gate; if anyone comes in through me, he will be
saved, and he will come in and come out and he will find pasture.
10 The thief does not come except to steal and to kill and to destroy;
I myself have come that they may have life and have (it) more
abundantly.
11 I myself am the good shepherd; the good shepherd lays down his
life for the sheep;
12 The hired-man and he who is not the shepherd, whose own the
sheep are not, beholds the wolf coming and leaves the sheep and
flees—and the wolf snatches and scatters them, 13 because he is a
hired-man and he has no concern for the sheep.
14 I myself am the good shepherd, and I know mine and mine know
me, 15 just as the Father knows me and I myself know the Father,
and I lay down my life for the sheep.
16 And other sheep I have which are not of this fold; and these too I
must bring, and they will hear my voice, and there shall be one flock,
one shepherd.
17 For this reason the Father loves me because I myself lay down my
life, in order that I may take it again. 18 Nobody takes it from me,
but I myself lay it down of myself. I have authority to lay it down,
and I have authority to take it again; this command I took from my

MT	LK	MK	JN 10:1-21
			Father.
			19 A division again took place among the Jews because of these words.
			20 And many of them said: He has a demon and is raving; why do you listen to him?
			21 Others said: These are not the words of one possessed by a demon. Can a demon open the eyes of the blind?
			(↓§270)

§202 A Samaritan Town Rejects Jesus

MT	LK 9:52-56	MK	JN
	(↑§192)		
	52 And he sent messengers before his face. And going they entered into a village of Samaritans in order to prepare for him.		
	53 And they did not receive him, because his face was (that of one) going to Jerusalem.		
	54 And the disciples James and John seeing said: Lord, do you want us to tell fire to come down from heaven and wipe them out as Elijah also did?*		
	55 But he turned and rebuked them.		
	And he said: You know not of what spirit you are. 56 For the Son of Man did not come to destroy the souls of men but to save.*		
	They went to another village.		

§203 On Following Jesus (§111)

MT 8:18-22	LK 9:57-62	MK	JN
18 And Jesus seeing large crowds about him gave orders to go off to the other side.			
19 And one scribe coming up said to him:	57 And as they were going on the way someone said to him:		
Teacher, I will follow you wherever you go,	I will follow you wherever you go, Lord.		
20 And Jesus says to him:	58 And Jesus said to him:		
The foxes have holes and the birds of the sky nests, but the Son of Man has nowhere to lay his head.	The foxes have holes and the birds of the sky nests, but the Son of Man has nowhere to lay his head.		
	59 And he said to another: Follow me.		
	And he said:		
21 And another of his disciples said to him:	Lord, allow me first to go off to bury my father.		
Lord, allow me first to go off and bury my father.	60 And he said to him:		
22 And Jesus says to him:	Let the dead bury their own dead. But, do you go off and announce the Kingdom of God.		
Follow me, and let the dead bury their own dead.			

MT 8:18-22	LK 9:57-62		MK	JN
	61 And another also said: I will follow you, Lord. But first allow me to take leave of those in my house. 62 And Jesus said to him: No one putting his hand on a plough, and looking back is fit for the Kingdom of God.			

§204 Mission of the Seventy-Two (§§121, 124, 125)

MT 9:37-38; 10:16, 9-10a, 11-13, 10b, 7-8a, 14, 15	LK 9:3-5	LK 10:1-12	MK 6:8-11	JN
(v. 11b)		1 And after these things, the Lord also appointed another seventy-two,* and sent them two by two before his face into every town and place where he himself was about to come.		
37 Then he says to his disciples: The harvest is great indeed but the workers few. 38 Pray therefore the Lord of the harvest that he will put out workers into his harvest.		2 And he said to them: The harvest is great indeed, but the workers few. Pray therefore the Lord of the harvest to put out workers into his harvest.		
10:16 Lo, I am sending you like sheep in the midst of wolves.		3 Go forth, Lo I am sending you like lambs in the midst of wolves.		
9 Do not procure gold or silver or copper for your belts, 10a nor a bag for the way, nor two coats, nor sandals, nor a staff.	3 Take nothing for the way, neither a staff nor a bag nor bread nor money, nor have two coats each.	4 Do not carry a purse nor a bag nor sandals;	8 And he commanded them to take nothing for the way, except a staff only, neither bread nor a bag nor copper in the belt, 9 but be shod with sandals and do not put on two coats.	
11 Into whichever city or village you enter, inquire if anyone in it is worthy; and remain there till you go away.	4 And into whichever house you enter,	and greet no one on the way. 5 Into whichever house you enter,	10 And he said to them: Wherever you enter into a house,	
	remain there and go away from there.	**(v. 7 below)**	remain there until you go away from there.	
12 And going into the house, greet it; 13 and if indeed the house be worthy, let your peace come upon it; but if it be not worthy, let your peace return upon you.		First say: Peace to this house. 6 And if a son of peace be there, your peace shall rest upon him; but if otherwise, it shall come back upon you.		

MT 9:37-38; 10:16, 9-10a, 11-13. 10b, 7-8a, 14, 15	LK 9:3-5	LK 10:1-12	MK 6:8-11	JN
		7 And remain in that house, eating and drinking what they have. For the workman is worthy of his wage. Do not transfer from house to house. 8 And into whichever city you enter and they receive you, eat what is laid before you, 9 And heal the sick in it, and say to them: The Kingdom of God has come upon you.		
10b *For the workman is worthy of his food.*				
7 *And as you go preach saying: The Kingdom of the Heavens has come near. 8a Heal the sick,*				
14 *And whoever does not receive you, and does not hearken to your words,* *going forth outside that house or city* *shake out the dust of your feet.*	5 *And whoever does not receive you,* *going forth from that city* *even shake off the dust from your feet* *as a witness against them.*	10 Into whichever city you enter, and they do not receive you, going forth into its streets say: 11 Even the dust from your city that adheres to our feet we wipe off at you. But know this that the Kingdom of God has come near. 12 I say to you, that it will be more tolerable in that day for Sodom than for that city.	11 *And whichever place does not receive you, and they do not hearken to you,* *going out thence* *shake out the earth that is under your feet* *as a witness to them.*	
15 *Amen I say to you that it will be more tolerable for the land of Sodom and Gomorrah in the day of judgement than for that city* (cf. 11:24).				

§205 Woes on the Unrepentant Cities (§§132, 183)

MT 11:21-23; 10:40	LK 10:13-16	MK 9:37b	JN
21 *Woe to you, Chorazin, Woe to you Bethsaida; for if in Tyre and Sidon were done the mighty deeds done in you, long ago they would have repented in sackcloth and ashes. 22 Indeed, I tell you, it will be more tolerable for Tyre and Sidon in the day of judgement than for you* (cf. Mt. 10:15). *23 And you, Capharnaum, shall you be exalted up to heaven? Unto Hades shall you go down.*	13 Woe to you, Chorazin, Woe to you, Bethsaida; for if in Tyre and Sidon had been done the mighty deeds done in you, long ago they would have repented, sitting in sackcloth and ashes. 14 Indeed, it will be more tolerable for Tyre and Sidon in the judgement than for you. 15 And you, Capharnaum shall you be exalted up to heaven? Unto Hades shall you go down.		
10:40 *He who receives you, receives me;*	16 He who listens to you, listens to me, and he		

MT 11:21-23; 10:40	LK 10:13-16	MK 9:37b	JN
and he who receives me, receives him who sent me.	who rejects you, rejects me, but he who rejects me, rejects him who sent me.	37b And whoever receives me, receives not me, but him who sent me.	

§206 Return of the Seventy-Two

MT	LK 10:17-20	MK	JN
	17 And the seventy-two* returned with joy, saying: Lord, even the demons are subject to us in your name (cf. 9:10). 18 And he said to them: I beheld Satan like a flash of lightning fall from heaven. 19 Behold I have given you the authority to tread upon snakes and scorpions and upon the whole might of the enemy, and in no way shall anything at all injure you. 20 Yet do not rejoice in this that the spirits are subject to you, but rejoice that your names have been inscribed in the heavens.	(cf. 6:30)	

§207 Jesus Thanks His Father (§133)

MT 11:25-27	LK 10:21-22	MK	JN
25 In that time Jesus answering said: I praise thee, Father, Lord of heaven and earth, because thou hast hidden these things from the wise and understanding and revealed them to babes. 26 Yes O Father, because thus it was pleasing before thee. 27 All things have been entrusted to me by my Father, and no one understands the Son but the Father nor does anyone understand the Father but the Son, and he to whom the Son wills to reveal him.	21 In that hour he rejoiced in the Holy Spirit and said: I praise thee, Father, Lord of heaven and earth, because thou hast hidden away these things from the wise and understanding, and revealed them to babes. Yes, O Father, because thus it was pleasing before thee. 22 *And turning to his disciples he said: All things have been entrusted to me by my Father, and no one knows who the Son is but the Father, and who the Father is but the Son, and he to whom the Son wills to reveal him.		

§208 "Blessed Are Your Eyes" (§146)

MT 13:16-17	LK 10:23-24	MK	JN
16 And blessed are your eyes because you see, and your ears because they hear. 17 Amen I say to you, many prophets and just men desired to	23 And turning to the disciples he said privately: Blessed are the eyes that see what you see. 24 For I say to you, many prophets and kings wanted to see the		

MT 13:16-17	LK 10:23-24	MK	JN
see the things you see and did not see them; and to hear the things you hear, and did not hear (them).	things you see and did not see them; and to hear the things you hear and did not hear (them).		

§209 The Lawyer's Question (Lk) (§302)

MT 22:34-39	LK 10:25-28	MK 12:28-31a, 34	JN
34 And when the Pharisees heard that he had silenced the Sadducees, they assembled in one place,			
35 And one of them, a lawyer, asked a question tempting him and saying:	25 And behold a certain lawyer arose tempting him, saying:	*28 And one of the Scribes coming up, having heard them debating, knowing that he had answered them well, asked him a question:*	
36 Teacher, which is the great commandment in the Law?	Teacher, what shall I do to inherit eternal life?	*Which is the first commandment of all?*	
37 And he said to him:	26 And he said to him: How do you understand what has been written in the Law? 27 And answering he said:	*29 Jesus answered: The first is: Hear, O Israel, the Lord our God is one Lord,*	
Thou shalt love the Lord thy God with thy whole heart and with thy whole soul	Thou shalt love the Lord thy God from thy whole heart and with thy whole soul and with thy whole strength	*30 and thou shalt love the Lord thy God from thy whole heart and from thy whole soul*	
and with thy whole mind. *38 This is the great and first commandment.* *39 The second is like to it:*	and with thy whole mind **(Dt. 6:5)**.	*and from thy whole mind and from thy whole strength.*	
Thou shalt love thy neighbour as thyself **(Lv. 19:18)**.	and thy neighbor as thyself **(Lv. 19:18)**.	*31a This the second: Thou shalt love thy neighbour as thyself.*	
	28 And he said to him: You have answered correctly. Do this and you shall live.	*34 And Jesus seeing that he had answered wisely, said to him: You are not far from the Kingdom of God.*	
(cf. 20:46)	**(cf. 20:40)**	**(cf. 12:34b)**	

§210 The Good Samaritan

MT	LK 10:29-37	MK	JN
	29 But he wishing to justify himself said to Jesus: And who is my neighbour? 30 And Jesus taking him up said: A certain man went down from Jerusalem to Jericho and fell in with robbers, who stripping and striking him went away leaving		

MT	LK 10:29-37		MK	JN

LK 10:29-37

him half-dead.

31 And by chance a certain priest was going down on that road and seeing him passed by on the other side.

32 Likewise also a Levite being by the place, coming and seeing him, passed by on the other side.

33 But a certain Samaritan on a journey came upon him and seeing him was moved with pity.

34 And coming up bound up his wounds pouring on oil and wine; and setting him on his own beast brought him to an inn and cared for him.

35 And on the following day taking out two denarii he gave them to the inn-keeper and said: Take care of him, and whatever you spend in addition I will pay you back on my return.

36 Which of these three do you think was the neighbour of the one who fell among thieves?

37 And he said: He who showed mercy to him.

And Jesus said to him:

Go you and do likewise.

§211 Martha and Mary

MT	LK 10:38-42		MK	JN

LK 10:38-42

38 And it happened on their journey that he entered into a certain village; and a certain woman, by name Martha, received him into the house.

39 And she had a sister called Mary, and she sitting down at the feet of the Lord was listening to his word.

40 But Martha was distracted with much serving, and coming up she said: Lord, do you not care that my sister has left me to serve alone? Therefore tell her to take her part in turn with me.

41 And the Lord answering said to her:

Martha, Martha, you worry and get upset about many things;*

42 there is need of one thing.* For Mary has chosen the good part, which will not be taken away from her.

§212 The Lord's Prayer (Lk) (§74)

MT 6:9-13	LK 11:1-4		MK	JN

MT 6:9-13

LK 11:1-4

1 And it happened that when he was in a certain place praying, when he ceased one of his disciples said to him:

Lord, teach us to pray just as John also taught his disciples.

2 And he said to them:

9 Pray you therefore thus: When you pray, say: **(11:25a)**

159

MT 6:9-13	LK 11:1-4	MK	JN
Our Father, who art in the heavens,	[Our] Father,* [who art in heaven],		
hallowed be thy name;	hallowed be thy name;		
10 thy Kingdom come;	thy Kingdom come.		
thy will be done, as in heaven so on earth.	[Thy will be done, as in heaven so on earth].		
11. our bread, that comes down, give us to-day;	3 Our bread, that comes down, give us day by day;		
12 and forgive us our debts, as we too have forgiven our debtors;	4 and forgive us our sins, for we ourselves also forgive everyone in debt to us;		
13 and lead us not into temptation,	and lead us not into temptation.		
but deliver us from the Evil One.	[but deliver us from the Evil One].		

§213 The Importunate Friend

MT	LK 11:5-8	MK	JN
	5 And he said to them:		
	Which of you will have a friend and will go to him at midnight		
	and say to him:		
	Friend, lend me three loaves of bread, 6 since my friend has come		
	along to me from a journey, and I have nothing to set before him.		
	7 And he from within answering will say:		
	Do not bother me; for now the door is shut and my children are		
	with me in bed. I cannot get up and give you.		
	8 I say to you, even if he will not get up and give him (them)		
	because he is his friend, yet because of his lack of consideration he		
	will get up and give him whatever he needs.		

§214 Encouragement to Pray (§83)

MT 7:7-11	LK 11:9-13	MK	JN
7 Ask and it shall be given to you;	9 And I say to you: Ask and it shall be given to you;		
seek and you will find; knock and it will be opened to you.	seek and you will find; knock and it will be opened to you.		
8 For everyone who asks receives,	10 For everyone who asks receives,		
and he who seeks finds,	and he who seeks finds,		
and to him who knocks it will be opened.	and to him who knocks it will be opened.		
9 Or what man of you is there, whom his son will ask for bread, will give him a stone?	11 And which one of you—the father—(if his) son shall ask for bread, will really give him a stone?		
10 Or again will ask for a fish, will give him a snake?	Or again* a fish, and instead of a fish will give him a snake?		
	12 Or again, will he ask for an egg, surely he will not give him a scorpion?		
11 If therefore you who are evil know how to give good gifts to your children,	13 If therefore you who are evil, know how to give good gifts to your children,		
by how much more will your Father who is in the heavens give good things to those who ask him.	by how much more will your Father who is from heaven give the Holy Spirit to those who ask him.		

MT 9:32-34	MT 12:22-30	LK 11:14-23	MK 3:22-27	JN
32 And as they were going out, behold, they brought to him a dumb man, demon-possessed. 33 And when the demon was cast out the dumb man spoke.	*22 Then there was brought to him one demon-possessed, blind and dumb. And he healed him so that the dumb man spoke and saw.*	14 And he was casting out a demon, and it was dumb. And it happened, when the demon had gone out, that the dumb (man) spoke.		
And the crowds marvelled, saying: Never in Israel has such a thing been seen. 34* But the Pharisees were saying:	*23 And all the crowds were amazed, and said: Surely this one is the Son of David? 24 But the Pharisees heard and said:*	And the crowds marvelled. 15 But some of them said:	22 And the Scribes who had come down from Jerusalem were saying:	
By the prince of the demons he casts out the demons.	*This one does not cast out the demons except by Beelzebul, prince of the demons.*	By Beelzebul the prince of the demons he casts out the demons.	He has Beelzebul, and: By the prince of the demons he casts out the demons.	
	(cf. 16:1)	16 But others tempting were seeking for a sign from heaven from him **(cf. 11:29)**.		
	25 But knowing their thoughts Jesus said to them:	17 But he knowing their intentions said to them:	23 And calling them up he said to them in parables: *How can Satan cast out Satan?*	
	Every kingdom divided against itself comes to ruin,	Every kingdom divided up against itself comes to ruin,	24 And if a kingdom is divided against itself, that kingdom cannot stand.	
	and every city or house divided over-against itself will not stand.	and house against house falls.	25 And if a house is divided against itself, that house will not be able to stand.	
	26 And if Satan casts out Satan, he is divided against himself; how therefore shall his kingdom stand?	18 And if Satan too is divided up against himself, how shall his kingdom stand? For you say that I cast out the demons by Beelzebul.	26 And if Satan has risen up against himself and is divided, he cannot stand but has an end.	
	27 And if I by Beelzebul cast out the demons, by whom do your sons cast them out? Wherefore they themselves shall be your judges. 28 But if by the Spirit of God I cast out the demons then upon you has fallen the Kingdom of God.	19 But if I by Beelzebul cast out the demons, by whom do your sons cast them out? Wherefore they themselves will be your judges. 20 But if by the finger of God I cast out the demons, then upon you has fallen the Kingdom of God.		
	29 Or how can anyone enter into the mansion of the Mighty One and steal his property, unless he first tie up the Mighty One? And then he will plunder his mansion.	21 When the Mighty One in full armour guards his own palace, his possessions are in peace. 22 But when a Mightier One than he comes up and overcomes him, he takes away his armour on	27 But no one can enter into the mansion of the Mighty One to plunder his property, unless he first tie up the Mighty One. And then he will plunder his mansion.	

MT 9:32-34	MT 12:22-30	LK 11:14-23	MK 3:22-27	JN
		which he relied, and distributes his spoils.		
	30 He who is not with me is against me; and he who gathers not with me, scatters.	23 He who is not with me is against me; and he who gathers not with me, scatters.	**(cf. 9:40)**	
		(cf. 9:50)		

§216 Return of the Unclean Spirit (Lk) (§141)

MT 12:43-45	LK 11:24-26	MK	JN
43 Now when the unclean spirit has gone out from the man, he goes through waterless places seeking rest, and does not find it. 44 Then he says: Into my house whence I came out I will return. And coming he finds it vacant and swept and in order. 45 Then he goes and takes with him seven other spirits worse than himself, and entering in dwells there, and the last things of that man become worse than the first. Thus also shall it be with this evil generation.	24 Now when the unclean spirit has gone out from the man, he goes through waterless places seeking rest; and not finding it, then he says: I will go back into my house whence I came out; 25 and coming he finds it vacant, swept and in order. 26 Then he goes and takes seven other spirits worse than himself, and entering in dwells there, and the last things of that man become worse than the first.		

§217 The Truly Blessed

LK 11:27-28	LK	MK	JN
27 And it happened that while he was saying these things, a certain woman from the crowd lifting up her voice said to him: Blessed is the womb that bore you and the breasts which you sucked. 28 But he said: Blessed rather are those who hear the word of God and keep it.			

§218 The Sign of Jonah (Lk) (§§140, 171)

MT 12:38-40, 42, 41	LK 11:29-32	MK 8:11-12	JN
38 Then some of the Scribes and Pharisees answered him, saying: Teacher, we want to see a sign from you **(cf. 16:1)**. *39 And answering he said to them: An evil and adulterous generation is seeking for a sign,*	29 And while the crowds were thronging him, he began to say: This generation is an evil generation; it is seeking for a sign;	*11 And the Pharisees went out and began to debate with him, asking from him a sign from heaven, tempting him. 12 And sighing deeply in his spirit he says: Why does this generation seek a sign?*	

MT 12:38-40, 42, 41	*LK 11:29-32*	*MK 8:11-12*	JN
and a sign shall not be given it, save the sign of Jonah the prophet. *40 For just as Jonah was in the belly of the sea-monster for three days and three nights, so shall the Son of Man be in the heart of the earth for three days and three nights.*	and a sign shall not be given it, save the sign of Jonah. 30 For even as Jonah became a sign to the Ninevites, so also will the Son of Man be to this generation.	*Amen I say to you—on no account shall a sign be given to this generation!*	
42 The queen of the south will rise in the judgement with this generation and will condemn it; *because she came from the ends of the earth to hear the wisdom of Solomon, and lo something greater than Solomon is here.*	31 The queen of the south will rise in the judgement with the men of this generation and will condemn them; because she came from the ends of the earth to hear the wisdom of Solomon, and lo something greater than Solomon is here.		
41 The men of Nineveh will rise up in the judgement with this generation and will condemn it; *because they repented at the preaching of Jonah and lo something greater than Jonah is here.*	32 The men of Nineveh will rise up in the judgement with this generation and will condemn it; because they repented at the preaching of Jonah, and lo something greater than Jonah is here.		

§219 Concerning Light (§§62, 104)

MT 5:15	*LK 11:33*	MK	JN
15 Nor do they light a lamp and put it under the measure, but upon the lampstand, and it shines for all who are in the house.	33 And no one kindling a lamp puts it into a cellar, nor under the measure, but upon the lampstand so that they who enter may see the light **(cf. 8:16)**.	**(4:21)**	

§220 The Sound Eye (Lk) (§78)

MT 6:22-23	*LK 11:34-36*	MK	JN
22 The lamp of the body is the eye. *If therefore thy eye is clear, thy whole body will be full of light.* *23 But if thy eye is evil then thy whole body will be full of darkness.* *If therefore the light that is in thee is darkness, how great the darkness!*	34 The lamp of the body is thy eye. When thy eye is clear then thy whole body is full of light. But if it is evil then thy body is also full of darkness. 35 Look out therefore that the light that is in thee is not darkness. 36 If therefore thy body is wholly full of light, not having any part dark, it will be wholly full of light, as when the lamp lights thee with its radiance.		

MT 23:25-26, 23, 1, 6-7, 27-28, 4, 29-31, 34-36, 14	LK 11:37-54	LK 20:45-46	MK 12:38-39	JN
	37 And while he was speaking a Pharisee invited him to dine with him; and entering he reclined. 38 And the Pharisee marvelled noticing that he did not first wash before the dinner. 39 And the Lord said to him:			
25 *Woe to you, Scribes and Pharisees, hypocrites, because you cleanse the outside of the cup and of the plate,*	Now it is you Pharisees who cleanse the outside of the cup and of the dish,			
but inside they are full of greed and license. 26 *O blind Pharisee, cleanse first the interior of the cup and the dish so that its exterior may be rendered clean.*	but your inside is full of greed and wickedness! 40 Fools, did not he who made the outside also make the inside? 41 Rather give as alms what is within, and lo all things are clean to you.			
23 *Woe to you, Scribes and Pharisees, hypocrites,*	42 But woe to you Pharisees,			
because you pay the tithe on mint and dill and cummin, and have left out the weightier things of the Law, judgement and steadfast love and faith.	because you pay the tithe on mint and rue and every herb, and pass over justice and the love of God.			
But you ought to have done the latter, without leaving out the former.	But you ought to have done the latter without passing over the former.			
1 *Then Jesus spoke to the crowds and his disciples,* 2 *saying:*		45 *And in the hearing of all the people he said to his disciples:*	38 *And in his teaching he was saying to them:*	
6 *For they like the first place at the banquets, and the first seats in the synagogues,* 7 *and the salutations at the market-places and to be called by men, Rabbi.*	43 Woe to you Pharisees, because you love the first place in the synagogues, and the salutations at market-places.	46 *Be wary of the Scribes who like to walk in long robes and love salutations in the market-places and first seats in the synagogues and first places in the banquets.*	*Beware of the Scribes who like walking in long robes and salutations in the market-places* 39 *and first seats in the synagogues and first places in the banquets.*	
27 *Woe to you, Scribes and Pharisees, hypocrites, because you are comparable to white-washed tombs, which outwardly indeed look fair, but inside are full of the bones of the dead and every uncleanness.* 28 *So also you outwardly appear to men just, but inwardly you are full of hypocrisy and wrong-*	44 Woe to you Scribes and Pharisees, hypocrites, because you are like concealed monuments, and the men that walk over them do not know.			

MT 23:25-26, 23, 1, 6-7, 27-28, 4, 29-31 34-36, 14

doing.

(cf. 23:2)

4 For they bind burdens heavy and hard to carry* and impose them on the shoulders of men, but they themselves do not wish to move them with their finger.

29 Woe to you, scribes and Pharisees, hypocrites.
because you build the tombs of the prophets, and decorate the monuments of the just,
30 and you say: If we had been in the days of our fathers, we would not have been their accomplices in the blood of the prophets.
31 Thus you are witnesses to yourselves

that you are the sons of those who slew the prophets.

34 Wherefore

Lo, I am sending to you prophets and wise men and scribes: (some) of them you will kill and crucify, and (some) of them you will beat in your synagogues, and will pursue from city to city;
35 in order that there should come upon you all the just blood shed upon the earth,

from the blood of Abel the Just to the blood of Zechariah son of Barachiah,
whom you slew between the holy place and the altar.
36 Amen, I say to you, all these

LK 11:37-54

45 And one of the lawyers answering says to him: Teacher, when you say those things you are also insulting us.
46 And he said:
Woe also to you lawyers, because you burden men with burdens hard to carry

but you yourselves do not touch the burdens with one of your fingers.
47 Woe to you,

because you build the monuments of the prophets,

but your fathers killed them.

48 Therefore you are witnesses, and you approve, of the deeds of your fathers,
for they indeed killed them, but you build their monuments.

49 Wherefore indeed the Wisdom of God said:
I will send to them prophets and apostles;
and (some) of them they will kill

and will pursue,
50 so that there will be required the blood of all the prophets, that has been shed from the foundation of the world, from this generation—
51 from Abel's blood to the blood of Zechariah,

who perished between the altar and the House.
Yes, I say to you, it shall be

LK 20:45-46

MK 12:38-39

JN

MT 23:25-26, 23, 1, 6-7, 27-28, 4, 29-31, 34-36, 14	LK 11:37-54	LK 20:45-46	MK 12:38-39	JN
things shall come upon this generation.	required from this generation.			
*14 *Woe to you, Scribes and Pharisees, hypocrites, because you shut the Kingdom of the Heavens in men's faces; for you do not go in, and you do not permit those about to enter, to enter in.*	52 Woe to you the lawyers, because you took away the key of knowledge; you yourselves did not go in, and you stopped those about to enter. 53 And as he was going out from there, the Scribes and the Pharisees began to be exceedingly resentful, and to draw him out about many things, 54 lying in wait for him to trap something from his mouth.			

§222 Leaven of the Pharisees (Lk) (§172)

MT 16:5-6	MT 16:11	LK 12:1	MK 8:14-15	JN
5 And when the disciples were coming to the other side, they forgot to take bread, 6 and Jesus said to them:		1 Meanwhile, as the myriads of the crowd were gathering together so as to trample on one another, he began to say to his disciples first:	*14 And his disciples forgot to take loaves and they had not even one loaf with them in the boat. 15 And he charged them saying:*	
	11 How do you not perceive that I spoke to you not about loaves? Beware of the leaven of the Pharisees and Sadducees.			
See and beware of the leaven of the Pharisees and Sadducees.		You yourselves beware of the leaven, that is, the hypocrisy of the Pharisees.	*See and watch out for the leaven of the Pharisees and the leaven of Herod.*	

§223 Call to Fearless Confession (Lk) (§§104, 126)

MT 10:26-33	LK 8:17	LK 12:2-9	MK 4:22	JN
26 Therefore do not be afraid of them: for there is nothing covered which will not be uncovered,	*17 For there is nothing hidden that will not become manifest;*	2 And there is nothing covered up which will not be uncovered,	*22 For there is nothing whatever hidden that will not be manifested;*	
and hidden which will not be made known.	*nor anything secret which will not become known and come to be manifested.*	and hidden, which will not be made known.	*nor that was secret but will come to be manifest.*	

MT 10:26-33	LK 8:17	LK 12:2-9	MK 4:22	JN
27 What I say to you in the dark, do you say in the light;		3 Wherefore, whatever you said in the dark, shall be heard in the light;		
and what you hear in the ear,		and what you spoke into the ear in the inner rooms,		
preach on the house-tops.		shall be preached on the house-tops.		
28 And do not be afraid of those who kill the body, but are not able to kill the soul;		4 And I say to you, my friends, do not be afraid of those who kill the body, and after that have no more they may do.		
but rather fear the one able to destroy both body and soul in Gehenna.		5 But I will show you whom you should fear; you should fear the one who after the killing has power to cast down into Gehenna. Yes, I say to you, fear this one.		
29 Are not two sparrows sold for a penny? And not one of them falls to the ground without your Father. 30 And even the hairs of your head are all numbered. 31 Therefore do not be afraid; you surpass many sparrows. 32 Everyone therefore who shall confess me before men,		6 Are not five sparrows sold for two pence? And not one of them is forgotten before God. 7 But even the hairs of your head have all been numbered **(21:18)**. Do not be afraid; you surpass many sparrows. 8 And I say to you, everyone whoever confesses me before men,		
I will confess him before my Father who is in the heavens. 33 But whosoever denies me before men, I too will deny him before my Father who is in the heavens (cf. **16:27).**		the Son of Man too will confess him before the angels of God. 9 But the one who denies me in front of men, will be denied in front of the angels of God **(cf. 9:26).**	**(cf. 8:38)**	

§224 Blasphemy against the Spirit (Lk) (§§98, 138)

MT 12:32	LK 12:10	MK 3:29	JN
32 And whoever shall say a word against the Son of Man, it shall be forgiven him; but whoever shall speak against the Holy Spirit it shall not be forgiven him, neither in this age nor in the one to come.	10 And everyone, who shall say a word against the Son of Man it shall be forgiven him; but to the one who blasphemes at the Holy Spirit, it shall not be forgiven.	*29 And whoever should blaspheme at the Holy Spirit has no forgiveness in the age, but is guilty of an ageless sin.*	

MT 10:19	LK 12:11-12	LK 21:14-15	MK 13:11	JN
19 When they betray you	11 But when they bring you before the synagogues and the authorities and the magistrates,	**(21:12)**	*11 And when they lead you, betraying you,*	
do not worry how or what you speak; ·	do not worry how or what defence you should make or what you should say:	*14 Fix therefore in your hearts not to premeditate your defence,*	*do not worry beforehand what you should speak,*	
for it will be given to you in that hour what you shall speak.	12 For the Holy Spirit will teach you in the very hour the things you are to say.	*15 for I will give you a mouth and wisdom, which all they who oppose you will not be able to withstand or contradict.*	*but whatever is given to you in that hour, speak that!*	

§226 Warning against Avarice

MT	LK 12:13-15	MK	JN
	13 And someone from the crowd said to him: Teacher, tell my brother to apportion the inheritance with me. 14 And he said to him: O man, who has appointed me judge or apportioner over you? 15 And he said to them: See and guard against all avarice; because not in someone's abundance of his possessions is his life.		

§227 Parable of the Rich Fool

MT	LK 12:16-21	MK	JN
	16 And he told them a parable saying: The land of a certain rich man yielded well. 17 And he debated in himself saying: What shall I do, for I have nowhere to store up my crops? 18 And he said: This I will do; I will pull down my barns and build larger ones, and there I will store up all the grain and my goods; 19 and I will say to my soul: Soul, you have many goods laid up for many years; take it easy, eat, drink, be happy. 20 But God said to him: Fool, this very night they will require your soul from you. —And the things you have prepared, whose will they be? 21 So (it is) with the one who hoards up for himself and is not rich towards God.		

MT 6:25-33	LK 12:22-32	MK	JN

MT 6:25-33

25 Wherefore I say to you:
Do not worry about your life, what you eat or what you drink,
nor about your body what you wear.
Is not the life more than the food, and the body than the clothing?
26 Look at the birds of the sky: they do not sow nor reap nor gather into barns,
yet your heavenly Father feeds them;
are not you worth more than they?
27 And which of you by worrying can add one cubit to his span?*
28 And why do you worry about clothing?

Learn from the lilies of the field how they grow; they toil not, neither do they spin.
29 And I say to you that not even Solomon in all his glory was arrayed like one of these.
30 And if the grass of the field that exists to-day and to-morrow is thrown into a furnace God so clothes, does he not by much more (clothe) you, O men of little faith?
31 Do not worry therefore, saying: What shall we eat? Or what shall we drink? Or what are we to wear?
32 For the nations are intent on all these things;
for your heavenly Father knows that you need all these things.
33 But first seek the Kingdom of God and his justice, and all these things will be added to you.

LK 12:22-32

22 And he said to his disciples:
Wherefore I say to you:
Do not worry about your life what you eat,
nor about your body what you wear.
23 For the life is more than the food, and the body than the clothing.
24 Consider the ravens: they neither sow nor reap,
nor have they a store room or a barn;
yet God feeds them;
how much more are you worth than the birds!
25 And which of you by worrying can add a cubit to his span?*

26 If therefore you cannot (do) the littlest thing, why do you worry about the remaining things?
27 Consider the lilies, how they grow; they neither toil nor spin.

And I say to you not even Solomon in all his glory was arrayed like one of these.
28 And if in a field the grass, that exists to-day and to-morrow is thrown into a furnace, God so clothes, by how much more you, O men of little faith!
29 And you, do not be seeking after what you may eat and what you may drink, and do not be anxious.
30 For the nations of the world are intent on all these things;
but your Father knows that you need these things.
31 Rather seek his Kingdom,
and all these things will be added to you.
32 Do not fear, little flock; for your Father is pleased to give you the Kingdom.

§229 Treasures in Heaven (Lk) (§77)

MT 6:19-21	LK 12:33-34	MK	JN

MT 6:19-21

19 Do not treasure for yourselves treasures upon earth,
where moth and rust corrode, and where thieves dig through and steal.
20 But treasure for yourselves treasures in heaven, where neither moth nor rust corrode, and where thieves do not dig through nor steal.
21 For where thy treasure is there too will be thy heart.

LK 12:33-34

33 Sell your possessions and give alms;
make for yourselves purses that do not become old,

an unfailing treasure in heaven, where thief does not come nigh, nor moth corrupt.

34 For where your treasure is, there too will be your heart.

§230 Watch with Lamps Lit (§317)

MT
(cf. 25: 1-13)

LK 12:35-38
35 Let your loins be girded round and (your) lamps lit.
36 And be you like men awaiting their lord when he returns from the wedding festivities, so that when he comes and knocks, they may open to him at once.
37 Blessed are those slaves whom the Lord, when he comes will find watching;
Amen I say to you, he will gird himself and will make them recline, and coming up he will minister to them.
38 And if he comes in the second watch, and even in the third, and finds them thus, blessed are they.

MK
(cf. 13: 33-35)

JN

§231 The Thief in the Night (Lk) (§315)

MT 24:43-44
43 And that know you, that if the master of the house had known at what watch the thief was coming, he would have watched and would not have allowed his house to be broken into.
44 Wherefore you too be prepared, because at the hour you do not imagine, the Son of Man is coming.

LK 12:39-40
39 And know you this, that if the master of the house had known at what hour the thief was coming, he would not have permitted his house to be broken into.

40 You too be prepared, because at the hour you do not imagine, the Son of Man is coming.

MK
(cf. 13: 35-37)

JN

§232 The Wise and Faithful Steward (§316)

MT 24:45-51

45 Then who is the faithful and wise slave whom the Lord has appointed over his household to give them food at the proper time?
46 Blessed is that slave whom his lord when he comes will find so doing,
47 Amen I say to you, that he will appoint him over all his possessions.
48 But if that slave, (being) bad, should say in his heart: My Lord is delaying,
49 and should begin to strike his fellow slaves, and were to eat and drink with the drunkards,
50 the lord of that slave will come on a day on which he is not expecting, and at an hour which he does not know,
51 and will dismember him and will put his portion with the hypocrites.

LK 12:41-48
41 And Peter said:
Lord are you telling this parable to us or also to all?
42 And the Lord said:
Then who is the faithful, the wise, steward whom the lord will appoint over his family to give the ration of corn at the proper time?
43 Blessed is that slave whom his lord when he comes will find so doing.
44 Truly I say to you, that he will appoint him over all his possessions.
45 But if that slave should say in his heart: My lord is delaying to come,
and should begin to strike the slave boys and girls, yea also to eat and drink and to get drunk,
46 the lord of that slave will come on a day on which he is not expecting, and at an hour which he does not know,
and will dismember him, and will put his portion with the unfaithful.
47 And that slave who knew the will of his lord and did not

MK

JN

MT 24:45-51	LK 12:41-48	MK	JN
	prepare or do according to his will, will be beaten severely. 48 But he who did not know, and did things deserving strokes, will be lightly beaten. For to everyone to whom much has been given, from him much will be required; and to whom much has been entrusted, they will demand of him much more.		

§233 The Divider of Households (§127)

MT 10:34-35	LK 12:49-53	MK	JN
	49 I came to cast fire upon the earth, and what do I want—if only it were already kindled? 50 I have a baptism to be baptised with, and how straitened I am until such time as it is accomplished.		
34 Do not suppose that I came to cast peace upon the earth; *I did not come to cast peace, but a sword.*	51 Do you imagine that I arrived to give peace on the earth? Not at all, I tell you, but rather division. 52 For from now on there will be five divided in one house, three against two and two against three.		
35 I came to antagonize a man against his father,	53 They shall be divided father against son and son against father,		
and daughter against her mother, *and a daughter-in-law against her mother-in-law,*	mother against daughter, and daughter against her mother, mother-in-law against her daughter-in-law, and daughter-in-law against her mother-in-law.		
and a man's enemies (will be) his own household.			

§234 The Signs of the Times (§171)

MT 16:2-3	LK 12:54-56	MK	JN
(cf. 12:38-39)		**(cf. 8: 11-12)**	
2 And he answering said to them: *When evening comes* you say, Good weather, for the sky is red,*	54 And he also said to the crowds: When you see a cloud rising over the west you say at once that a shower is coming, and so it happens.		
3 And in the early morning: Stormy to-day, for the sky is red and overcast. *While you know how to descry the face of the sky,*	55 And when (you see) a south wind blowing, you say that it will be a scorching heat, and it happens. 56 Hypocrites, you know how to discern the face of the earth and of the sky,		
yet the signs of the times you cannot.	but how do you not discern this time?		

MT 5:25-26

*25 Get on good terms quickly with your accuser whilst you are
still with him on the way,
lest perhaps the accuser hand you over to the judge,
and the judge hand you over to the attendant,
and you be cast into prison.
26 Amen I say to you, you shall not go out thence, until you
have paid up the last penny.*

LK 12:57-59
57 And why too do you not judge by yourselves what is just?
58 For as you go off with your accuser before a magistrate,
on the way take pains to settle with him;
lest perhaps he drag you along to the judge,
and the judge will hand you over to the constable,
and the constable will cast you into prison.
59 I say to you, you shall not go out thence until you have paid
up even the last halfpenny.

§236 Repentance or Destruction

MT   LK 13:1-5   MK   JN

1 Now there were some present at that time reporting to him
about the Galileans whose blood Pilate had mingled with their
sacrifices.
2 And answering, he said:
Do you imagine that these Galileans were sinners above all the
Galileans because they suffered these things?
3 No, I tell you, but unless you repent, you will all likewise perish.
4 Or those eighteen upon whom the tower fell in Siloam and
killed them; do you imagine that they were debtors above all the
men dwelling in Jerusalem? 5 No, I tell you, but unless you repent
you will all likewise perish.

§237 The Barren Figtree

MT
**(cf. 21:
18-19)**

LK 13:6-9
6 And he used to tell this parable:
A certain person had a fig-tree planted in his vineyard, and he
came seeking fruit on it and did not find it.
7 And he said to the vinedresser: Lo, for three years I have been
coming seeking fruit on this fig-tree, and have not found it; I will
therefore cut it down. For why should it waste the ground?
8 But he answering says to him: Sir, leave it just for this year,
whilst I dig round it and spread manure. 9 And if it should bear
fruit in the coming year? And if not, you shall cut it down.

MK
**(cf. 11:
12-14,
19-27)**

JN

MT	LK 13:10-17	MK	JN

LK 13:10-17

10 And he was teaching in one of the synagogues on the Sabbath.
11 And lo a woman, who had a spirit of infirmity eighteen years, and was bent double and was not able at all to stand erect.
12 And seeing her Jesus called (her) up and said to her: O woman, you have been freed from your infirmity.
13 And he laid his hands upon her, and at once she was made erect again, and glorified God.
14 And the synagogue-president answering, being indignant that Jesus had healed on the Sabbath, said to the crowd: There are six days on which it is proper to work; on them therefore come and be healed and not on the Sabbath day.
15 And the Lord answered him and said: Hypocrites, does not each one of you on the Sabbath loose his ox or ass from the stall, and leading it off, give it to drink? **(cf. 14:5)**.

(cf. 12: 11-12)

16 And this woman being a daughter of Abraham, whom Satan has bound for eighteen years, was it not proper (for her) to have been loosed from this bond on the Sabbath day?
17 And when he said this all his opponents were put to shame, and the whole crowd rejoiced over all the glorious things being done by him.

§239 The Mustard Seed (Lk) (§§106, 149)

MT 13:31-32	LK 13:18-19	MK 4:30-32	JN

MT 13:31-32

31 Another parable he put before them saying: The Kingdom of the Heavens is like

a grain of mustard which a man took and sowed in his field,

32 which is indeed smaller than all the seeds,

but when it is grown is greater than the plants and becomes a tree, so that the birds of the sky come and roost in its branches.

LK 13:18-19

18 Therefore he used to say: Like to what is the Kingdom of God? And to what shall I liken it?
19 It is like a grain of mustard which a man took and sowed in his own garden,

and it grew

and became a great tree, and the birds of the sky roosted on its branches.

MK 4:30-32

30 And he used to say: How may we liken the Kingdom of God? Or in what parable may we put it? 31 As a grain of mustard, which when it is sowed upon the earth—

being smaller than all the seeds that are on the earth— 32 and when it is sowed, it rises up and becomes greater than all the plants and produces great branches, so that under its shade the birds of the sky are able to roost.

§240 The Leaven (Lk) (§150)

MT 13:33	LK 13:20-21

MT 13:33

33 Another parable he spoke to them: The Kingdom of the Heavens is like leaven

LK 13:20-21

20 And again he said: To what shall I liken the Kingdom of God?

MT 13:33

which a woman took and covered up in three measures of flour until all was leavened.

LK 13:20-21
21 It is like leaven
which a woman took and covered in three measures of flour until all was leavened.

MK   JN

§241 Exclusion from the Kingdom (§§87, 91, 279, 316-318)

MT 7:13-14; 25:10b-12; 7:22-23; 8:11-12; 20:16

LK 13:22-30
22 And he was going through town after town and village after village teaching and making his way to Jerusalem.
23 And someone said to him: Lord, those to be saved—are they few? And he said to them:
24 Strive hard to enter through the narrow gate;

MK   JN

7:13 Enter through the narrow gate; for broad is the gate and wide open the way that leads off to destruction,
and many there are who enter through it;
14 How narrow (is) the gate and constricted the way that leads off to life,
and few there are who find it.

because many, I tell you, will seek to enter

and will not be able.

25:10b . . . the bridegroom came and those ready entered with him into the wedding feast, and the door was shut.
11 And later the rest of the virgins also came saying:

Lord, Lord open to us.
12 But he answering said: Amen I say to you, I know you not.

25 When the master of the house has risen and shut up the door,

then you will begin to stand outside and knock on the door saying:
Lord, Lord, open to us;
and answering he will say to you: I know you not whence you are.

7:22 Many will say to me in that day:
Lord, Lord, did we not prophesy in your name, and in your name cast out demons, and in your name work many miracles?
23 And then I shall declare to them:
I never knew you;
depart from me, you who work lawlessness.

26 Then you will begin to say:
We ate and drank in your presence, and you taught in our streets.
27 And saying he will say to you:
I know you not whence you are;
stand away from me, all you workers of unrighteousness.

(cf. 8:12 below)

8:11 And I say to you, that many will come from east and west and will recline with Abraham and Isaac and Jacob in the Kingdom of the Heavens;
12 but the sons of the Kingdom will be cast out into the exterior darkness;

28 Weeping and gnashing of teeth shall be there,

(cf. v. 29)
when you see Abraham and Isaac and Jacob, and all the prophets, in the Kingdom of God,
but you (yourselves) cast out without.

(see v. 11 above)

Weeping and gnashing of teeth shall be there.

29 And they will come from east and west and from north and south and will recline in the Kingdom of God.

20:16 Thus the last will be first and the first last **(cf. 19:30)**.

30 And behold those who will be first are last, and those who will be last are first.

(10:31)

MT	LK 13:31-33	MK	JN
	31 At that very hour some Pharisees came up, saying to him: Go out and go from here, for Herod wants to kill you. 32 And he said to them: Go and tell this fox; behold I cast out demons and effect cures to-day and to-morrow, and on the third day I am finished (with my task). 33 However I have to journey today and tomorrow and the next, because it is not possible for (the) prophet to perish outside Jerusalem.		

§243 Lament over Jerusalem (Lk) (§305, cf. §289)

MT 23:37-39	LK 13:34-35	MK	JN
37 Jerusalem, Jerusalem, thou who killeth the prophets and stoneth the ones sent to thee, *how often I wished to gather thy children,* *just as a hen gathers her chicks under her wings, and you would not.* *38 Behold your House is left to you desolate.**	34 Jerusalem, Jerusalem, thou who killeth the prophets and stoneth the ones sent to thee, how often I wished to have gathered thy children, just as a hen her own brood under her wings, and you would not. 35 Behold your House is left to you desolate.*		
39 For I say to you, by no means may you see me from now, until you say: Blessed is he who comes in the name of the Lord.	And I say to you, by no means may you see me until it shall come when you say: Blessed is he who comes in the name of the Lord.		

§244 A Dropsical Man Healed

MT	LK 14:1-6	MK	JN
	1 And it happened that on his coming into the house of one of the rulers of the Pharisees on a Sabbath to eat bread, they watched him closely. 2 And behold in front of him was a man with dropsy. And Jesus answering said to the lawyers and Pharisees: Is it lawful to heal on the Sabbath or not? 4 But they kept silent. And taking him he healed him and let him go. 5 And answering he said to them:		
(cf. 12:11)	Of which one of you will an ass* or an ox fall into a well, and he will not at once haul it up on the Sabbath-day? **(cf. 13:15)**. 6 And they could not answer back these things.	**(cf. 13:15)**	

§245 Advice to Guests (§304)

MT 23:12	LK 14:7-11	MK	JN
	7 And he told the guests a parable, noting how they selected the first places, saying to them:		
	8 When you are invited by someone to a marriage-feast, do not recline in the first place, lest someone more honourable than you may have been invited by him, 9 and he who invited both you and him coming shall say to you, Give place to this person; and then you will begin with shame to take the lowest place.		
	10 But when you are invited, go and sit in the last place, so that when he who invited you comes, he will tell you: Friend, go up higher. Then you will have honour before all your fellow-guests.		
12 And whoever shall exalt himself shall be humbled, and whoever shall humble himself shall be exalted.	11 For everyone who exalts himself shall be humbled, and he who humbles himself shall be exalted (cf. 18:14b).		

§246 Advice to a Host

MT	LK 14:12-14	MK	JN
	12 And he said to him who had invited him:		
	When you give a lunch or a dinner, do not invite your friends nor your brothers, nor your relations nor rich neighbours, lest they also invite you back and recompense be made to you.		
	13 But when you give a reception, invite the poor, the maimed, the lame, the blind, 14 and you will be blessed because they have nothing to recompense you, for you will be recompensed in the resurrection of the just.		

§247 The Great Supper (cf. §299)

MT (cf. 22:1-10)	LK 14:15-24	MK	JN
	15 And one of the table-companions hearing these things said to him:		
	Whoever shall eat bread in the Kingdom of God is blessed.		
	16 But he said to him:		
	A certain man started to give a great dinner and invited many.		
	17 And he sent his slave at the hour of the dinner to tell the guests: Come, for all is now ready.		
	18 And they one and all began to make excuses.		
	The first said to him: I have bought an estate and I have urgently to go out and see it. I beg you, hold me excused.		
	19 And another said: I have bought five yoke of oxen, and I am going to test them. I beg you, hold me excused.		
	20 And another said: I have married a wife, and therefore I cannot come.		

MT	LK 14:15-24	MK	JN
	21 And the slave came and reported these things to his lord. Then the master of the house got angry and said to his slave: Go out quickly into the thoroughfares and streets of the city and bring in here the poor and the maimed and the blind and the lame. 22 And the slave said: Lord, what you ordered has been done, and there is still room. 23 And the lord said to the slave: Go out into the roads and hedges and oblige them to come in, that my house may be filled. 24 For I say to you that none of those men that were invited shall taste my supper.		

§248 Conditions of Discipleship (§§127, 177)

MT 10:37-38	LK 14:25-27	MK	JN
37 He who loves father or mother above me is not worthy of me. And he who loves son or daughter above me is not worthy of me. *38 And he who does not take his cross and follow after me is not worthy of me.*	25 And great crowds were travelling with him, and turning he said to them: 26 If anyone comes to me, and does not hate his father and mother and wife and children and brothers and sisters and besides also his own life, he cannot be my disciple. 27 Whoever does not carry his own cross and come after me cannot be my disciple.		
(cf. 16:24)	**(cf. 9:23)**	**(cf. 8:34)**	

§249 The Tower Builder

MT	LK 14:28-33	MK	JN
	28 For which of you wanting to build a tower, does not first sit down and count the cost, if he has (enough) for completion? 29 Lest, when he has laid the foundation and is not able to finish, all the onlookers begin to mock him, 30 saying: This man began to build but could not finish. 31 Or what king, going to engage another king in battle, will not first sit down and deliberate whether he is able with ten thousand to meet the one coming against him with twenty thousand? 32 And if not, while he is a long way off, he will send an embassy asking for peace. 33 So therefore everyone of you who does not take leave of all his own possessions cannot be my disciple.		

§250 The Salt (Lk) (§§61, 186)

MT 5:13	LK 14:34-35	MK 9:49-50	JN
13 You are the salt of the earth.		49 *Everyone shall be salted with fire, and every offering shall be salted with salt.**	
	34. Salt therefore is good.	50 *Salt is good;*	
But if the salt should be spoilt, how shall it be salted?	But if even the salt should be spoilt, how shall it be restored?	*but if the salt should become un-salty, how shall you restore it?*	
For nothing is it still of value,	35 Neither for the ground nor for manure is it suitable;		
except for being thrown outside to be trodden down by men.	they throw it outside.		
(cf. Mt. 11:15)	He that hath ears to hear, let him hear.	*Have salt in yourselves and be at peace with one another.*	

§251 The Lost Sheep (Lk) (§187)

MT 18:12-13	LK 15:1-7	MK	JN
	1 Now all the tax-collectors and the sinners were drawing near to him to hear him.		
	2 But both the Pharisees and the Scribes were grumbling saying: This man receives sinners and eats with them.		
	3 And he told them this parable, saying:		
12 What think you? If some man should own a hundred sheep, and one of them should stray,	4 Some man among you having a hundred sheep, and losing one of them,—		
will he not leave the ninety-nine on the mountains and go and seek the one gone astray?	does he not forsake the ninety-nine in the desert and go after the lost one, until he find it?		
13 And should he happen to find it,	5 And having found (it) he sets (it) upon his shoulders rejoicing,		
	6 and coming into the house, he invites (his) friends and neighbours, saying to them: Rejoice with me, because I have found my sheep that was lost.		
Amen, I say to you, that he rejoices over it more	7 I say to you that so there will be joy in heaven over one sinner repenting, (more)		
than over the ninety-nine that have not strayed.	than over the ninety-nine just ones who have no need of repentance.		

§252 The Lost Coin

MT	LK 15:8-10	MK	JN
	8 Or what woman having ten drachmae, if she were to lose one drachma,—does she not light a lamp and sweep the house and search carefully until she finds it?		
	9 And having found (it) she invites (her) friends and neighbours saying: Rejoice with me, because I have found the drachma which I lost.		

MT   LK 15:8-10   MK   JN
            10 Thus I say to you, there is joy before the angels of God over
            one sinner repenting.

§253 The Prodigal Son

MT   LK 15:11-32   MK   JN
            11 And he said:
            A certain man had two sons. 12 And the younger of them said to
            (his) father: Father, give me the portion of the property that falls
            (to me). And he divided the living for them.
            13 And after not many days the younger son having gathered up
            everything departed for a distant region, and there he squandered
            his property, living extravagantly.
            14 And when he had spent everything, a severe famine came upon
            that region, and he himself began to be in need.
            15 And he went and attached himself to one of the citizens of that
            region, and he sent him on to his estates to feed pigs.
            16 And he longed to fill his belly from the pods on which the
            swine were feeding, and no one gave to him.
            17 And coming to himself he said: How many employees of my
            father abound in bread; but here am I perishing with famine. 18 I
            will rise up and go to my father, and I will say to him: Father, I
            have sinned against heaven and before you; 19 no longer am I
            worthy to be called your son; make me as one of your employees.
            20 And rising up he came to his own father.
            And while he was yet far away, his father saw him and was moved
            with pity, and running he fell upon his neck and kissed him.
            21 And the son said to him: Father, I have sinned against heaven
            and before you; I am no longer worthy to be called your son;
            make me like one of your employees.
            22 And his father said to his slaves: Bring out quickly the first
            robe and put it on him, and put a ring on his hand and sandals on
            (his) feet. 23. And bring the fatted calf, slaughter (it), and let us
            eat and be merry. 24 For this son of mine was dead and has come
            to life, he was lost and been found. And they began to make
            merry.
            25 Now his elder son was on the estate, and as he drew near
            coming to the house, he heard music and dancing; 26 and
            summoning one of the boys he inquired what it might be.
            27 And he said to him: Your brother has come, and your father
            has slaughtered the fatted calf because he has got him back in
            good health.
            28 And he got angry and would not go in. And his father going
            out appealed to him.
            29 But he answering said to his father: Behold I serve you so
            many years and have never transgressed your command, and you

MT	LK 15:11-32	MK	JN

never gave me a goat for me to make merry with my friends.
30 But when this son of yours who has devoured your living with
harlots has come, you have slaughtered for him the fatted calf.
31 And he said to him: Child, you are always with me, and all my
things are yours. 32 But it was right to make merry and rejoice
because this brother of yours was dead and has come to life, has
been lost and is found.

§254 The Dishonest Steward (cf. §§191, 316)

MT	LK 16:1-12	MK	JN
(cf. 18:23-25; 24:45ff.)			

1 And he said also to his disciples:
There was a certain rich man who had a manager, and he was
accused to him of squandering his possessions.
2 And calling him, he said to him: What (is) this I hear about
you? Render an account of your managership; for you can no
longer manage.
3 And the manager said to himself: What shall I do, because my
master is taking the managership away from me? To dig I am not
able; to beg I am ashamed.
4 I know what I will do, so that when I am removed from the
managership they will receive me into their own houses.
5 And summoning each one of his master's debtors, he said to the
first: How much do you owe my master? 6 And he said: A
hundred barrels of oil. And he said to him: Take your bill and sit
down quickly and write fifty.
7 Then he said to another: And how much do you owe? And he
said: A hundred measures of wheat. He says to him: Take your
bill and write eighty.
8 And the master praised the manager with regard to the injustice,
that he had acted with foresight. For the sons of this age are more
farseeing than the sons of light with regard to their own
generation.
9 And I say to you, make for yourselves friends of the Mammon
of injustice, so that when it fails they may receive you into the
everlasting tents.
10 The one who is faithful in the least thing is also faithful in the
great, and the one who is unjust in the least thing is also unjust in
the great.
11 If therefore you were not faithful in the unjust Mammon, who
will entrust you with the true one?
12 And if you were not faithful in what belongs to another, who
will give you what is yours?

§255 On Serving Two Masters (Lk) (§79)

MT 6:24
24 Nobody can serve two masters;
for either he will hate the one and love the other,
or he will be attached to one and despise the other.
You cannot serve God and Mammon.

LK 16:13
13 No house-slave can serve two masters;
for either he will hate the one and love the other,
or he will be attached to one and despise the other.
You cannot serve God and Mammon.

MK

JN

§256 The Pharisees Reproved

MT

LK 16:14-15
14 Now the Pharisees being money-lovers heard all these things,
and scoffed at him.
15 And he said to them:
You are the ones who justify yourselves before men, but God
knows your hearts, for what is exalted among men (is) an
abomination before God.

MK

JN

§257 The Kingdom Violently Treated (§131)

MT 11:12-13

(cf. v. 13 below)

12 But from the days of John the Baptist until now
the Kingdom of the Heavens suffers violence and the violent
snatch it away.
13 For all the Prophets and the Law prophesied as far as John.

LK 16:16
16 The Law and the Prophets (were) until John;

from then
the Kingdom of God is evangelized, and everyone uses violence
against it.

(cf. v. 16 above)

MK

JN

§258 The Law Will Endure (§63)

MT 5:18
18 For amen I say to you, until the heaven and the earth pass
away,
not one iota or one pen-stroke of the Law will pass away, until
all things be done.

LK 16:17
17 But it is easier for the heaven and the earth to pass away,

than for one pen-stroke of the Law to fall.

MK

JN

MT 5:32	LK 16:18	MK	JN
32 But I say to you, that everyone who divorces his wife, except for the reason of incest,	18 Everyone who divorces his wife	(10:11-12)	
makes her commit adultery,	and marries another commits adultery,		
and whoever would marry a divorced woman	and he who marries a woman divorced from her husband		
commits adultery **(cf. 19:9)**.	commits adultery.		

§260 The Rich Man and Lazarus

MT	LK 16:19-31	MK	JN
	19 Now there was a certain rich man and he wore purple and fine linen, feasting sumptuously every day. 20 And a certain poor man called Lazarus lay at his gate covered with sores, 21 and longing to be satisfied with the crumbs that fell from the table of the rich man; moreover the dogs came and licked his sores. 22 And the poor man went and died and was carried up by the angels into Abraham's bosom. And the rich man also died and was buried. 23 And lifting up his eyes in Hell, being in torment he sees Abraham from afar and Lazarus in his bosom. 24 And calling out he said: Father Abraham, have pity on me and send Lazarus to dip the tip of his finger in water and cool my tongue, because I am tormented in this flame. 25 And Abraham said: Child, remember that you received your good things in your life and Lazarus likewise bad things. But now he is comforted here, and you are tormented. 26 And in addition to all these things, between us and you a great chasm has been fixed, so that those who want to pass across hence to you cannot, nor may they cross over thence to us. 27 And he said: Then I beseech you, father, to send him to my father's house; 28 for I have five brothers, so that he may warn them lest they too should come into this place of torment. 29 And Abraham says: They have Moses and the Prophets; let them listen to them. 30 And he said: No, father Abraham, but if someone should come to them from the dead, they would repent. 31 But he said to him: If they do not listen to Moses and the Prophets, neither will they be persuaded if someone should rise from the dead.		

§261 A Warning against Scandals (Lk) (§185)

MT 18:7, 6

7 Woe to the world from scandals; for it is necessary for scandals to come, but woe to that man through whom the scandal comes.

6 And whoever should scandalize one of these little ones who believe in me, it is advantageous for him for an ass's mill-stone to be suspended round his neck and to be submerged in the depth of the sea.

LK 17:1-3a

1 And he said to his disciples:

It is impossible for scandals not to come, but woe (to him) through whom they come.

2 It were better for him if a mill-stone were hung round about his neck and he had been thrown into the sea, (rather) than that he should scandalize one of these little ones.
3a Mind yourselves!

MK 9:42

42 And whoever should scandalize one of these little ones who believe in me, it is good for him rather if an ass's mill-stone were hung round about his neck, and he had been cast into the sea.

JN

§262 On Forgiveness (§188)

MT 18:15, 21-22
15 And if your brother should sin against you, go off, reprove him between you and him alone. If he should hear you, you have gained your brother.

21 The Peter came up and said to him: Lord how many times shall my brother sin against me and I shall forgive him? Up to seven times? 22 Jesus says to him: I do not say to you, up to seven times, but up to seventy-seven times.

LK 17:3b-4
3b If your brother should sin, rebuke him;

and if he should repent, forgive him.

4 And if he should sin against you seven times a day, and seven times turn back to you saying, I repent, you shall forgive him.

MK

JN

§263 On Faith (§§180, 295)

MT 17:20
20 And he says to them: Because of the littleness of your faith.

For Amen I say to you, if you have faith like a grain of mustard seed, you shall say to this mountain, Remove hence to there, and it will be removed and nothing will be impossible to you.

(cf. 21:22)

LK 17:5-6
5 And the apostles said to the Lord: Increase our faith.
6 And the Lord said:
If you have faith like a grain of mustard seed,

you would say to this mulberry tree, Be uprooted and planted in the sea, and it would obey you.

MK

(cf. 11:22)

JN

§264 The Unprofitable Servant

MT	LK 17:7-10	MK	JN

LK 17:7-10

7 And one of you having a slave who ploughs or shepherds, will he say to him as he comes in from the farm: Come at once and sit at table?

8 But will he not rather say to him: Prepare something that I may dine, and gird yourself and serve me until I eat and drink, and afterwards you shall eat and drink?

9 Does he thank the slave because he has done the things commanded him? I think not!

10 Thuswise also you, when you have done everything commanded you, say: We are unprofitable servants, we have done what we had to do.

§265 The Healing of Ten Lepers

MT	LK 17:11-19	MK	JN

LK 17:11-19

11 And it came to pass as he was going to Jerusalem, that he was passing through the border between Samaria and Galilee.

12 And as he was coming into a certain village there met him ten men, lepers, who stood at a distance.

13 And they raised a cry saying: Jesus, master, have pity on us.

14 And seeing he said to them: Go and show yourselves to the priests.

And it happened as they went they were cleansed.

15 And one of them seeing that he was cured, returned praising God with a loud voice, 16 and he fell on his face at his feet thanking him; and he was a Samaritan.

17 And Jesus answering said: Were not ten cleansed? And where are the nine? 18 Were none found returning to give glory to God except this foreigner?

19 And he said to him: Rise and go; your faith has saved you.

§266 On the Coming of the Kingdom

MT	LK 17:20-21	MK	JN
(cf. 24:26)			

LK 17:20-21

20 And being asked by the Pharisees when the Kingdom of God was coming, he answered them and said:

The Kingdom of God does not come with watching; 21 nor will they say, Lo here, or There! For lo the Kingdom of God is within you (cf. 17:23).

MT 24:23, 27, 37-39, 17-18; 10:39; 24:41, 40, 28	LK 17:22-37	MK 13:21, 15-16	JN
	22 And he said to his disciples: Days will come when you will desire to see one of the days of the Son of Man, and you will not see (it).		
23 Then if anyone should say to you: Behold, here (is) the Christ, or: Here!, do not believe.	23 And they will say to you: Behold there! or: Behold, here! Do not go off, or pursue.	21 And then if anyone should say to you: See, here (is) the Christ, See there! Believe not.	
27 For just as the lightning comes forth from the east and appears as far as the west, so shall be the Advent of the Son of Man.	24 For just as the lightning flashing from one (end) of the heaven to the other shines out, so shall be the Son of Man in his day. 25 But first he must suffer many things and be rejected by this generation.		
37 For just as the days of Noah, so also shall be the Advent of the Son of Man.	26 And as it happened in the days of Noah, so shall it be also in the days of the Son of Man;		
38 For as they were in the days that were before the flood, feasting and drinking, marrying and giving in marriage, up to the day on which Noah entered into the ark, 39 and they knew not until the flood came and took away everyone,	27 they were eating, they were drinking, they were marrying, they were giving in marriage, up to the day on which Noah entered into the ark, and the flood came and destroyed all.		
	28 Likewise, as it happened in the days of Lot; they were eating, they were drinking, they were buying, they were selling, they were planting, they were building. 29 And on the day that Lot went forth from Sodom, it rained fire and brimstone from heaven and destroyed all.		
so also shall be the Advent of the Son of Man.	30 Just the same will it be on the day the Son of Man is revealed.		
17 Let him on the roof-top not come down to take away the things from his house, 18 and let him in the field not turn back to take his coat,	31 On that day he who shall be on the roof-top and his belongings in the house, let him not come down to take them away, and let him in the field likewise not turn back.	15 And let him on the roof-top not come down nor enter in to take away any things out of his house, 16 and let him at the field not turn back to the things behind to take his coat.	
10:39 He who has found his life, will lose it, and he who has lost his life for my sake will find it (cf. 16:25).	32 Remember Lot's wife! 33 Whoever would seek to preserve his life will lose it, and whoever will lose (it) will cause it to come alive (cf. 9:24). 34 I say to you, on that night there will be two (men) in one bed;	(cf. 8:35)	

MT 24:23, 27, 37-39, 17-18; 10:39; 24:41, 40, 28	LK 17:22-37	MK 13:21, 15-16	JN
	the one will be taken, and the other will be left.		
24:41 two women grinding at the mill, one is taken, and one is left.	35 There will be two women grinding together, the one will be taken, but the other will be left;		
40 Then there will be two men in the field, one is taken, and one is left;	36* two men in a field, one will be taken and the other will be left. 37 And answering they say to him: Where, Lord? And he said to them:		
28 Wherever the corpse may be, there the eagles will be gathered.	Where the body is, there too will the eagles be gathered together.		

§268 The Unjust Judge and the Widow

MT	LK 18:1-8	MK	JN
	1 And he spoke a parable to them about having to pray always and not to grow weary, 2 saying: In a certain city there was a judge who did not fear God or respect man. 3 And in that city there was a widow, and she came to him, saying: Give me justice from my accuser. 4 And he refused for a long time. But subsequently he said to himself: Though I neither fear God nor respect man, 5 yet because of the bother this widow gives me, I will give her justice lest continually coming she wear me out. 6 And the Lord said: Hear what the unjust judge says. 7 For will not God certainly effect the vindication of his Elect who cry to him day and night, and will he delay over them? 8 I say to you that he will speedily effect their vindication. However, when the Son of Man comes will he really find faith on the earth?		

§269 The Pharisee and the Tax-Collector (§304)

MT 23:12	LK 18:9-14	MK	JN
	9 And he spoke also this parable to some who had persuaded themselves that they were just and who despised the rest. 10 Two men went up to the Temple to pray, the one a Pharisee and the other a tax-collector. 11 The Pharisee stood and prayed these things to himself: O		

186

MT 23:12

LK 18:9-14   MK   JN

God, I thank thee that I am not as the rest of men, grasping, unjust, adulterers, or even like this tax-collector. 12 I fast twice a week, I tithe all I possess.
13 But the tax-collector keeping at a distance would not even raise his eyes to heaven, but beat his breast saying: O God, have mercy on me, sinner that I am.
14 I say to you, the latter went down to his house justified, rather than the other.

12 For whoever shall exalt himself shall be humbled,
and whoever shall humble himself shall be exalted (cf. 18:4).

For everyone who exalts himself shall be humbled,
but he who humbles himself shall be exalted (cf. 14:11).

(↓ §276)

§270 Jesus Is Consecrated

MT   LK   MK   JN 10:22-39

(↑ §201)

22 There took place then the Dedication in Jerusalem; it was winter.
23 And Jesus was walking in the Temple in the porch of Solomon.
24 The Jews therefore surrounded and said to him: How long do you hold us in suspense? If you are the Christ, tell us openly.
25 Jesus answered them:
I have told you and you do not believe; the works which I myself do in the name of my Father, these bear witness about me;
26 But you yourselves do not believe, because you are not my own sheep.
27 My own sheep listen to my voice, and I know them and they follow me,
28 and I give them eternal life, and they will never perish, and no one shall snatch them from my hand.
29 What my Father has given me is greater than all, and nobody can snatch (them) from my Father's hand.
30 I and the Father—we are one.
31 The Jews therefore fetched stones to stone him.
32 Jesus answered them:
Many good works of my Father I have shewn you; for which of these works are you stoning me?
33 The Jews answered him:
We are not stoning you for a good work, but for blasphemy, and because you being a man, make yourself God.
34 Jesus answered them: Does it not stand written in your Law: I said, you are gods? (Ps. 81[82]:6).
35 If it said those (were) gods to whom the word of God came, and the Scripture cannot be undone, 36 do you say to the one

MT	LK	MK	JN 10:22-39

whom the Father has sanctified and sent into the world: You are blaspheming; because I said: I am the Son of God?

37 If I do not do the works of my Father, believe me not; 38 but if I do, even if you do not believe me, go on believing the works, so that you should know and may know that the Father (is) in me and I (am) in the Father.

39 Therefore they tried again to arrest him; and he went out from their hands.

§271 Jesus Re-crosses the Jordan

MT	LK	MK	JN 10:40-42

40 And he went off again across the Jordan to the place where John was baptizing at first, and remained there.

41 And many came to him and said: John indeed did no sign, but everything John said about this one was true.

42 And many believed in him there.

§272 Jesus Raises Lazarus

MT	LK	MK	JN 11:1-44
	(cf. 7: 36f)		

1 Now there was a certain sick (man), Lazarus from Bethany, from the village of Mary and Martha her sister.

2 And Mary was she who had anointed the Lord with myrrh and wiped his feet with her hair, whose brother Lazarus had got sick.
    (cf. 12:3).

3 The sisters therefore sent to him, saying: Lord, see, he whom you love is sick.

4 And Jesus hearing said:
This sickness is not unto death, but (is) for the glory of God, so that the Son of God may be glorified through it.

5 Now Jesus loved Martha and her sister and Lazarus.

6 When therefore he heard that he was sick, he then still remained in the place where he was for two days.

7 Then after this he says to his disciples:
Let us go again to Judea.

8 The disciples say to him: Rabbi, the Jews were just now seeking to stone you, are you then going up there again?

9 Jesus answered:
Are there not twelve hours in the day? If anyone walks in the day, he does not stumble, because he sees the light of this world;

10 but if anyone walks in the night, he stumbles, because the light is not in it.

MT	LK	MK	JN 11:1-44

11 These things he said and after this he says to them:
Lazarus our friend has gone to sleep; but I go to wake him up.
12 The disciples therefore said to him: Lord, if he has gone to
sleep, he will be saved.
13 But Jesus had spoken about his death. But they themselves
thought that he was speaking of the rest of sleep.
14. Then therefore Jesus said to them openly: Lazarus is dead.
15 And I am glad because of you, that I was not there, so that
you may believe; but let us go to him.
16 Thomas, the one called Didymus, said therefore to his co-
disciples: Let us go too so that we may die with him.
17When Jesus therefore had come he found that he had already
been four days in the tomb.
18 Now Bethany was close to Jerusalem, about the distance of
fifteen stadia.
19 Now many of the Jews had come to Martha and Mary to
console them about their brother.
20 When therefore Martha had heard that Jesus was coming she
met him; but Mary stayed in the house.
21 Martha therefore said to Jesus:
Lord, if you had been here, my brother would not have died;
22 but now I know that whatever you will ask of God, God will
give you.
23 Jesus says to her:
Your brother will be raised.
24 Martha says to him:
I know that he will be raised up in the resurrection on the last
day.
25 Jesus said to her:
I myself am the resurrection and the life. He who believes in me,
even if he has died, will live. 26 And everyone who lives and
believes in me does not ever die. Do you believe this?
27 She says to him:

**(cf.
16:
16)**

Yes, Lord; I fully believe that you are the Christ the Son of God,
he who is to come into the world.
28 And having said these things, she went off and called Mary her
sister secretly saying:
The Teacher is here, and is calling you.
29 And when the latter heard she arose speedily and came to him:
30 For Jesus had not yet come into the village, but was still in the
place where Martha had met him.
31 The Jews therefore who were with her in the house and
consoling her, seeing Mary rise with speed and go out, followed
her, thinking that she was going away to the tomb in order to
weep there.
32 When Mary then had come where Jesus was, seeing him she
fell at his feet, saying to him:
Lord, if you had been here, my brother would not have died.
33 So when Jesus saw her weeping he was greatly distressed in his

MT	LK	MK	JN 11:1-44
			spirit and troubled himself,
			34 and said:
			Where have you laid him?
			They said to him: Lord, come and see.
			35 Jesus shed tears.
			36 The Jews therefore said:
			See how he loved him.
			37 And some of them said:
			Could not this (man) who opened the eyes of the blind (man)
			cause that this (man) should not die?
		(cf.	38 Jesus therefore again being greatly distressed in himself comes
		15:	to the tomb; now it was a cave and a stone was laid against it.
		47)	39 Jesus says:
			Take the stone away.
			Martha the sister of the dead man says to him:
			Lord, already he smells, for it is four days ago.
			40 Jesus says to her:
			Did I not say to you that if you will believe, you will see the glory
			of God.
			41 So they took the stone away.
			And Jesus raised his eyes upwards and said:
			O Father: I give thee thanks that thou hast heard me.
			42 And I know that thou hearest me always; but I have spoken
			because of the crowd standing around, so that they may believe
			that thou hast sent me.
			43 And having said these things, he cried with a loud voice:
			Lazarus, come out.
			44 The dead man came out with his feet and hands bound with
			bandages. And his face was bound round with a sweat-cloth.
			Jesus says to them:
			Loose him and let him go.

§273 The Sanhedrin Condemns Jesus (§§294, 325)

MT	LK 19:47-48	MK 11:18	JN 11:45-54
(cf. 26: 1-5)	47 *And he was teaching day by day in the Temple,*		45 Therefore many of the Jews, who had come to Mary, and having beheld what he had done, believed in him.
	and the high-priests and the scribes sought to destroy him, and the chief men of the people, 48 *and they did not find how to do it;*	18 *And the high priests and the Scribes heard and they sought how they might destroy him; for they feared him.*	46 But some of them went off to the Pharisees and told them what Jesus had done. 47 Therefore the high priests and the Pharisees got together a Council and said: What do we do, because this man is working many signs?
	for the whole people heard and hung upon him.	*For the whole crowd was amazed at his teaching.*	48 If in this manner we let him, all will believe in him, and the Romans will come and take away both our place and our race.

190

MT	LK 19:47-48	MK 11:18	JN 11:45-54

JN 11:45-54

49 Now a certain one of them, Caiaphas, being the high-priest of that year, said to them:
50 You yourselves know nothing, nor are you considering that it is expedient for you that one man should die for the people and that the whole race should not be destroyed.
51 Now this he did not say from himself; but being high-priest of that year he prophesied that Jesus was going to die for the race, 52 and not for the race alone, but also that he might gather together into one the children of God who have been scattered.
53 From that day therefore they planned to kill him.
54 Jesus therefore no longer continued to walk openly among the Jews, but went away thence into the country near the desert, to a city called Ephraim, and there he remained with the disciples.

(↓ §285)

§274 A Question about Divorce (cf. §67)

MT 19:3-9

(↑ §192)

3 And the Pharisees came up to him tempting him and saying: Is it lawful for a man to put away his wife for any reason?

4 And he answering said:
Have you not read that

the creator from the beginning made them male and female.
(Gen. 1:27)
5 And he said:
For this reason a man will leave father and his mother and will be joined to his wife, and the two shall be in one flesh **(Gen. 2:24)**;
6 and so they are no longer two but one flesh. For what God has yoked together, let man not separate.

7 They say to him:
Why then did Moses command to give a document of divorce and to put her away?

LK

MK 10:2-12

(↑ §192)

2 And the Pharisees coming up questioned him whether it is lawful for a husband to put away a wife, tempting him.
3 And he answering said to them:
What did Moses command you?

---

6 But from the beginning of creation, God made them male and female;

7 for this reason a man will leave his father and mother and will be joined to his wife. 8 and the two shall be in one flesh;

and so they are no longer two but one flesh. 9 For what God has yoked together, let man not separate.

---

4 And they said:
Moses permitted to write a document of divorce and to put away.

JN

MT 19:3-9	LK	MK 10:2-12	JN
8 He says to them: Moses, because of your hard-heartedness, permitted you to put away your wives; but from the beginning it has not been so. **vv. 5-6.**		5 And Jesus said to them: Because of your hard-heartedness he wrote for you this commandment. 6 But from the beginning of creation God made them male and female; 7 for this reason a man will leave his father and mother; and will be joined up to his wife. 8 and the two shall be in one flesh, and so they are no longer two but one flesh. 9 For what God has yoked together, let man not separate. 10 And in the house again his disciples questioned him about this.	
9 I say to you, that whosoever puts away his wife, except for incest, and marries another, commits adultery, and he who marries her who has been put away commits adultery.		11 And he says to them: Whosoever puts away his wife, and marries another, commits adultery against her. 12 And if she being put away from her husband marries another she commits adultery. (↓ §276)	

§275 Teaching on the Single Life

MT 19:10-12	LK	MK	JN
10 The disciples say to him: If the case of a man with his wife is like this, it is not expedient to marry. 11 But he said to them: Not all can take this saying, but to whom it has been given. 12 For there are eunuchs who from the mother's womb were born so, and there are eunuchs who were made eunuchs by men, and there are eunuchs who have made themselves eunuchs for the Kingdom of the Heavens. He who can take it, let him take it.			

§276 "Let the Children Come" (cf. §183)

MT 19:13-15	LK 18:15-17	MK 10:13-16	JN
	(↑ §269)	(↑ §274)	
13 Then were brought to him little children, to lay hands on them and pray (cf. 18:4-6).	15 And they brought to him also the babes, to touch them (cf. 9:48).	13 And they brought to him little children to touch them (cf. 9:36).	

MT 19:13-15	LK 18:15-17	MK 10:13-16	JN
But the disciples rebuked them. 14 But Jesus said to them: Let the little children and do not stop them coming to me; for of such is the Kingdom of the Heavens. **(cf. 18:3)** 15 And laying (his) hands on them, he went thence.	And the disciples seeing began to rebuke them. 16 But Jesus called them up saying: Let the little children come to me, and do not stop them; for of such is the Kingdom of God. 17 Amen I say to you, whosoever does not receive the Kingdom of God as a little child, shall by no means enter into it.	And the disciples rebuked them. 14 And Jesus seeing was upset and said to them: Let the little children come to me; do not stop them; for of such is the Kingdom of God. 15 Amen I say to you, whosoever does not receive the Kingdom of God as a little child, shall by no means enter into it. 16 And embracing them, he blessed them, laying (his) hands on them.	

§277 The Rich Young Man (cf. §302)

MT 19:16-22	LK 18:18-23	MK 10:17-22	JN
16 And behold one coming to him said: Teacher, what good thing* shall I do to possess eternal life? 17 And he said to him: Why do you ask me about the Good? The Good is One.* If you wish to enter into life, keep the commandments. 18 He says to him: Which? And Jesus said: Thou shalt not murder, thou shalt not commit adultery, Thou shalt not steal, Thou shalt not bear false witness, 19 honour father and mother, and thou shalt love thy neighbour as thyself **(Ex. 20:12-16; Dt. 5:16-20)**. 20 The young man says to him: All these things I have done from my youth; what do I still lack? 21 Jesus said to him: If you wish to be perfect, Go off, sell your goods, and give to the poor, and you shall have treasure in the heavens; and come follow me. 22 And hearing this word the young man went away sad, for he had many possessions.	18 And some ruler questioned him, saying: Good Teacher, what do I do to inherit eternal life? 19 And Jesus said to him: Why do you call me Good? No one is Good but one, God. 20 You know the commandments: Do not commit adultery, do not murder, do not steal, do not bear false witness, honour thy father and thy mother. 21 And he said: All these things I have done from my youth. 22 And Jesus hearing said to him: Still one thing is wanting to you. Sell all that you have and give away to the poor, and you shall have treasure in the heavens; and come follow me. 23 And hearing these things he became very sad, for he was exceedingly rich.	17 And as he was setting out on the road one running up knelt to him and began to question him: Good Teacher, what shall I do to inherit eternal life? 18 And Jesus said to him: Why do you call me Good? No one is Good but one, God. 19 You know the commandments: Do not murder, do not commit adultery, do not steal, do not bear false witness, do not defraud, honour thy father and mother. 20 And he said to him: Teacher, All these things I have done from my youth. 21 And Jesus, looking on him, loved him, and said to him: One thing is lacking to you. Go off, sell whatever you have, and give to the poor, and you shall have treasure in heaven; and come follow me. 22 And his face falling at this word he went away sad, for he had many possessions.	

193

MT 19:23-29	LK 18:24-30	*LK 22:28-30*	MK 10:23-30	JN
23 But Jesus said to his disciples: Amen I say to you, that a rich man with difficulty will enter into the Kingdom of the Heavens. 24 Again I say to you,	24 But Jesus, seeing him become sad, said: With what difficulty do those who have possessions go into the Kingdom of God.		23 And Jesus looking around says to his disciples: With what difficulty will those who have possessions enter into the Kingdom of God. 24 And the disciples were astounded at his words. But Jesus again answering says to them: Children, how difficult it is for those who trust in riches* to enter into the Kingdom of God.	
that it is easier for a camel to pass through the eye of a needle than for a rich man (to pass) into the Kingdom of God. 25 And when the disciples heard they were exceedingly amazed saying: Who then can be saved? 26 And Jesus looking upon (them) said to them: With men this is impossible, but with God all things are possible.	25 For it is easier for a camel to pass through the eye of a sewing needle than for a rich man to pass into the Kingdom of God. 26 And they that heard said: Who indeed can be saved? And he said: The things impossible with men are possible with God.		25 It is easier for a camel to go through the eye of a needle than for a rich man to pass into the Kingdom of God. 26 And they were above measure exceedingly amazed saying to one another: Who indeed can be saved? 27 But Jesus looking upon them says: With men it is impossible, but not with God. For all things are possible with God.	
27 Then Peter answering said to him: Behold, we left all things and followed you, what then shall we have? 28 And Jesus said to them: Amen I say to you that you who have followed me, in the rebirth, when the Son of Man has taken his seat on the throne of his glory,	28 And Peter said: Behold, we leaving our own followed you. 29 And he said to them: Amen I say to you that		28 Peter began to say to him: Behold, we left all things and followed you. 29 Jesus said: Amen, I say to you,	
		28 And you are the ones who have stayed with me in my trials. *29 And I bequeath to you as my Father has bequeathed to me a Kingdom, 30 so that you will eat and drink at my table in my Kingdom,*		
you yourselves too shall sit on twelve thrones, judging the twelve tribes of Israel.		*and you will sit on thrones judging the twelve tribes of Israel.*		
29 And everyone, whosoever has left houses, or brothers or sisters, or father or mother or wife,* or children or lands, for the sake of my name,	there is no one who has left house or wife, or brothers, or parents, or children, for the sake of the Kingdom of God,		there is no one who has left house, or brothers or sisters, or father or mother, or wife,* or children or lands, for my sake and for the sake of the Gospel,	

MT 19:23-29	LK 18:24-30	LK 22:28-30	MK 10:23-30	JN
will receive a hundredfold	30 who indeed will not get back manyfold in this time,		30 who will not get a hundredfold in this time, houses and brothers and sisters and mothers and children and lands, with persecutions,	
and will inherit eternal life.	and in the age to come eternal life.		and in the age to come eternal life.	
	(↓ §280)		(↓ §280)	

§279 The Labourers in the Vineyard

MT 19:30-20:16	LK	MK 10:31	JN
30 And many first will be last and last first **(cf. 20:16)**.	**(cf. 13:30)**	31 And many first will be last and the last first.	

MT 19:30-20:16 (continued):

20:1 The Kingdom of the Heavens is like a man, an estate-owner, who went out early in the morning to hire labourers for his vineyard.
2 And having agreed with the labourers for a denarius for the day, he sent them into his vineyard.
3 And going out about the third hour he saw others standing in the market-place unemployed, 4 and he said to them: Go off, you also into the vineyard, and I will give you whatever is just. 5 And they went.
And again going out about the sixth and ninth hours he did the same.
6 And going out about the eleventh hour, he found others standing and he says to them: Why have you stood here the whole day unemployed? 7 They say to him: Because no one has hired us. He says to them: Go off you also into the vineyard.
8 And when evening came, the lord of the vineyard says to his agent. Summon the labourers and pay out the wage to them, beginning from the last down to the first.
9 And they that came at the eleventh hour received a denarius each.
10 And they that came first thought that they would receive more; but they themselves also received a denarius each.
11 And receiving (it) they began to grumble against the estate-owner, saying: 12 These who were last worked one hour, and you have made them equal to us who have borne the burden of the day and the heat.
13 And he, answering one of them, said:
Comrade, I do you no injustice; did you not agree with me on a denarius? 14 Take what is yours and go off. But I wish to give this last the same as to you. 15 Or is it not lawful for me to do what I wish in my own affairs? Or is your eye evil because I am good?

MT 19:30-20:16
16 Thus the last will be first and the first last. For many are called but few are chosen* (cf. 19:30; 22:14).

LK
(cf. 13:30)

MK 10:31
(cf. 10:31 above)

JN

§280 The Third Passion Prediction

MT 20:17-19

17 And Jesus, as he was going up to Jerusalem,

took his twelve disciples aside and on the way he said to them:
18 Behold, we are going up to Jerusalem, and the Son of Man will be betrayed to the high priests and scribes and they will condemn him to death,
19 and they will betray him to the Gentiles, for mocking
and scourging and crucifying.
and on the third day he will be raised.

LK 18:31-34
(↑ §278)
(cf. 9:51)

31 And taking the Twelve he said to them:

Behold, we are going up to Jerusalem, and all the things written by the prophets regarding the Son of Man will be accomplished;
32 for he will be betrayed to the Gentiles and he will be mocked and insulted and spat upon,
33 and having scourged they will kill him and on the third day he will be raised up.
34 But they themselves perceived none of these things, and this utterance was hidden from them, and they did not understand what was said.
(↓ §282)

MK 10:32-34
(↑ §278)

32 And they were on the way going up to Jerusalem, and Jesus was leading them, and they were astounded, but they who followed were afraid.
And taking again the Twelve he began to tell them the things about to happen to him:
33 Behold, we are going up to Jerusalem, and the Son of Man will be betrayed to the high priests and the scribes and they will condemn him to death,
and they will betray him to the Gentiles 34 and they will mock him and spit on him, and they will scourge and kill him, and after three days he will be raised up.

JN

§281 Request of the Sons of Zebedee (§334)

MT 20:20-28
20 Then the mother of the sons of Zebedee, with her sons, came up to him worshipping and asking something from him.

21 And he said to her: What do you want?

She says to him: Say that these two sons of mine shall sit one on your right and one on your left in your Kingdom.
22 And Jesus answering said:
You know not what you are asking. Can you

LK 22:24-27

MK 10:35-45
35 And James and John, the two sons of Zebedee go up to him, saying to him: Teacher, we want you to do for us whatever we ask you.
36 And he said to them: What do you want me to do for you?
37 And they said to him: Grant us that one shall sit on your right and one on your left in your glory.
38 And Jesus said to them:
You know not what you are asking. Can you

JN

MT 20:20-28	LK 22:24-27	MK 10:35-45	JN
drink the cup which I am about to drink?		drink the cup, which I am drinking? Or be baptized with the baptism with which I am being baptized?	
They say to him: We can. 23 He says to them: You shall drink my cup indeed,		39 And they said to him. We can. And Jesus said to them: You shall drink the cup which I drink, and you shall be baptized with the baptism with which I am being baptized,	
but to sit on my right and left, this is not mine to give, but for whom it has been prepared by my Father. 24 And when they heard, the ten were indignant about the two brothers.	*24 And there also took place a contention among them about whom they thought to be the greatest among them.*	40 but to sit on my right and left, is not mine to give, but for whom it has been prepared. 41 And when they heard, the ten began to be indignant about James and John.	
25 But Jesus calling them up said: You know that they who rule over the nations lord (it) over them and the magnates exercise authority over them. 26 It will not be so among you; but whoever wants to become great among you, shall be your servant **(18:1-5)**; 27 and whoever wants to be first among you, shall be your slave.	*25 And he said to them: The kings of the nations lord it over them, and those in authority over them are called Benefactors. 26 But you yourselves not so, but let the greatest among you become as the junior, and the ruler as the servant **(9:46)**. 27 For who is greatest, the one who reclines, or the one who serves? Is it not the one who reclines?*	42 And Jesus calling them up says to them: You know that they who are thought to rule over the nations lord (it) over them, and their magnates exercise authority over them. 43 But it is not so among you; but whoever wants to become great among you, shall be your servant; 44 and whoever wants to be first among you, shall be slave of all.	
28 Just as the Son of Man did not come to be served, but to serve, and to give his life a ransom for many.	*Yet I myself am in your midst as the one who serves.*	45 For the Son of Man too did not come to be served, but to serve, and to give his life a ransom for many.	

§282 Healing of the Blind Beggar(s) (§118)

MT 9:27-31	MT 20:29-34	LK 18:35-43	MK 10:46-52	JN
		(↑ §280)		
And as Jesus passed along from there, there followed him	29 And as they were going out of Jericho, a great crowd followed him.	35 And it happened that when he was near to Jericho,	46 And they come into Jericho. And as he was going out of Jericho, and his disciples and a large crowd,	
two blind men	30 And behold two blind men sitting by the road,	a certain blind man sat by the road begging.	the son of Timaeus, Bar-timaeus, a blind beggar sat by the road.	
crying out and saying:	hearing that Jesus was passing by, cried out, saying:	36 And hearing a crowd passing by, he inquired why this was. 37 And they told him that Jesus the Nazarene was passing by; 38 and he bellowed saying:	47 And hearing that it was Jesus of Nazareth, he began to shout and to say:	
Have pity on us, Son of David.	Lord, have pity on us, Son of David.	Jesus, Son of David, have pity on me.	Son of David, Jesus, have pity on me.	

MT 9:27-31	MT 20:29-34	LK 18:35-43	MK 10:46-52	JN
	31 And the crowd rebuked them that they should be silent;	39 And those going in front rebuked him that he should keep quiet;	48 And many rebuked him that he should be silent;	
	but they cried out the more saying: Lord, have mercy on us, Son of David.	but he all the more cried out: Son of David, have mercy on me.	but he all the more cried out: Son of David, have mercy on me.	
28 And as he was going into the house, the blind men came up to him,	32 And Jesus stopping called them	40 And Jesus stopping ordered him to be led to him.	49 And Jesus stopping said: Call him. And they call the blind man, saying to him: Take heart, get up, he is calling you. 50 And he throwing off his cloak, jumping up came to Jesus.	
and Jesus says to them:	and said:	And when he came near he questioned him,	51 And Jesus answering said to him:	
Do you believe that I can do this thing? They say to him: Yes, Lord.	What do you want me to do for you? 33 They say to him: Lord, that our eyes may be opened.	41 What do you want me to do for you? And he said: Lord, that I may see.	What do you want me to do for you? And the blind man said to him: Rabbouni, that I may see.	
29 Then he touched their eyes, saying: Be it done to your according to your faith. 30 And their eyes were opened. And Jesus charged them saying: Look, let nobody know. 31 But they going out made him known in all that land.	34 And Jesus moved with compassion, touched their eyes, and at once they saw and followed him. (↓ §288)	42 And Jesus said to him: Have sight. Your faith has saved you. 43 And immediately he saw, and followed him, glorifying God. And all the people seeing gave praise to God.	52 And Jesus said to him: Go off; your faith has saved you. And at once he saw and followed him on the road. (↓ §288)	

§283 Jesus and Zacchaeus (§§187, 251)

MT	LK 19:1-10	MK	JN
	1 And having entered, he passed through Jericho. 2 And behold a man by name called Zacchaeus, and he was chief tax-collector and he (was) rich. 3 And he tried to see who Jesus was, and he was unable to because of the crowd, for he was small in stature. 4 And running on ahead, he got up on a sycamore in order to see him, because he was going to pass that way. 5 And as he came upon the place, Jesus looking up said to him: Zacchaeus, get down quickly, for to-day it suits me to stay in your house. 6 And he got down quickly and received him with joy. 7 And all who saw began to murmur, saying: He has gone in to lodge with a man a sinner. 8 But Zacchaeus stood and said to the Lord: Lo, the half of my possessions, Lord, I give to the poor; and if I have defrauded		

MT	LK 19:1-10		MK	JN
	anyone of anything I repay fourfold.			
	9 And Jesus said to him: Today, salvation has come to this house,			
	because he too is a son of Abraham.			
	10 For the Son of Man has come to seek and to save what has			
(cf. 18:11)	been lost **(cf. 15:6)**.			

§284 Parable of the Ten Mnas (§318)

MT 25:14-30	LK 19:11-28	MK	JN
	11 And as they heard these things, he added another parable, because of his being near Jerusalem, and their imagining that the Kingdom of God was about to appear immediately,		
	12 He therefore said:		
14 As for instance, a man going abroad	A certain nobleman went to a distant region to receive for himself a kingdom and to return.		
called his own slaves and handed his property over to them.	13 And calling his ten slaves he gave them ten mnas, and he said to them: Trade until I come.		
15 And to one he gave five talents and to another two and to another one, to each according to his ability, and he went abroad.			
Immediately 16 he who had received five talents invested them and earned another five. 17 In the same way, he who had the two earned another two. 18 But he who had received the one, went off and dug the earth and hid his lord's money.			
	14 But his citizens hated him, and sent an embassy after him saying: We do not want this man to rule over us.		
19 And after a long time the lord of those slaves comes and settles account with them.	15 And it happened on his return after receiving the kingdom, and he said that these slaves should be called to whom he had given the money so that everyone should know the result of the trading.		
20 And the one who had received five talents came up and brought another five talents saying:	16 And the first arrived saying:		
Lord, you handed over to me five talents, behold I have gained another five talents.	Lord, your mna has gained ten mnas.		
21 The lord said to him:	17 And he said to him:		
Well done, good and faithful slave: you were faithful over few, I will put you over many; enter into the joy of your lord.	Well done, good slave, because you were faithful in the least, have authority over ten cities.		
22 And the one with two talents came up and said:	18 And the second came, saying:		
Lord, you handed two talents over to me, see, I have gained two more talents.	Your mna, Lord, has made five mnas.		
23 The lord said to him: Well done, good and faithful slave, you were faithful over few, I will set you over many. Enter into the joy of your lord.	19 And he said to this one too: And do you be over five cities.		
24 And now the one who had the one talent coming up, said:	20 And the other came, saying:		
Lord, I know that you are a hard man, reaping where you did not sow, and gathering together where you did not winnow.	Lord, behold your mna, which I have had hidden in a cloth. 21 For I was afraid of you, because you are a hard man, taking up what you did not put down, and reaping what you did not sow.		
25 And being afraid I went and hid your talent in the ground;			

199

MT 25:14-30	*LK 19:11-28*	**MK**	**JN**
see, you have what is yours.	22 He says to him:		
26 And his lord answering said to him:	Out of your mouth I will condemn you, evil slave;		
Evil and lazy slave,	You knew that I was a hard man, taking up what I did not put		
You knew that I reap, where I did not sow and gather up where	down and reaping what I did not sow?		
I did not winnow?			
27 It was your duty then to deposit my money with the bankers;	23 Why then did you not give my money to a bank, and then		
then when I came I would receive back what is mine with	when I came I would have claimed it with interest?		
interest.			
	24 And to the attendants he said:		
28 Take therefore the talent from him and give to him who has	Take the mna from him and give to him who has the ten mnas.		
the ten talents.			
	25* And they said to him: Lord, he has ten mnas.		
29 For to everyone that has shall be given and he will have	26 I say to you that to everyone who has shall be given;		
more:			
but from him who has not, even what he has shall be taken away	but from him who has not, even what he has shall be taken away	(cf. 4:25)	
from him (cf. 13:12).	(cf. 8:18).		
30 And throw the unprofitable slave into the exterior darkness;	27 As for these enemies of mine who refuse to let me rule over		
for weeping and gnashing of teeth shall be there (22:13).	them, bring them here and slay them before me.		
	28 And having said these things he went before going up to		
	Jerusalem.		
	(↓ §288)		

§285 The Expectancy of the Jews

MT	LK	MK	JN 11:55-57
			(↑ §273)
			55 Now it was near the Passover of the Jews; and many went up to Jerusalem from the country before the Passover in order to purify themselves.
			56 They were therefore seeking Jesus and said to one another as they stood in the Temple: What do you think? That he will not come to the Festival?
			57 For the high-priests and the Pharisees had given orders that if anyone knew where he was, he should inform so that they might arrest him.

§286 Jesus Anointed in Bethany (§§95, 326)

MT	LK	MK	JN 12:1-8
(cf. 26:10-13)	(cf. 7:36f)	(cf. 14:3-9)	1 Jesus therefore six days before the Passover came to Bethany, where was Lazarus, the one who had died,* whom Jesus had raised

MT	LK	MK	JN 12:1-8

from the dead.

2 So they made a banquet for him there, and Martha was serving, and Lazarus was one of the ones reclining with him;

3 Mary therefore, taking a pound of perfume, expensive pure nard, anointed the feet of Jesus and wiped his feet with her hair; and the house was filled with the odour of the perfume.

4 And Judas the Iscariot, one of his disciples, the one about to betray him, says:

5 Why was this perfume not sold for three hundred denarii and given to the poor?

6 But he said this not because he cared about the poor, but because he was a thief and having the begging-bag took what was dropped into it.

7 Jesus therefore said:

Leave her, so that she may perform this (deed) for the day of my interment; 8 for the poor you have with you always, but me you do not have always.

§287 A Plot against Lazarus

MT	LK	MK	JN 12:9-11

9 Now a great crowd of the Jews knew that he was there, and they came not for Jesus only but also in order to see Lazarus whom he had raised from the dead.

10 And the high-priests planned to kill Lazarus as well, 11 for many of the Jews, because of him, began to withdraw and to believe in Jesus.

VII. Jesus Teaches in Jerusalem
§§ 288-324

MT 21:1-9	LK 19:29-40	MK 11:1-10	JN 12:12-19
(↑ §282)	(↑ §284)	(↑ §282)	
1 And when they drew near to Jerusalem and came to Bethphage, towards the Mount of Olives, then Jesus sent two disciples 2 saying to them: Go into the village that is opposite you, and immediately you will find an ass tied up and a colt with it; untying, lead (it) to me. 3 And if anyone should say anything to you, you shall say that the Lord has need of them; and at once he will send them. 4 Now this happened that the saying spoken by the prophet would be fulfilled that says: 5 Say to the daughter of Sion: Behold, thy king cometh to thee meek and riding on an ass, and upon a colt, foal of an ass (Zech. 9:9). 6 And the disciples went and did just as Jesus had instructed them.	29 And it happened as he drew near to Bethphage and Bethany, towards the Mount that is called of Olives, he sent two of the disciples, 30 saying: Go off into the village opposite, going into which you will find a colt tied up, upon which no man has ever yet sat, and untying lead it. 31 And if anyone asks you: Why are you untying it?, thus you shall say: The Lord has need of it.	1 And when they draw near to Jerusalem to Bethphage and Bethany, towards the Mount of Olives, he sends two of his disciples 2 and says to them: Go off into the village that is opposite you. and immediately going into it you will find a colt tied up upon which no man has yet sat; untie and bring it. 3 And if anyone should say to you: Why are you doing this? say: The Lord has need of it, and is sending it back again here at once.	
	32 And those sent went away and found just as he had told them. 33 And while they were untying the colt, its owners said to them: Why are you untying the colt? 34 And they said: The Lord has need of it. 35 And they led it to Jesus, and laying their garments upon the colt they put Jesus upon (it).	4 And they went away and found a colt tied up at the door, outside on the street and they untie it. 5 And some of those who stood there said to them: What are you doing untying the colt? 6 And they said to them just as Jesus told them; and they permitted them. 7 And they bring the colt to Jesus, and they throw on it their garments	
7 They led the ass and the colt, and they put their garments on them, and he sat upon them. 8 And the enormous crowd strewed their garments on the road, and some cut branches from the trees and strewed them on the road.	36 And as he went they were strewing their garments on the road. 37 And when he drew near now to the descent of the Mount of Olives, the entire multitude of the disciples rejoicing began to praise God with loud voice for all the mighty deeds which they had seen 38 saying:	and he sat upon it. 8 And many strewed their garments onto the road, and others bunches, cutting (them) from the fields,	12 On the morrow the great crowd that came to the feast, hearing that Jesus was coming to Jerusalem, 13 took the branches of the palm-trees and went out to meet him.
9 And the crowds who went in front of him and those who followed cried saying:		9 And those who went in front and those who followed cried:	and they cried out:

MT 21:1-9	LK 19:29-40	MK 11:1-10	JN 12:12-19
Hosanna to the Son of David! Blessed is he who comes in the name of the Lord. Hosanna in the highest! **(cf. 21:7)** (↓ §290)	Blessed is he who comes, the king, in the name of the Lord; in heaven peace, and glory in the highest! **(cf. 11:7)**	Hosanna! Blessed is he who comes in the name of the Lord; blessed the coming kingdom of our father David; Hosanna in the highest! **(cf. 19:35)** (↓ §290)	Hosanna! Blessed is he who comes in the name of the Lord, even the king of Israel. 14 And Jesus having found a young ass, sat upon it, according as it is written: 15 Fear not, daughter of Sion; behold your king comes, seated on the foal of an ass **(Zech. 9:9)**. 16 These things his disciples did not know at first, but when Jesus was glorified, then they remembered that these things had been written about him, and these things they did to him. 17 The crowd therefore bore witness— the one that was with him when he summoned Lazarus from the tomb and raised him from the dead. 18 On account of this too, the crowd met him, because they had heard he had done this sign.
	39 And some of the Pharisees from the crowd said to him: Teacher, rebuke your disciples.		19 The Pharisees therefore said to one another: You perceive that you profit nothing. See, the world has gone after him. (↓ §322)
(cf. 21:15-16)	40 And he answering said: I say to you, if these shall keep silent, the stones will cry out.		

§289 Jesus Weeps over the City (cf. §243)

MT	LK 19:41-44	MK	JN
	41 And as he drew near, seeing the city he wept over it, 42 saying: If you had known, in this your day - even you - the things for your peace! But now they are hidden from your eyes. 43 For days will come upon you and your enemies will invest you with a rampart and will encircle you and compress you on all sides **(cf. 21:20)**. 44 And they will level you and your children in you and they will not leave a stone upon a stone in you, because you did not know the time of your visitation.		

§290 Jesus in Jerusalem (Mt, Mk) (§30)

MT 21:10-11

(↑ §288)

10 And when he entered into Jerusalem the whole city was shaken, saying: Who is this one?

11 And the crowds said: This one is the prophet Jesus who is from Nazareth of Galilee.

LK

MK 11:11

(↑ §288)

11 And he entered into Jerusalem into the Temple, and looking over everything, as it was already the evening hour, he went out to Bethany with his disciples.

(↓ §292)

JN 2:13

13 And the Passover of the Jews was near and Jesus went up to Jerusalem.

§291 Jesus Cleanses the Temple (Mt, Lk) (§§30, 293)

MT 21:12-17

12 And Jesus entered into the Temple of God,

and he cast out all the sellers and buyers in the Temple,

and the tables of the money-changers he overturned and the chairs of the sellers of the doves,

13 And he says to them:

It it written: My House shall be called a House of Prayer,

but you make it a den of thieves! **(Is. 56:7; 60:7; Jer. 7:11)**.

14 And the blind and the lame came up to him in the Temple, and he healed them.

15 And the high-priests and the Scribes seeing the wonders he did and the children crying out in the Temple and saying: Hosanna to the Son of David, were indignant;

16 and they said to him: Do you hear what these are saying?

LK 19:45-46

(↑ §289)

45 And entering into the Temple,

he began to cast out the sellers and buyers in it,

46 saying to them:

It is written: Indeed my House shall be a House of Prayer,

but you made it a den of thieves! **(Is. 56:7; Jer. 7:11)**.

(↓ §294)

(cf. 19:40)

MK 11:15b-17

15b And entering into the Temple

he began to cast out the sellers and the buyers in the Temple,

and the tables of the money-changers and the chairs of the sellers of the doves he overturned; 16 and he did not permit anyone to carry a burden through the Temple.

17 And he was teaching and saying to them:

Is it not written: My House shall be called a House of Prayer for all the nations?

But you have made it a den of thieves!

JN 2:14-16, 23-25

14 And in the Temple he found the sellers of cattle and sheep and doves and the money-changers sitting,

15 and making a sort of whip of little cords he cast them all out of the Temple, both the sheep and the cattle;

and he poured out the coins of the money-changers and overturned the tables;

16 and to the sellers of doves he said: Take these things away;

do not make my Father's House a house of trade.

23 Now when he was in Jerusalem at the Passover at the Feast, many believed in his name, beholding his signs which he did;

24 but Jesus himself did not trust himself to them, because he knew all men,

25 and because he had no need that anyone should witness about man, for he knew what was in man.

MT 21:12-17
And Jesus says to them:
Yes; did you never read:
Out of the mouths of babes and
sucklings I will establish praise?
(Ps. 8:3, [LXX]).
17 And leaving them, he went forth
out of the city to Bethany, and
lodged there.

LK 19:45-46

MK 11:15b-17

JN 2:14-16, 23-25

§292 The Cursing of the Figtree (§237)

MT 21:18-19ab
18 But going up early into the city he was
hungry.
19 And seeing a single figtree by the road,

he came up to it and found nothing on it but
only leaves,
and he says to it:
May no fruit ever come from you again.

(↓ §295)

LK 13:6
6 And he used to tell this parable.

*A certain person had a figtree planted in his
vineyard, and he came seeking fruit on it*

and did not find it.

MK 11:12-14
12 And on the morrow when they went from
Bethany he was hungry.
13 And seeing a figtree from a distance having
leaves, he came if perhaps he might find
something on it;
and coming up to it, he found nothing but
leaves; for it was not the season for figs.
14 And answering he said to it:
May no one eat fruit from you ever again.
And his disciples heard.

JN

§293 The Cleansing of the Temple (Mk) (§§30, 291)

MT 21:12-13

*And Jesus entered into the Temple of
God and he cast out all the sellers
and buyers in the Temple.*

*and the tables of the money-changers
he overturned and the chairs of the
sellers of the doves,*

and he says to them:

It is written: My House shall be

LK 19:45-46

*45 And entering into the Temple he
began to cast out those who sold and
bought in it,*

46 saying to them:

It is written: And my House shall be

MK 11:15-17
15 And they come into Jerusalem.

And entering into the Temple he
began to cast out the sellers and the
buyers in the Temple,

and the tables of the money-changers
and the chairs of the sellers of the
doves he overturned.
16 And he did not permit anyone to
carry a burden through the Temple.
17 And he was teaching and saying to
them:
Is it not written that my House shall

JN 2:13-16
*13 And the Passover of the Jews was
near and Jesus went up to Jerusalem.
14 And he found in the Temple those
selling cattle and sheep and doves, 15
and making a sort of scourge of little
cords he cast them all out of the
Temple, both the sheep and the
cattle.
and he poured the coins of the
money-changers and overturned the
tables,*

*16 and to the sellers of the doves he
said:*

MT 21:12-13	LK 19:45-46	MK 11:15-17	JN 2:13-16
called a House of Prayer,	*a House of Prayer,*	be called a House of Prayer for all the nations **(Is. 56:7; Jer. 7:11)**,	
but you make it a den of thieves.	*but you made it a den of thieves.*	but you have made it a den of thieves?	*Take these things away; do not make my Father's House a house of trade.*

§294 The Plot of the Priests (§§273, 325)

MT	LK 19:47-48	MK 11:18-19	JN
	(↑ §291)		
(cf. 26:3-5)	47 And he was teaching day by day in the Temple; and the high priests and the Scribes sought to destroy him, and the chief men of the people, 48 and they did not find how to do it, for the whole people heard and hung upon him.	18 And the high priests and the Scribes heard, and they sought how they might destroy him; for they feared him. For the whole crowd was amazed at his teaching. 19 And when evening came, he went forth out of the city.	**(cf. 11:47-48)**
	(↓ §296)		

§295 The Withered Figtree (§§74, 75, 212, 292)

MT 21:19c-22; *6:15*	LK	MK 11:20-27a	JN
(↑ §292)			
19c And the tree immediately withered away.		20 And passing by early they saw the figtree withered **away** from the roots.	
20 And when the disciples saw it they wondered saying: How did the figtree wither away immediately? 21 And Jesus answering said to them: Amen I say to you, if you have faith and do not waver, not only will you do it to the figtree, but if you were to say to this mountain: Be lifted up and cast into the sea, it will be done.		21 And Peter remembered and says to him: Rabbi, see, the tree you cursed has withered away. 22 And Jesus answering says to them: Have faith in God. 23 But I say to you that whoever would say to this mountain: Be lifted up and cast into the sea—and does not waver in his heart but believes that what he says is done—it will be (done) for him.	
22 And all things whatsoever you ask in prayer, when you believe, you will receive. **(cf. 5:23-24; 6:9a-14)**		24 Wherefore I say to you, all things whatever you pray and ask for, believe that you have received, and it will be (done) for you. 25 And when you stand praying, forgive if you have anything against anyone, so that your Father who is in the heavens may forgive you your trespasses. 26* But if you do not forgive, neither will your Father who is in the heavens forgive your trespasses. 27 And they come again into Jerusalem **(cf. 11:15)**.	
6:15 But if you do not forgive men their trespasses; neither will your Father forgive you your trespasses.			

MT 21:23-27	LK 20:1-8	MK 11:27b-33	JN
	(↑ §294)		

MT 21:23-27

23 And as he came into the Temple,

there came up to him as he was teaching the high priests and the elders of the people saying:
By what authority are you doing these things?

And who has given you this authority?

24 And Jesus answering said to them:
I too will ask you one question,
which if you tell me, I too will tell you by what authority I do these things.
25 The baptism that was John's, whence was it? From heaven or from men?
But they argued among themselves, saying:

If we were to say 'From heaven', he will say to us: Why then did you not believe him?
26 And if we were to say 'From men', we fear the crowd;
for all hold John as a prophet.

27 And answering they said to Jesus: We do not know.
He then said to them:
Neither do I tell you by what authority I do these things.

LK 20:1-8

1 And it happened on one of the days, while he was teaching the people in the Temple and evangelizing,
the high priests and the Scribes, with the elders stood by, 2 and they spoke saying to him:
Tell us by what authority are you doing these things?
Or who is it who gave you this authority?

3 And answering he said to them:
I too will ask you a question;
now tell me,

4 The baptism of John—was it from heaven or from men?
5 But they argued together among themselves, saying:
If we were to say 'From heaven', he will say: Why did you not believe him?
6 And if we were to say 'From men', the whole people will stone us;
for it has been persuaded that John is a prophet.
7 And they answered that they did not know whence (it was).
8 And Jesus said to them:
Neither do I tell you by what authority I do these things.

(↓ §298)

MK 11:27b-33

27b And while he was walking in the Temple,

there come to him the high priests and the Scribes and the elders 28 and they said to him:

By what authority are you doing these things?

Or who has given you this authority to do these things?
29 And Jesus said to them:
I too will further ask you one question,
now answer me - and I will tell you by what authority I do these things.
30 The baptism that was John's - was it from heaven or from men? Answer me.
31 And they argued among themselves saying: What do we say?
If we were to say 'From heaven', he will say: Why then did you not believe him?
32 But were we to say 'From men', - they feared the crowd,
for all held that John was really a prophet.

33 And answering they say to Jesus: We do not know.
And Jesus says to them:
Neither do I tell you by what authority I do these things.

(↓ §298)

§297 The Parable of the Two Sons

MT 21:28-32	LK	MK	JN

MT 21:28-32
28 Now what do you think?
A certain man had two sons.
Coming to the first he said:
Son, go off to-day and work in my vineyard.
29* And he answered and said:
I (go) Lord; and he did not go.
30* And coming to the second, he said the same.
And he answered and said:
I am not willing. Later he changed his mind and went.
31 Which of the two did his father's will?

MT 21:28-32   LK   MK   JN
They say: The latter.
Jesus says to them:
Amen I say to you, that the taxcollectors and the harlots are
preceding you into the Kingdom of God,
32 For John came to you in the way of righteousness, and you did
not believe him; but the tax-collectors and the harlots believed
him. But you having seen would not later change your mind and
believe him.

§298 The Wicked Tenants

MT 21:33-46	LK 20:9-19	MK 12:1-12	JN
	(↑ §296)	(↑ §296)	
33 Hear another parable. There was a man, owner of an estate, who planted a vineyard and put round it a hedge, and dug in it a pit and built a tower. and let it to tenants and went abroad.	9 And he began to tell the people this parable. A certain man planted a vineyard and let it to tenants and went abroad for a long time.	1 And he began to speak to them in parables. A man planted a vineyard, and put round a hedge and dug a trough and built a tower and let it to tenants, and went abroad.	
34 And when the season of the fruits drew near he sent his slaves to the tenants to receive his fruits.	10 And at the season he sent a slave to the tenants that they should give him of the fruit of the vineyard.	2 And he sent a slave to the tenants at the season that he might receive of the fruits of the vineyard from the tenants.	
35 And the tenants taking his slaves, flogged one, and killed another, and stoned another. 36 Again he sent other slaves more than the first, and they treated them the same way.	But the tenants flogged him and sent him away empty-handed. 11 And he proceeded to send another slave; but they flogged and insulted that one and sent him away empty-handed. 12 And he proceeded to send a third; and this one too they wounded and threw out.	3 And they took and flogged him and sent him empty-handed. 4 And again he sent them another slave; and they stoned and hit that one on the head and insulted (him). 5 And he sent another, and that one they killed. and many others, flogging some and killing others.	
(cf. 21:35)			
37 And finally he sent them his son, saying: They will respect my son. 38 But the tenants seeing the son, said in themselves: This one is the heir; come, let us kill him, and let us possess his inheritance. 39 And taking him they threw him out without the vineyard and killed (him). 40 When therefore the owner of the vineyard comes, what will he do to those tenants?	13 And the owner of the vineyard said: What shall I do? I will send my son the beloved one. Surely they will respect him. 14 But the tenants seeing him, argued with one another saying: This one is the heir; let us kill him, that the inheritance may become ours. 15 And throwing him out without the vineyard they killed (him). What therefore will the owner of the vineyard do to them?	6 He still had one, the beloved son; he sent him to them last, saying: They will respect my son. 7 But those tenants said to themselves: This one is the heir; come, let us kill him; and we shall have the inheritance. 8 And they took and killed him, and threw him out without the vineyard. 9 What therefore will the owner of the vineyard do?	

MT 21:33-46	LK 20:9-19	MK 12:1-12	JN
41 They say to him: He will put those bad men to a bad end, and will let out the vineyard to other tenants,who will render to him the fruits in their seasons.	16 He will come and destroy these tenants, and will give the vineyard to others.	He will come and destroy the tenants, and will give the vineyard to others.	
42 Jesus says to them: Did you never read in the Scriptures: The stone which the builders rejected, has become the head of the corner; This was the Lord's doing and it is wonderful in our eyes? **(Ps. 117[118]: 22-23).** 43 Wherefore I say to you, that the Kingdom of God shall be taken away from you, and shall be given to a nation producing its fruits.	And when they had heard they said: Heaven forbid. 17 And he looking on them said: What then is this that is written: The stone which the builders rejected has become the head of the corner? **(Ps. 117 [118]:22).**	10 Did you not read this writing: The stone which the builders rejected, has become the head of the corner; 11 This was the Lord's doing and it is marvellous in our eyes? **(Ps. 117 [118]:22-23).**	
44* And he who falls upon this stone shall be crushed; but upon whomsoever it falls it will grind him to powder.	18 Everyone who falls upon that stone shall be crushed; but upon whomsoever it falls, it will grind him to powder.		
45 And when the high priests and Pharisees had heard his parables, they knew that he was speaking about them;	**(cf. v. 19b)**	**(cf. v. 12b)**	
46 and seeking to seize him,	19 And the Scribes and the high priests sought to lay hands upon him in that very hour, and they feared the people;	12 And they sought to seize him, and they feared the crowd;	
they feared the crowds, since they held him as a prophet.	for they knew that he spoke this parable against them.	for they knew that he spoke the parable against them. And leaving him they went away.	
	(↓ §300)	(↓ §300)	

§299 The Marriage Feast (§247)

MT 22:1-14	LK 14:15-24	MK	JN
1 And Jesus answering again spoke to them in parables, saying:	*15 And when one of those at table had heard these things, he said to him: Blessed is he who eats bread in the Kingdom of God. 16 But he said to him:*		
2 The Kingdom of the Heavens has been likened to a man, a king, who made a marriage for his son.	*A certain man made a great supper and invited many.*		
3 And he sent his slaves to invite the guests to the supper, and they would not come.	*17 And he sent his slave at the hour of the supper*		
4 Again he sent other slaves saying: Tell the guests: Lo, I have prepared my dinner, my oxen and fat cattle have been killed	*to tell the guests:*		
and all is ready. Come to the marriage.	*Come, because it is now ready.*		

212

MT 22:1-14

5 But they not caring went off,
one to his own estate,

and another to his business.

6 And the rest seizing his slaves insulted and killed (them).
7 Then the king became angry, and sending his troops he destroyed those murderers and burned their city.
8 Then he says to his slaves: The marriage indeed is ready, but the guests were not worthy.
9 Go therefore to the junctions of the roads, and call to the marriage whoever you find.

10 And those servants went out onto the roads and gathered together all they found, evil and good,

and the wedding-hall was filled with those at table.

11 And the king entering in to look at those at table saw a man there not wearing a wedding garment.
12 And he says to him: Comrade, how did you come in here not having a wedding garment? And he was silent.
13 Then the king said to the attendants: Bind his hands and feet and throw him out into the exterior darkness.
Weeping and gnashing of teeth shall be there (cf. 8:11-12).
14 For many are called, but few (are) chosen (cf. 20:16).

LK 14:15-24

18 And with one accord they began to make excuses.
The first said to him: I have bought an estate and I have an obligation to go out and see it; I beg you hold me excused.
19 And another said: I have bought five yoke of oxen and I go to test them; I beg you, hold me excused.
20 And another said: I have married a wife, and therefore I cannot come.
21 And the slave came and reported these things to his lord.

Then the master of the house got angry and

said to his slave:

Go out quickly into the thorough-fares and streets of the city, and bring in here the poor and the maimed and the blind and the lame.
22 And the slave said: Lord, what you have ordered has been done and there is still room.
23 And the lord said to the slave: Go out into the roads and hedges and oblige them to come in,
that my house may be filled.
24 For I say to you that none of those men that were invited shall taste my supper.

(cf. 13:28-30)

MK

JN

§300 Tribute To Caesar

MT 22:15-22

15 Then the Pharisees went and held a council how they might snare him in speech.
16 And they send him their disciples, with the Herodians,

saying:
Teacher, we know that you are truthful and teach the way of God in truth, and are not swayed by anyone,

LK 20:20-26

(↑ §298)

20 And having carefully watched they sent spies pretending they were just, so that they might entrap him in speech, so as to betray him to the government and to the authority of the governor.
21 And they questioned him, saying:
Teacher, we know that you speak and teach with honesty,

MK 12:13-17

(↑ §298)

13 And they send to him some of the Pharisees and the Herodians in order to catch him by speech.

14 And coming, they say:
Teacher, we know that you are truthful

and are not swayed by anyone,

JN

MT 22:15-22	LK 20:20-26	MK 12:13-17	JN
for you do not have regard to the person of men. 17 Tell us therefore, what your opinion is; Is it lawful to pay tax to Caesar, or not? 18 And Jesus knowing their wickedness said: Why do you tempt me, hypocrites? 19 Show me the coin of the tax. And they brought up to him a denarius. 20 And he says to them: Whose image and superscription is this? 21 They say to him: Caesar's. Then he says to them: Render therefore the things that are Caesar's to Caesar and the things that are God's to God. 22 And having heard they were amazed, and leaving him they went away.	and that you do not consider a person, but according to truth teach the way of God. 22 Is it lawful for us to pay tribute to Caesar, or not? 23 And divining their stratagem he said to them: 24 Hand me a denarius. Whose image and superscription has it? And they said: Caesar's 25 And he said to them: Render then the things that are Caesar's to Caesar and the things that are God's to God. 26 And they were unable to entrap his speech before the people, and being amazed at his reply they were silent.	for you do not have regard to the person of men, but according to truth teach the way of God. Is it lawful to pay tax to Caesar, or not? do we give or do we not give? 15 And he perceiving their hypocrisy, said to them: Why do you tempt me? Bring me a denarius for me to see. 16 And they brought (one). And he says to them: Whose image and superscription is this? And they said to him: Caesar's. 17 And Jesus said to them: Render the things that are Caesar's to Caesar and the things that are God's to God. and they were amazed at him.	

§301 How Do the Dead Rise?

MT 22:23-33	LK 20:27-39	MK 12:18-27	JN
23 On that day Sadducees came up to him who say there is no Resurrection. And they questioned him, 24 saying: Teacher, Moses said: If a man should die not having children, his brother shall marry his wife, and shall raise offspring for his brother **(Gen. 38:8; Dt. 25:5)**. 25 Now there were with us seven brothers: and the first, having married expired, and not having offspring left his wife to his brother. 26 In the same way the second also, and the third, until the seven. 27 And last of all the wife died too. 28 In the resurrection then, of which of the seven will she be wife? For they all had her. 29 And Jesus answering said to them:	27 And some of the Sadducees coming up, who deny there is a Resurrection, questioned him, 28 saying: Teacher, Moses wrote for us: If a man's brother, having a wife, should die, and he himself were childless, that his brother should take his wife and raise up offspring for his brother. 29 So there were seven brothers; and the first, having taken a wife, died childless. 30 The second also 31 and the third took her, and similarly too the seven did not leave behind children, and they died. 32 And the wife died last. 33 The wife then, in the resurrection, of which of them does she become wife? For the seven had her as wife. 34 And Jesus answering said to them:	18 And the Sadducees come to him, those who say there is no Resurrection. And they started to question him, saying: 19 Teacher, Moses wrote for us: If a man's brother should die, and leave a wife, and not leave a son, that his brother should take his wife and raise up offspring for his brother. 20 There were seven brothers: and the first took a wife, and dying did not leave offspring. 21 The second also took her and died, not leaving behind offspring, and the third similarly; 22 and the seven did not leave offspring. At the end of all the wife died. 23 In the resurrection, when they rise, of which of them will she be wife? For the seven had her as wife. 24 And Jesus said to them:	

MT 22:23-33	LK 20:27-39	MK 12:18-27	JN
You are wrong, neither knowing the Scriptures nor the power of God.		Are you not wrong for this reason, neither knowing the Scriptures nor the power of God?	
30 For in the resurrection	The sons of this world marry and are given in marriage,		
	35 but the ones counted worthy to obtain that world and the resurrection from the dead	25 When therefore they rise from the dead	
they neither marry nor are given in marriage,	neither marry nor are given in marriage,	they neither marry nor are given in marriage,	
	36 neither indeed can they die any more,		
but are like angels in heaven.	for they are equal to the angels, and are sons of God, being sons of the resurrection.	but are like angels in the heavens.	
31 But about the resurrection of the dead, have you not read what was spoken to you by God, saying:	37 But that the dead are raised, Moses too indicated at the Bush when he says	26 But about the dead, that they are raised, have you not read in the book of Moses at the Bush how God said to him, saying:	
32 I am the God of Abraham and the God of Isaac and the God of Jacob **(Ex. 3:6)**.	that he is the Lord God of Abraham and God of Isaac and God of Jacob.	I (am) the God of Abraham and the God of Isaac and the God of Jacob.	
He is not the God of the dead but of the living.	38 And he is not God of the dead but of the living. For all live to him.	27 He is not the God of the dead but of the living. You are very wrong.	
33 And when the crowds heard, they were astonished at his teaching.	39 And some of the Scribes answering said: Teacher, you have spoken well.	**(cf. 12:28)**	

§302 The Lawyer's Question (Mt, Mk) (§§209, 303)

MT 22:34-40	LK 10:25-28; 20:40	MK 12:28-34	JN
34 And when the Pharisees heard that he had silenced the Sadducees, they assembled in one place,		28 And one of the Scribes coming up, having heard them debating, knowing that he had answered them well, asked him a question:	
35 and one of them, a lawyer, asked a question tempting him: and saying:	*25 And behold a certain lawyer arose tempting him, saying:*	Which is the first commandment of all?	
36 Teacher, which is the great commandment in the Law?	*Teacher, What shall I do to inherit eternal life?*	29 Jesus answered: The first is: Hear O Israel, the Lord our God is one Lord,	
37 And he said to him:	*26 And he said to him:*	30 and thou shalt love the Lord thy God from thy whole heart	
Thou shalt love the Lord thy God with thy whole heart and with thy whole soul and with thy whole mind **(Dt. 6:5)**.		and from thy whole soul and from thy whole mind and from thy whole strength **(Dt. 6:4-5)**.	
38 This is the great and first commandment. 39 The second is like to it: Thou shalt love thy neighbor as thyself **(Lev. 19:18)**.		31 This the second: Thou shalt love thy neighbor as thyself **(Lv. 19:18)**. There is no other commandment greater than these.	
40 On these two commandments the whole Law depends, and the Prophets.	*How do you understand what has been written in the Law?*		

MT 22:34-40	LK 10:25-28; 20:40	MK 12:28-34	JN
	27 And he answering said:	32 And the Scribe said to him: Teacher, in truth you have said well, that God is one and there is none other but him:	
(22:37)	*Thou shalt love the Lord thy God* *from thy whole heart* *and with thy whole soul* *and with thy whole strength* *and with thy whole mind* *and thy neighbour and thyself.*	33 and to love him, from the whole heart and from the whole understanding and from the whole strength and to love the neighbour as oneself, is more than all the holocausts and sacrifices (**1 Sam. 15:22**).	
	28 And he said to him: You have answered correctly; *Do this and you shall live.*	34 And Jesus seeing that he had answered wisely, said to him: You are not far from the Kingdom of God.	
(22:46)	20:40 No longer therefore did anyone dare to question him at all.	And nobody any longer dared to question him.	

§303 How Is Jesus David's Son?

MT 22:41-46	LK 20:41-44, *40*	MK 12:35-37a; *12:34c*	JN
41 And when the Pharisees were assembled Jesus questioned them, 42 saying: What is your opinion about the Christ? Whose son is he? They say to him: David's. 43 He says to them: How then does David in the Spirit call him Lord, saying: 44 The Lord said to my Lord, Sit thou at my right hand, until I put thy enemies under thy feet? (**Ps. 109[110]:1**). 45 If David therefore calls him Lord, how is he his Son?	41 And he said to them: How say they that the Christ is the Son of David? 42 For David himself says in the Book of the Psalms: The Lord said to my Lord, Sit thou at my right hand, 43 until I put thy enemies a footstool for thy feet (**Ps. 109[110]:1**). 44 David therefore calls him Lord; how then is he his Son?	35 And Jesus answering said, while teaching in the Temple: How say the Scribes that the Christ is the Son of David? 36 David himself said in the Holy Spirit: The Lord said to my Lord, Sit thou at my right hand, until I put thy enemies under thy feet (**Ps. 109[110]:1**). 37a David himself says he is Lord; whence then is he his Son?	
46 And no one was able to answer him a word, nor did anyone dare from that day to question him any more.	*40 No longer therefore did anyone dare to question him at all.*	*34c And nobody any longer dared to question him.*	

MT 23:1-36	LK 20:45-47	LK 11:46, 43, 52, 42, 39-40, 44, 47-51	MK 12:37b-40	JN
1 Then Jesus spoke to the crowds and his disciples, 2 saying:	45 And in the hearing of all the people, he said to his disciples:		37b And the large crowd heard him gladly, 38 and in his teaching he was saying to them:	
Upon the chair of Moses the Scribes and Pharisees continue to sit. 3 Hence do whatever they tell you, and keep it, but according to their deeds do not do. For they talk but do not do.	46 Be wary of the Scribes,		Beware of the Scribes,	
4 For they bind burdens heavy and hard to carry* and lay them on men's shoulders but they themselves are unwilling to move them with their finger.		*46 And he said: Woe also to you lawyers, because you burden men with burdens hard to carry, but you yourselves do not touch the burdens with one of your fingers.*		
5 For they do all their deeds to be seen by men; for they broaden their phylacteries and enlarge their fringes.	who like to walk in long robes.		who like walking in long robes,	
6 And they love the first place at the banquets and the first chairs in the synagogues, 7 and the salutations in the market-places, and to be called by men, Rabbi.	and love salutations in the market-places and first seats in the synagogues and first places at the banquets;	*43 Woe to you Pharisees because you love the first place in the synagogues and the salutations in the market-places.*	and salutations in the market-places, 39 and first seats in the synagogues and first places at the banquets,	
8 But do not yourselves be called Rabbi; for One is your teacher, and you are all brothers. 9 And do not call any one your Father upon earth, for you have one Father, the heavenly one. 10 Neither be called instructors, for one is your instructor, the Christ.				
11 He who is the greatest among you shall be your servant **(Mt 20:26-27)**.	**(cf. 22:26)**		**(cf. 10:43, 44)**	
12 For whoever shall exalt himself shall be humbled, and whoever shall humble himself shall be exalted.	**(cf. 14:11; 18:14)**			
13* But woe to you, Scribes and Pharisees, hypocrites, because you devour the houses of the widows, while praying with great pretence; for which reason you will receive a greater condemnation.	47 who devour the houses of the widows and pray with great pretence; these will receive a greater condemnation.		40 the devourers of the houses of the widows and orphans, while praying with great pretence; these will receive a greater condemnation.	
14* But woe to you, Scribes and Pharisees, hypocrites.	(↓ §306)	*52 Woe to you lawyers,*	(↓ §306)	

217

MT 23:1-36	LK 20:45-47	LK 11:46, 43, 52, 42, 39-40, 44, 47-51	MK 12:37b-40	JN

MT 23:1-36

because you shut the Kingdom of
the Heavens in men's faces;
for you yourselves do not enter,
and you do not permit those
about to enter to enter in.
15 Woe to you Scribes and
Pharisees, hypocrites, for you go
about the sea and the land to
make one proselyte, and when he
is made, you make him twice as
much a son of Gehenna as
yourselves.
16 Woe to you, blind guides who
say: Whoever swears by the
sanctuary it is nothing; but
whoever swears by the gold of the
sanctuary is in debt.
17 Blind fools, for which is
greater? The gold or the
sanctuary that sanctifies the gold?
18 And: Whoever swears by the
altar, it is nothing; but whoever
swears by the gift on the altar is
in debt.
19 Foolish and blind ones, which
therefore is greater? The gift, or
the altar that sanctifies the gift?
20 For he who swears by the
altar, swears by it and by
everything on it.
21 And he who swears by the
sanctuary, swears by it and by
him who dwells in it.
22 And he who swears by heaven,
swears by the throne of God and
by him who sits upon it.
23 Woe to you, Scribes and
Pharisees hypocrites,
because you pay the tithe on mint
and dill and cummin,
and have left out the weightier
things of the Law, judgement and
steadfast love and faith;
and you ought to have done the
latter without leaving out the
former.
24 Blind guides, who strain out
the gnat, but swallow the camel.

LK 11:46, 43, 52, 42, 39-40, 44, 47-51

*because you took away the key of
knowledge,
you yourselves did not enter, and
you stopped those about to enter.*

42 But woe to you, Pharisees,

*because you pay the tithe on mint
and rue and every herb,
and pass over judgement and the
love of God.*

*And you ought to have done the
latter without passing over the
former.*

MT 23:1-36	LK 20:45-47	LK 11:46, 43, 52, 42, 39-40, 44, 47-51	MK 12:37b-40	JN

MT 23:1-36

25 Woe to you Scribes and
Pharisees, hypocrites,
because you cleanse the outside of
the cup and the dish,
but inside they are full of greed
and intemperance.
26 Blind Pharisee, cleanse first
the inside of the cup and the dish,
that its outside also may be made
clean.
27 Woe to you, Scribes and
Pharisees, hypocrites,
because you are comparable to
white-washed tombs,
which outwardly indeed look fair,
but within are full of the bones
of the dead and every
uncleanness.
28 So also you outwardly appear
just to men, but inwardly you are
full of hypocrisy and wrong-
doing.
29 Woe to you, Scribes and
Pharisees, hypocrites,
because you build the tombs of
the prophets, and decorate the
tombs of the just.
30 And you say: If we had been
in the days of our fathers, we
would not have been their
accomplices in the blood of the
prophets.
31 Thus you are witnesses to
yourselves that you are the sons
of those who slew the prophets.

32 Fill up, then, yourselves, the
measure of your fathers.
33 Serpents, offspring of vipers,
how will you escape from the
condemnation of Gehenna?
34 Wherefore, behold I am
sending to your prophets and
wise men and scribes;
and some of them you will kill
and crucify
and some of them you will beat
in your synagogues,
and will pursue from city to city,

LK 11:46, 43, 52, 42, 39-40, 44, 47-51

39 And the Lord said to him:
Now you Pharisees
cleanse the outside of
the cup and the dish,
but your inside is full of greed
and wickedness.
40 Fools, did not he who made
the outside also make the inside?

44 Woe to you, Scribes and
Pharisees,
because you are like concealed
monuments,
and the men who walk over them
do not know.

47 Woe to you,

because you build the monuments
of the prophets,

but your fathers killed them.

48 So you are witnesses and you
approve the deeds of your fathers,
for they indeed killed them, but
you build their monuments.

(cf. 3:7)

49 Wherefore indeed the Wisdom
of God said: I will send to them
prophets and apostles;
and some of them they will kill

and will pursue,

219

MT 23:1-36	LK 20:45-47	LK 11:46, 43, 52, 42, 39-40, 44, 47-51	MK 12:37b-40	JN
35 in order that there should come upon you all the just blood that was shed upon the earth,—		*50 so that there will be required the blood of all the prophets, that has been shed from the foundation of the world, from this generation—*		
from the blood of Abel the just to the blood of Zechariah the son of Barachiah, whom you slew between the sanctuary and the altar.		*51 from the blood of Abel to the blood of Zechariah,*		
36 Amen, I say to you, all these things shall come upon this generation.		*who perished between the altar and the House. Yes, I say to you, it shall be required from this generation.*		

§305 Lament over Jerusalem (Mt) (§243)

MT 23:37-39	LK 13:34-35	MK	JN
37 Jerusalem, Jerusalem, thou who killeth the prophets and stoneth the ones sent to thee, how often I wished to gather thy children, just as a hen gathers her chicks under her wings, and you would not.	*34 Jerusalem, Jerusalem, thou who killeth the prophets, and stoneth the ones sent to thee, how often I wished to have gathered thy children, just as a hen her own brood under her wings, and you would not.*		
38 Behold, your House is left to you desolate*.	*35 Behold, your House is left to you desolate.*		
39 For I say to you, by no means may you see me from now, until you say: Blessed is he who comes in the name of the Lord.	*And I say to you, by no means may you see me until it shall come when you say: Blessed is he who comes in the name of the Lord.*		
(↓ §307)			

§306 The Widow's Mite

MT	LK 21:1-4	MK 12:41-44	JN
	(↑ §304)	(↑ §304)	
	1 And looking up he saw the rich putting their gifts into the treasury.	41 And while sitting opposite the treasury, he was watching how the crowd was putting money into the treasury, and many rich men were putting much.	
	2 And he saw a certain destitute widow putting therein two lepta.	42 And one poor widow coming put in two lepta, which is a quadrans.	
	3 And he said: Truly I say to you that this poor widow has put in more than	43 And calling up his disciples he said to them: Amen I say to you that this poor widow has put in more than all	

220

MT	LK 21:1-4	MK 12:41-44	JN

LK 21:1-4
all.
4 For all these put into the gifts of God out of their superfluity, but she out of her penury put in all the livelihood she had.

MK 12:41-44
who put into the treasury.
44 For all put in out of their superfluity; but she out of her penury put in all whatever she had, her whole livelihood.

§307 Prediction of the Temple's End

MT 24:1-2

(↑ §305)

1 And Jesus, coming out of the Temple, was passing,
and his disciples came up to point out to him the buildings of the Temple.

2 And answering he said to them:
Do you not see all these things?
Amen I say to you, not a stone upon a stone will be left here which will not be overthrown.

LK 21:5-6

5 And while some were speaking about the Temple, that it had been adorned with beautiful stones and trophies,
he said:
6 All the things you behold,
days will come in which not a stone upon a stone will be left which will not be overthrown **(cf. 19:44).**

MK 13:1-2

1 And as he was passing out of the Temple,
one of his disciples says to him: Teacher, see, what wonderful stones and what wonderful buildings!
2 And Jesus said to him:
Do your see these great buildings?
Not a stone upon a stone will be left here which will not be overthrown.

JN

§308 Signs Preceding the End of the Age

MT 24:3-8
3 Now while he was sitting upon the Mount of Olives
his disciples came up to him privately saying:

Tell us, when shall these things be?
And what (shall be) the sign of your Advent and the completion of the Age?
4 And Jesus answering said to them:
See that no one deceives you!
5 For many will come in my name, saying: I am the Christ,
and will deceive many.
6 And you will come to hear of wars and rumours of wars.
See you are not disturbed;
for these things have to happen, but the end is not yet.

7 For nation shall rise against nation, and

LK 21:7-11

7 And they questioned him, saying:

Teacher, when then shall these things be?
And what (shall be) the sign when these things are about to happen?
8 And he said:
See that you be not deceived!
For many will come in my name saying: I am, and: The time has come.
Do not go after them.
9 And when you hear of wars and rebellions,

do not be frightened;
for these thing have first to happen, but the end is not at once.
10 Then he said to them:
Nation shall rise against nation, and kingdom

MK 13:3-8
3 And while he was sitting on the Mount of Olives opposite the Temple,
Peter questioned him privately, and James and John and Andrew:
4 Tell us, when shall these things be?
And what (shall be) the sign when all these things are about to be completed?
5 And Jesus began to say to them:
See that no one deceives you!
6 For many will come in my name, saying: I am,
and will deceive many.
7 And when you hear of wars and rumours of wars,
be not disturbed;
for they have to happen, but not yet the end.

8 For nation shall rise against nation, and

JN

MT 24:3-8	LK 21:7-11	MK 13:3-8	JN
kingdom against kingdom. and there will be famines and plagues and earthquakes in various places.	against kingdom, 11 and there will be great earthquakes, and in various places famines and plagues and there will be terrors and great signs from heaven.	kingdom against kingdom; there will be earthquakes in various places, there will be famines and troubles.	
8 And all these things are a beginning of birth pangs.		These things are a beginning of birth pangs.	

§309 Persecutions Foretold (§§125, 225)

MT 24:9-14	*MT 10:17-22*	LK 21:12-19	*LK 12:11-12*	MK 13:9-13	JN
		12 But before all these things, they will lay their hands upon you, and persecute (you),			
	17 Be wary of men!	**(20:46)**		9 But you yourselves look out **(12:38)**!	
9 Then they will betray you to affliction,	*For they will betray you to councils, and in their synagogues they will scourge you, 18 and you will be led before governors and kings too for my sake,*	betraying (you) to the synagogues and prisons, (you) being led away before kings and governors for the sake of my name;		They will betray you to councils, and to synagogues; you will be beaten, and you will stand before governors and kings for my sake,	
	for a witness to them	13 for you it will be an occasion for a witness.		for a witness to them.	
(cf. 24:14)	*and to the nations.*			10 And first the gospel must be preached to all the nations.	
	19 And when they betray you,		*11 But when they bring you in before the synagogues and the authorities and the magistrates,*	11 And when they lead you, betraying you,	
	do not worry how or what you should speak; for it will be given to you in that hour what you shall speak;	14 Fix therefore in your hearts not to premeditate your defence; 15 for I will give you a mouth and wisdom which all those opposed to you will be unable to withstand or to contradict.	*do not worry how or what defence you should make, or what you should say; 12 for the Holy Spirit will teach you in the very hour the things you are to say.*	do not worry beforehand what you should speak; but whatever is given to you in that hour, speak that!	
	20 For it is not you who speak but the Spirit of your Father which speaks			For you are not the ones speaking but the Holy Spirit.	

MT 24:9-14	MT 10:17-22	LK 21:12-19	LK 12:11-12	MK 13:9-13	JN
	in you. *21 And brother will betray brother to death and (the) father (his) son,*	16 And you will be betrayed even by parents and brothers and relatives and friends,		12 And brother will betray brother to death and (the) father (his) son,	
	and children will rise up against parents, and will put them to death;			and children will rise up against parents, and will put them to death;	
and they will kill you;		and they will put to death some of you;			
and you will be hated by all the nations for my name's sake. 10 And then many will be scandalized, and will betray one another, and will hate one another. 11 And many false prophets will arise and will deceive many. 12 And because of the increase of wrong-doing the love of the many will grow cold.	*22 and you will be hated by all for my name's sake.*	17 and you will be hated by all for my name's sake.		13 and you will be hated by all for my name's sake.	
		18 And not by any means will a hair of your head perish.			
13 But he who perseveres to the end, he will be saved. 14 And this gospel of the Kingdom will be proclaimed in the whole inhabited world, as a witness to all the nations, and then the end will come.	*But he who perseveres to the end he will be saved.*	19 In your perseverance you will gain your souls.		But he who perseveres to the end, he will be saved. **(cf. 13:10)**	

§310 A Prophecy of Calamity (§267)

MT 24:15-22	LK 21:20-24: *17:31*	MK 13:14-20	JN
15 When therefore you see the Abomination of the Desolation, spoken of through Daniel the prophet, standing in the holy place—he that reads let him understand **(Dn. 9:27; 11:31)**. 16 Then let those in Judea flee to the mountains.	20 And when you see Jerusalem encircled by military camps, know then that its desolation is at hand **(cf. 19:43)**. 21 Then let those in Judea flee to the mountains, and let those in its midst get out,	14 And when you see the Abomination of the Desolation standing where he ought not—he that reads let him understand **(Dn. 9:27; 11:31)**— then let those in Judea flee to the mountains.	

MT 24:15-22 | LK 21:20-24; *17:31* | MK 13:14-20 | JN

LK:
and those in the country-side not enter into it,
22 because these are days of vengeance for the
fulfilment of all that has been written.

MT:
17 Let him on the roof-top not come down to
take away things out of his house,

LK:
*17:31 On that day he who shall be on the roof-
top and his belongings in the house, let him
not come down to take them away;*

MK:
15 And let him on the roof-top not come
down nor enter in to take away anything out
of his house;

MT:
18 and let him in the field not turn back to
take his coat.

LK:
and let him in the field likewise not turn back.

MK:
16 and let him at the field not turn back to the
things behind to take his coat.

MT:
19 And woe to those who are pregnant and
are breast-feeding in those days;
20 and pray that your flight does not happen
in winter, nor on a Sabbath.
21 For then there shall be great affliction such
as has not been from the beginning of the
world
until now, nor will ever happen.

LK:
23 And woe to those who are pregnant and
are breast-feeding in those days;

for there shall be great distress upon the earth

and wrath for this people.
24 And they shall fall by the edge of the sword
and they shall be taken captive to all the
nations;
and Jerusalem shall be trodden down by the
nations, until the times of the nations have
been fulfilled.

(↓ §312)

MK:
17 And woe to those who are pregnant and
are breast-feeding in those days;
18 and pray that your flight does not happen
in winter.
19 For those days will be an affliction of such
a kind as has not been from the beginning of
the creation which God created
until now, and will not ever happen.

MT:
22 And if those days had not been shortened,
no flesh would be saved;
but because of the elect those days will be
shortened.

MK:
20 And if the Lord had not shortened the
days, no flesh would be saved;
but because of the elect whom he has chosen
he has shortened the days.

§311 Warning against False Christs (§267)

MT 24:23-28 | LK 17:23-24, 37b | MK 13:21-23 | JN

MT:
23 Then if anyone should say to you:
Behold, here (is) the Christ, or: Here,
do not believe.
24 For false Christs and false prophets will
arise, and will give great signs and wonders so
as to deceive, if possible, even the elect.
25 Behold I have foretold you.

26 If therefore they should say to you: Behold,
he is in the desert!, do not go out; Behold, (he
is) in the inner rooms, do not believe.
27 For just as the lightning comes out of the
east and appears as far as the **west**,
so also shall be the Advent of the Son of Man.

LK:
*23 And they will say to you:
Behold, there!, or : Behold, here!,
do not go off nor pursue.*
(cf. 21:8)

*24 For just as the lightning flashing from (one
end) of the sky to the other, shines out,
so also shall be the Son of Man in his day.*

MK:
21 And then if anyone should say to you:
See, here (is) the Christ, see, there,
believe not.
22 And false Christs and false prophets will
arise, and will perform signs and wonders in
order to lead astray, if possible, even the elect.
23 And do you beware! I have foretold you all
things.

MT 24:23-28	LK 17:23-24, 37b	MK 13:21-23	JN
28 Wherever the corpse may be, there will the eagles be gathered.	*37b And he said to them: Where the body is, there too will the eagles be gathered together.*		

§312 The Coming of the Son of Man

MT 24:29-31	LK 21:25-28	MK 13:24-27	JN
29 Now immediately after the tribulation of those days the sun will be darkened and the moon will not give its light, and the stars will fall from heaven.	(↑ §310) 25 And there will be signs in the sun and moon and stars, and upon the earth distress of nations in perplexity at the sound of the sea and the surf, 26 while men will be withering away from fear and expectation of the things to come upon the inhabited world;	24 But in those days after that tribulation the sun will be darkened and the moon will not give its light, 25 and the stars will be falling out of heaven,	
and the powers of the heavens will be shaken.	for the powers of the heavens will be shaken.	and the powers that are in the heavens will be shaken.	
30 And then will appear the sign of the Son of Man in heaven, and then all the tribes of the earth will mourn, and they will see the Son of Man coming upon the clouds of heaven with power and much glory. 31 And he will send his angels with a great trumpet and sound,* and they will gather up his elect from the four winds, from end to end of the heavens.	27 And then they will see the Son of Man coming on a cloud with power and much glory.	26 And then they will see the Son of Man coming upon clouds with much power and glory. 27 And then he will send the angels and he will gather up his elect from the four winds, from the end of the earth to the end of heaven.	
	28 And when these things begin to happen, stand up and lift up your heads, for your redemption is near.		

§313 The Time of the Coming

MT 24:32-36	LK 21:29-33	MK 13:28-32	JN
32 And from the fig-tree learn the parable; when now its branch becomes tender and sprouts the leaves, you know that summer is nigh; 33 so you too when you see all these things,	29 And he spoke a parable to them: See the fig-tree and all the trees; 30 when now they burst out, (as you see for yourselves) you know that summer is already near; 31 so you too when you see these things	28 And from the fig-tree learn the parable; when now its branch becomes tender and sprouts the leaves, you know that summer is nigh; 29 so you too when you see these things	

MT 24:32-36
you know that it is near at the doors.

34 Amen I say to you that this generation will by no means pass away until all these things be done.
35 Heaven and earth will pass away, but my words may by no means pass away.
36 But regarding that day and hour no one knows, neither the angels of the heavens, nor the Son, except the Father alone.

LK 21:29-33
happening you know that the Kingdom of God is near.
32 Amen I say to you that this generation will by no means pass away until all things be done.
33 Heaven and earth will pass away, but my words will by no means pass away.

(↓ §320)

MK 13:28-32
happening, you know that it is near at the doors.
30 Amen I say to you that this generation will by no means pass away, till all these things be done.
31 Heaven and earth will pass away, but my words will by no means pass away.
32 But regarding that day or hour no one knows, neither the angels in heaven, nor the Son, except the Father.

(↓ §320)

JN

§314 The Suddenness of the Coming (§267)

MT 24:37-42
37 For just as the days of Noah,
so also shall be the Advent of the Son of Man,

38 For as they were in the days that were before the Flood,
feasting and drinking, marrying and giving in marriage,
up to the day on which Noah entered into the ark,
39 and they knew not until the Flood came and took away everyone,

so also shall be the Advent of the Son of Man.

(cf. 24:17-18)

(cf. 10:39)

LK 17:26-34, 36, 35
26 And as it happened in the days of Noah, so shall it be also in the days of the Son of Man,

27 they were eating, they were drinking, they were marrying and giving in marriage,
up to the day on which Noah entered into the ark,
and the Flood came and destroyed all.

28 Likewise as it happened in the days of Lot; they were eating, they were drinking, they were buying, they were selling, they were planting, they were building;
29 and on the day that Lot went forth from Sodom, it rained fire and brimstone from heaven and destroyed all.
30 Just the same will it be on the day on which the Son of Man will be revealed.
31 On that day he who shall be on the rooftop, and his belongings in the house let him not come down to take them away, and let him in the field likewise not turn back.
32 Remember Lot's wife.
33 Whoever shall seek to preserve his life shall lose it, and whosoever will lose (it), will cause it to come alive.
34 I say to you, on that night there will be two (men) in one bed, the one will be taken, and

MK 13:35

(13:15-16)

JN

MT 24:37-42	LK 17:26-34, 36, 35 *the other will be left.*	MK 13:35	JN
40 Then there will be two men in the field, one is taken and one is left;	36* *Two men in a field, one will be taken, and the other will be left.*		
41 two women grinding at the mill, one is taken and one is left.	35 *There will be two women grinding together, the one will be taken, but the other will be left.*		
42 Watch therefore, because you do not know on what day your Lord will come.		35 *Watch therefore, for you know not when the lord of the house comes, whether evening or midnight or cockcrow or morning.*	

§315 The Thief in the Night (§231)

MT 24:43-44	LK 12:39-40	MK	JN
43 And know that (thing), that if the house-owner knew in which watch the thief was to come, he would have watched and would not have allowed his house to be dug through.	39 *And know this, that if the house-owner knew at which hour the thief was to come, he would not have permitted his house to be dug through.*		
44 Wherefore you too be prepared, because at the hour you do not imagine, the Son of Man is coming.	40 *You too be prepared because at the hour you do not imagine, the Son of Man is coming.*	(cf. 13:35)	

§316 The Faithful Steward (§232)

MT 24:45-51	LK 12:41-46; 13:28	MK	JN
	41 *And Peter said to him: Lord, are you telling this parable to us, or also to all?* 42 *And the Lord said:*		
45 Who then is the faithful and wise slave whom the lord has appointed over his household. to give them food at the proper time?	*Who then is the faithful, the wise steward whom the lord will appoint over his family to make proper provision at the proper time?*		
46 Blessed is that slave whom his lord when he comes will find so doing.	43 *Blessed is that slave whom his lord when he comes will find doing so.*		
47 Amen I say to you, that he will appoint him over all his possessions.	44 *Truly I say to you that he will appoint him over all his possessions.*		
48 But if that slave, (being) bad, should say in his heart: My lord is delaying,	45 *But if that slave should say in his heart: My Lord is delaying to come,*		
49 and should begin to strike his fellow-slaves, and also to eat and drink with the drunkards,	*and should begin to strike the slave boys and girls, yea, also to eat and drink and to get drunk,*		
50 the lord of that slave will come in a day in which he is not expecting and in an hour which he does not know.	46 *the lord of that slave will come in a day which he is not expecting, and in an hour which he does not know,*		

MT 24:45-51

51 and will dismember him, and will put his portion with the hypocrites.

Weeping and gnashing of teeth shall be there **(cf. 25:30)**.

LK 12:41-46; 13:28

and will dismember him, and will put his portion with the unfaithful.

13:28 Weeping and gnashing of teeth shall be there.

MK JN

§317 The Ten Virgins (§§230, 241)

MT 25:1-13

1 Then the Kingdom of the Heavens will be likened to ten virgins who took their lamps and went forth to meet the bridegroom and the bride.
2 And five of them were foolish and five wise.
3 Now the foolish when they took their lamps did not take oil with them;
4 But the wise took oil in the flasks with their lamps.
5 And as the bridegroom delayed they all dozed and slept.
6 And in the middle of the night there was a shout: Behold the bridegroom; go out to meet him.
7 Then all those virgins got up and trimmed their lamps;
8 and the foolish said to the wise: Give us some of your oil, because our lamps are extinguished.
9 And the wise answered saying: No, lest there be not enough for us and for you. Go rather to the vendors and buy for yourselves.
10 And as they were going off to buy, the bridegroom came, and those who were ready entered with him into the wedding feast, and the door was shut.
11 And later the rest of the virgins also come, saying: Lord, Lord, open to us.
12 But he answering said: Amen I say to you, I know you not.
13 Watch therefore because you know not the day nor the hour **(cf. 24:42)**.

LK 12:35-40; 13:25-27

35 Let your loins be girded round and (your) lamps lit.
36 And be you like men awaiting their lord when he returns from the wedding festivities, so that when he comes and knocks they may open to him at once.
37 Blessed are those slaves whom the lord, when he comes, will find watching. Amen I say to you, he will gird himself and will make them recline, and coming up he will minister to them **(cf. Jn. 13:5)**.
38 And if he comes in the second watch, and even in the third, and finds them thus, blessed are they.
39 And know you this, that if the master of the house had known at what hour the thief was coming, he would not have permitted his house to be broken into.
40 You too be prepared, because at the hour you do not imagine the Son of Man is coming.

13:25 From (the time) when the master of the house has risen and locked up the door, and you have begun to stand outside, and to knock on the door, saying: Lord, lord, open to us.
And answering he will say to you: I know you not whence you are.
26 Then you will begin to say: We ate and drank in your presence and you taught in our streets.
27 And saying he will say to you: I know you not whence you are; stand away from me, all you workers of unrighteousness.

MK JN

§318 The Talents (§§241, 284)

MT 25:14-30

LK 19:11-27; 13:28

11 And when they heard these things, he added a parable, because they were near Jerusalem and were imagining that the kingdom was going to appear straight away.

MK JN

MT 25:14-30	LK 19:11-27; 13:28	MK	JN

MT 25:14-30

14 As for instance, a man going abroad.

called his own slaves and handed his property over to them, 15 and to one he gave five talents, and to another two and to another one, to each according to his ability, and he went abroad.

16 Immediately he who had received five talents invested them and earned another five.
17 In the same way, he who had the two earned another two.
18 But he who had received the one, went off and dug the earth and hid his lord's money.
19 And after a long time the lord of those slaves comes and settles account with them.

20 And the one who had received five talents came up and brought another five talents saying:
Lord, you handed over to me five talents, behold I have gained another five talents.
21 The Lord said to him:
Well done, good and faithful slave, you were faithful over few, I will put you over many; enter into the joy of your Lord.
22 And the one with the two talents came up and said:
Lord, you handed two talents over to me, see, I have gained two more talents.
23 The Lord said to him:
Well done, good and faithful slave, you were faithful over few, I will set you over many. Enter into the joy of your Lord.
24 And now the one who had received one talent coming up, said:
Lord, I knew you that you are a hard man, reaping where you did not sow and gathering up where you did not winnow.
25 And being afraid I went and hid your talent in the ground; see, you have what is yours.

26 And his lord answering said to him:
Evil and lazy slave;
You knew that I reaped where I did not sow and gather up where I did not winnow?
27 It was your duty then to deposit my money with the bankers; then when I came I would receive back what is mine with interest.

28 Take therefore the talent from him and give to him who has the ten talents.

29 For to everyone that has shall be given and he will have

LK 19:11-27; 13:28

12 He therefore said: A certain nobleman went into a far region to receive a kingdom for himself and to return.
13 And calling his ten slaves he gave them ten mnas and said to them: Trade until I come.

14 But his citizens hated him and sent an embassy after him, saying: We do not want this man to rule over us.

15 And it happened on his return after receiving the kingdom that he said that these slaves should be called to whom he had given the money so that he should know what they had traded.
16 And the first arrived saying:

Lord, your mna has gained ten mnas.

17 And he said to him:
Well done, good slave, because you were faithful in the least, have authority over ten cities.
18 And the second came saying:
Your mna, Lord, has made five mnas.

19 And he said to this one too:
And do you be over five cities.

20 And the other came saying:

Lord, behold your mna, which I have had hidden in a cloth.

21 For I was afraid of you, because you are a hard man, taking up what you did not put down, and reaping what you did not sow.
22 He says to him:
Out of your mouth I will condemn you, evil slave;
You knew that I was a hard man, taking up what I did not put down and reaping what I did not sow?
23 Why then did you not give my money to a bank, and then when I came I would have demanded it with interest?

24 And to the attendants he said:
Take the mna from him and give to him who has ten mnas.

25* And they said to him: Lord, he has ten mnas.
26 I say to you that to everyone who has shall be given;

MK

(cf. 13:34)

229

MT 25:14-30

more;

but from him who has not, even what he has shall be taken away from him **(cf. 13:12)**.

30 And throw the unprofitable slave into the exterior darkness;

Weeping and gnashing of teeth shall be there **(22:13; 26:51)**.

LK 19:11-27; 13:28

but from him who has not, even what he has shall be taken away **(cf. 8:18)**.

13:28 Weeping and gnashing of teeth shall be there.

27 As for these enemies of mine who refuse to let me rule over them, bring them here and slay them before me.

MK

(cf. 4:25)

JN

§319 The Last Judgement

MT 25:31-46

31 When the Son of Man comes in his glory, and all his angels with him, then he will sit upon the throne of his glory.
32 And all the nations will be gathered together before him, and he will separate them from one another, just as the shepherd separates the sheep from the goats. 33 And he will place the sheep on his right and the goats on the left.
34 Then the king will say to those on his right;
Come ye blessed of my Father,
inherit the Kingdom prepared for you from the foundation of the world.
35 For I was hungry and you gave me to eat,
I was thirsty and you gave me to drink,
I was a stranger and you entertained me,
36 naked and you clothed me,
I was sick and you watched over me,
I was in prison and you came to me.
37 Then the just will answer him, saying:
Lord, when did we see you hungry, and fed you, or thirsty and gave you to drink?
38 When did we see you a stranger and entertain you? Or naked and clothed you?
39 When did we see you sick or in prison, and came to you?
40 And the king answering will say to them:
Amen I say to you, as often as you did it to one of these the least of my brethren, you did it to me.
41 Then the king will say to those on the left:
Go from me, cursed ones, into the eternal fire that has been prepared for the devil and his angels.
42 For I was hungry and you did not give me to eat;
I was thirsty and you did not give me to drink;
43 I was a stranger and you did not entertain me;
naked, and you did not clothe me;

LK   MK   JN

MT 25:31-46	LK	MK	JN
sick and in prison and you did not watch over me. 44 Then they too will answer saying: Lord, when did we see you hungry or thirsty, or a stranger, or naked, or sick, or in prison, and we did not minister to you? 45 And he will answer them, saying: Amen, I say to you, as often as you did not do it to one of these, the least ones, neither did you do it to me. 46 And these shall go off into eternal punishment, but the just into eternal life. (↓ §325)			

§320 Jesus' Final Warnings (Lk, Mk)(§314)

MT	LK 21:34-36	MK 13:33-37	JN
	(↑ §313)	(↑ §313)	
(cf. 24:37-39)	34 But be wary of yourselves, lest ever your hearts should be weighed down with surfeiting and drunkenness and with worries of life,	(cf. 13:9)	
(cf. 24:44;48-50)	and that day should come upon you suddenly 35 like a snare; for it will come upon all who dwell upon the face of the whole earth.		
(cf. 24:20)	36 And keep awake at every season, praying that you may be able to escape all these things that are going to happen,	(cf. 13:33)	
(cf.24:32)	and to stand before the Son of Man.		
(cf. 25:1-3)	(21:36)	33 Look out , keep awake, and pray,	
(cf. 24:44)		for you know not when the time is (cf. 13:9).	
(cf. 25:14-30)	(cf. 19:12f)	34 Like a man going abroad, leaving his house and giving authority to his slaves, to each one his work;	
(cf. 24:45-47)		he also commanded the doorkeeper to watch.	
(cf. 24:39-44; 25:1-13)	(cf. 12:35-40)	35 Watch therefore, for you know not when the lord of the house comes, either evening, or midnight, or cockcrow, or dawn, 36 lest suddenly coming he should find you sleeping.	
(cf. 24:42)		37 And what I say to you I say to all: Watch. (↓ §325)	

§321 Jesus Teaches in the Temple

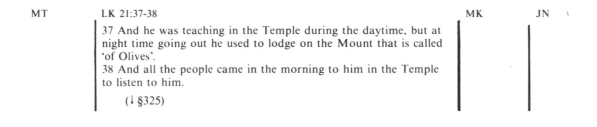

MT   LK 21:37-38   MK   JN

37 And he was teaching in the Temple during the daytime, but at night time going out he used to lodge on the Mount that is called 'of Olives'.
38 And all the people came in the morning to him in the Temple to listen to him.

(↓ §325)

§322 Some Greeks Ask for Jesus

MT   LK   MK   JN 12:20-26

(↑ §288)

20 Now among those who went up to worship at the Festival were some Greeks;
21 These then came up to Philip who was from Bethsaida in Galilee, and asked him, saying: Sir, we want to see Jesus.
22 Philip comes and tells Andrew;
Andrew comes, and Philip, and they tell Jesus.
23 Jesus therefore answers them, saying:
The hour has come for the Son of Man to be glorified.
24 Amen amen I say to you, if the grain of wheat does not fall on the ground and die, it remains alone; but if it dies, it bears much fruit.
25 He who loves his life loses it, and he who in this world hates his life shall guard it for eternal life.
26 If anyone serves me, let him follow me, and where I myself am there also my own servant shall be; if anyone serves me my Father will honour him.

§323 Jesus Prophesies His Crucifixion

MT   LK   MK   JN 12:27-36

27 Now my soul is troubled. And what should I say? O Father, save me from this hour; but for this I have come to this (very) hour. 28 O Father, glorify thy name.
There came then a voice from heaven:
Indeed I have glorified (it) and will glorify (it) again.
29 Therefore the crowd that stood and listened said that there had been thunder; others said: An angel has spoken to him.
30 Jesus answered and said:
Not for my sake has this voice occurred but for yours.
31 Now is (the) judgement of this world; now shall the ruler of

MT	LK	MK	JN 12:27-36

this world be cast out outside.

32 And I, if I am lifted up from the earth, will draw all (men) to myself.

33 Now he said this signifying by what kind of death he was going to die.

34 The crowd therefore answered him: We ourselves have heard from out of the Law that the Christ remains for ever, and how do you say that the Son of Man will have to be lifted up? Who is this Son of Man?

35 Jesus therefore said to them:

Yet a little while the light is among you. Walk while you have the light, so that the darkness does not overtake you; and he who walks in the darkness does not know where he is going. 36 While you have the light, believe in the light, so as to become sons of light.

These things Jesus spoke, and going off hid from them.

§324 Jesus Is Sent by the Father

MT	LK	MK	JN 12:37-50

37 Now though he had done such signs before them, they did not believe in him, 38 so that the word of Isaiah the prophet was fulfilled which he spoke:

O Lord, who has believed our report?

And the arm of the Lord, to whom has it been revealed? **(Is. 53:1)**.

39 For this (reason) they could not believe, because again Isaiah has said:

40 He has blinded their eyes,

and has hardened their hearts,

lest they see with their eyes

and understand with their heart,

and be converted, and I will heal them.

41 These things Isaiah said **(Is. 6:10)**, because he saw his glory and spoke about him.

42 Nevertheless, however, many even of the rulers believed in him, but because of the Pharisees did not confess, lest they be put out of the synagogue.

43 For they loved the glory of men rather than the glory of God.

44 But Jesus exclaimed and said:

He who believes in me believes not in me but in him who sent me.

45 And he who beholds me beholds him who sent me.

46 I have come into the world (as) a light, so that everyone who believes in me may not remain in the darkness.

47 And if anyone should hear my words and not retain them, I myself do not judge him; for I did not come to judge the world,

MT	LK	MK	JN 12:37-50

JN 12:37-50
but to save the world.
48 He who rejects me, and who does not receive my words, has one who judges him; the word that I have spoken, that will judge him at the last day.
49 Because I have not spoken from myself, but the Father who has sent me, he has given me commandment what to say and what to speak.
50 And I know that his commandment is eternal life; therefore whatever I myself speak, I so speak just as the Father has spoken to me.

(↓ §332)

VIII. The Passion, Death, and Resurrection of Jesus
§§ 325-376

MT 26:1-5	LK 22:1-2	MK 14:1-2	JN
(↑ §319)	(↑ §321)	(↑ §320)	
			(cf. 11:45f)
1 And it happened that when Jesus had ended all these words, he said to his disciples:			
2 You know that after two days the Passover comes, and the Son of Man will be handed over to be crucified.	1 And the feast of the Azymes drew near which is called the Passover.	1 Now it was the Passover and the Azymes after two days.	
3 Then were gathered together the high-priests and the elders of the people into the court of the high-priest who was called Caiaphas,	2 And the high-priests and the scribes	And the high-priests and the scribes	
4 And they held a council together in order to lay hold of Jesus by cunning and kill him.	sought how to do away with him;	sought how to lay hold of him by cunning and kill him.	
5 And they said: Not on the feast, lest a riot occur among the people.	For they feared the people.	2 For they said: Not on the feast, lest perhaps there will be a riot of the people.	
	(↓ §327)		

§326 Jesus Anointed in Bethany (Mt, Mk) (§§95, 286)

MT 26:6-13	LK 7:36-38	MK 14:3-9	JN 12:1-8
6 Now Jesus happening to be in Bethany in the house of Simon the leper,	36 And someone of the Pharisees asked him to eat with him, and entering into the house of the Pharisee he reclined at table.	3 And when he was in Bethany in the house of Simon the leper,	1 Jesus therefore six days before the Passover came into Bethany where was Lazarus the one who died*, whom Jesus had raised from the dead. 2 So they made a banquet for him there, and Martha was serving, but Lazarus was one of the ones reclining with him;
7 there came up to him a woman having an alabaster phial of very expensive perfume,	37 And behold there was a certain woman in the city, a sinner; and learning that he was at table in the house of the Pharisee, bringing an alabaster phial of perfume,	while he was reclining, there came a woman having an alabaster phial of very costly pure nard perfume.	3 Mary therefore taking a pound of perfume, very expensive pure nard,
and poured it over his head as he was reclining at table.	38 and standing behind at his feet weeping, she began to wash his feet with her tears, and wiped them with the hair of her head, and kissed his feet and anointed (them) with the perfume.	Breaking the alabaster phial, she poured it over his head.	anointed the feet of Jesus and wiped his feet with her hair; and the house was filled with the odour of the perfume.
8 And his disciples seeing were irritated saying: Why this waste?		4 And there were some who were irritated among themselves and saying: Why has this waste of perfume happened?	4 And Judas, the Iscariot, one of his disciples, the one about to betray him says:
9 For this could have been sold for a large sum,		5 For this perfume could have been sold for above three hundred denarii	5 Why was this perfume not sold for three hundred denarii

237

MT 26:6-13	LK 7:36-38	MK 14:3-9	JN 12:1-8
		and given to the poor; and they were angry with her.	*and given to the poor?*
			6 Now he said this not because he cared about the poor, but because he was a thief, and having the begging-bag took what was dropped into it.
10 And Jesus knowing said to them: Why do you make trouble for the woman? For she has worked a good work for me; 11 for the poor you have with you always,		6 And Jesus said: Leave her; why do you make trouble for her? for she has worked a good work on me; 7 for the poor you have with you always, and when you wish you can do good to them,	*7 Jesus therefore said: Leave her;* *that she may perform this (deed) for the day of my interment; 8 for the poor you have always with you,*
but me you do not always have. 12 For when she poured this perfume over my body, she did it for my entombing. 13 Amen I say to you, wherever this gospel shall be preached in the whole world so too what she has done will be spoken of as a memorial of her.		but me you do not always have. 8 She did what she had; she has anticipated anointing my body for my entombment. 9 And Amen I say to you, wherever this gospel shall be preached in the whole world, so also what she has done will be spoken of as a memorial of her.	*but me you do not always have.*

§327 The Betrayal of Jesus

MT 26:14-16	LK 22:3-6	MK 14:10-11	JN
	(↑ §325)		
14 Then one of the Twelve, the one called Judas Iscariot, going to the high-priests, 15 said:	3 And Satan entered into Judas the one called Iscariot, being of the number of the Twelve; 4 And going off, he conferred with the high-priests and the temple-police as to how he might betray him to them.	10 And Judas Iscariot, one of the Twelve, went off to the high-priests in order to betray him to them.	
What will you give me, and I will betray him to you? And they fixed for him thirty pieces of silver.	5 And they rejoiced and agreed to give him money. 6 And he fully consented,	11 And they rejoiced when they heard and promised to give him money,	
16 And from then he was looking for an opportunity to betray him.	and was looking for an opportunity to betray him to them apart from the crowd.	and he was looking for how he might opportunely betray him.	

MT 26:17-20	LK 22:7-14	MK 14:12-17	JN
17 And on the first of the Azymes,	7 And the day of the Azymes came, on which the Passover had to be sacrificed. 8 And he sent Peter and John, saying: Go and prepare for us to eat the Passover.	12 And on the first day of the Azymes, when they sacrificed the Passover,	
the disciples came up to Jesus saying: Where do you want us to prepare for you to eat the Passover?	9 And they said to him: Where do you want us to prepare?	his disciples say to him: Where do you want us to go off and prepare for you to eat the Passover? 13 And he sends two of his disciples,	
18 And he said: Go up into the city	10 And he said to them: Behold, when you enter into the city, a man will encounter you carrying a pitcher of water; follow him into the house into which he enters;	and says to them: Go up into the city, and a man will meet you carrying a pitcher of water; follow him, 14 and wherever he enters in,	
to the one-you-know and say to him:	11 and you shall say to the house-owner of the house:	say to the house-owner:	
The Teacher says: My time is near. With you I make the Passover with my disciples.	The Teacher says to you: Where is the dining-room where I eat the Passover with my disciples? 12 And that (man) will show you a great upper room spread; and prepare there.	The Teacher says: Where is my dining-room where I eat the Passover with my disciples? 15 And he himself will show you a great upper room spread ready; and prepare there for us.	
19 And the disciples did as Jesus had instructed them, and they prepared the Passover. 20 Now when evening came he reclined with the twelve disciples.	13 And they went off and found it just as he had told them, and they prepared the Passover. 14 And when the hour came, he sat down, and the apostles with him.	16 And the disciples went out, and came into the city and found it just as he said to them, and they prepared the Passover. 17 And when evening came, he comes with the Twelve.	
(↓ §330)		(↓ §330)	

§329 The First Cup (§331)

MT	LK 22:15-18	MK	JN
	15 And he said to them: With desire I have desired to eat this Passover with you before my Passion. 16 For I say to you, that I do not eat it any more until it has been fulfilled in the Kingdom of God. 17 And taking up the cup giving thanks he said: Take this and share it out among you.		
(26:29)	18 For I say to you, that I will not drink as from now of the fruit of the vine, until the Kingdom of God has come.	(14:25)	
	(↓ §331)		

MT 26:21-25	LK 22:21-23	MK 14:18-21	JN 13:21-26
(↑ §328)		(↑ §328)	
21 And while they were eating, he said: Amen I say to you, that one of you will betray me.		18 And while they were reclining and eating Jesus said: Amen I say to you, that one of you will betray me, who is eating with me.	*21 Having said then these things, Jesus was troubled in spirit and witnessed and said:* *Amen I say to you, that one of you will betray me.*
22 And being exceedingly grieved they began to say to him each one: It is not I, O Lord?		19 They began to be grieved and to say to him one after the other: Not I?	*22 The disciples began to look at one another, perplexed about whom he was speaking.* *23 One of his disciples whom Jesus loved was reclining on Jesus's bosom.* *24 Simon Peter therefore nods to this one and says to him: Say who it is, about whom he is speaking.* *25 So he, leaning back thus on the breast of Jesus, says to him: Lord, who is it?*
23 But he answering said: The one who dipped his hand with me in the dish, he will betray me.	*21 However, behold the hand of the one who betrays me upon the table with me!*	20 But he said to them: One of the Twelve, the one dipping with me into the dish.	*26 Jesus therefore answers:* *He is that one to whom I shall dip the morsel and give to him.* *Dipping therefore the morsel, he takes and gives (it) to Judas of Simon Iscariot.*
24 For the Son of Man indeed goes away according as it has been written about him, but woe to that man by whom the Son of Man is betrayed. It were good for him if that man had not been born.	*22 For the Son of Man indeed goes in accordance with what has been decreed.* *However, woe to that man by whom he is betrayed.* *23 And they began to debate among themselves as to which of them was the one about to do this.*	21 For the Son of Man indeed goes away according as it has been written about him. but woe to that man through whom the Son of Man is betrayed. It were good for him if that man had not been born.	
25 And Judas, who betrayed him, answering said: It is not I, Rabbi? He says to him: Thou hast said it.			

§331 Institution of the Eucharist (cf. §329)

MT 26:26-30	LK 22:19-20. *18*	MK 14:22-26	JN	1 COR 11:23b-25
	(↑ §329)			
26 Now while they were eating,	19a And	22 And while they were eating		*23b for the Lord Jesus, on the*

MT 26:26-30

Jesus, taking the bread and blessing (it) broke (it), and giving to the disciples said:
Take, eat; this is my Body.

27 And taking the cup

and giving thanks he gave to them, saying: Drink from it, all;

28 for this is my Blood of the new* covenant,
that is being shed for many unto remission of sins.

29 And I say to you, I will not drink from now of this fruit of the vine,
until that day when I shall drink it new with you in the Kingdom of my Father.
30 And having sung the hymn, they went out onto the Mount of Olives.

(↓ §336)

LK 22:19-20; *18*

taking bread giving thanks he broke and gave to them saying:

This is my Body, 19b* that has been given for you; do this unto my remembrance.
20 And the cup in like manner after supping,
saying:

This cup (is) the new covenant in my Blood,
that is being shed for you.

(↓ §333)

*18 For I say to you, I will not drink as from now of the fruit of the vine,
until the Kingdom of God has come.*

MK 14:22-26

taking the bread blessing he broke and gave to them, and said:

Take, eat;* this is my Body.

23 And taking the cup,

giving thanks he gave to them and all drank from it.
24 And he said to them:
This is my Blood of the covenant,

that is being shed for many.

25 Amen I say to you that I will not drink any more of the fruit of the vine,
until that day when I shall drink it new in the Kingdom of God.

26 And having sung the hymn, they went out onto the Mount of Olives.

(↓ §336)

JN

1 COR 11:23b-25

night on which he was betrayed, took bread 24 and giving thanks he broke (it) and said:

*Take, eat; this is my Body that has been broken for you; do this unto my remembrance.
25 In like manner also the cup after supping
saying:*

This cup is the new covenant in my Blood.

Do this; for as often as you drink, (it is) unto my remembrance.

§332 Jesus Washes His Disciples' Feet

MT   **LK**   **MK**   **JN 13:1-20**

(↑ §324)

1 And before the Festival of the Passover,
Jesus knowing that his hour had come that he should pass from this world to the Father,
having loved his own who were in the world, he loved them utterly.
2 And during supper, the devil having already put into the heart of Judas Simon Iscariot to betray him,
3 knowing that the Father had given all things into his hands, and that he had gone forth from God and was going back to God,
4 he rises from the supper and puts off his garments, and taking a towel girded himself.
5 Then he pours water into the wash-bowl, and began to wash the

MT	LK	MK	JN 13:1-20

feet of the disciples and to wipe (them) with the towel with which
he was girded.
6 He comes therefore to Simon Peter, who says to him:
7 Lord, are you washing my feet?
Jesus answered and said:
What I am doing you do not know now, but you will know
hereafter.
8 Peter says to him:
You shall never wash my feet.
Jesus answered him:
Unless I wash you, you have no part with me.
**9 Simon Peter says to him: Lord, not only my feet but also (my)
hands and head.**
10 Jesus says to him:
The one who has been washed has no need except to have the feet
washed but is wholly clean. And you yourselves are clean, but not
all.
11 For he knew the one who was to betray him; for that reason he
said: You are not all clean.
12 When therefore he had washed their feet and had taken his
garments, and again reclined he said to them:
Do you know what I have done to you? 13 You yourselves call me
the teacher and the Lord; and you say rightly, for I am. 14 If
therefore I myself—the Teacher and the Lord—have washed your
feet, you ought also to wash one another's feet.
15 For I have given you an example so that just as I have done to
you, you also should do.
16 Amen, amen I say to you, a servant is not greater than his
lord, nor an apostle greater than the one who sent him.
17 If you know these things, you are blessed, if you do them.
18 I am not speaking of all of you; I myself know the ones I have
chosen; but that the Scripture shoud be fulfilled:
He who eats bread with me has lifted up his heel against me **(Ps.
41:9)**.

19 I tell you now before it comes to pass, so that when it happens
you may believe that I myself am.

(10:39)

20 Amen, amen I say to you, he who receives whoever I send
receives me. And he who receives me, receives him who sent me

§333 Jesus Announces His Betrayal (Lk, Jn) (§330)

MT	LK 22:21-23	MK	JN 13:21-30
	(↑ §331)		
(26:21-25)	21 However, behold the hand of the one who betrays me upon	**(14:18-21)**	21 Having said these things Jesus was troubled in spirit and

MT	LK 22:21-23	MK	JN 13:21-30

the table with me! 22 For the Son of Man goes in accordance with what has been determined. However, woe to that man by whom he is betrayed.

23 And they began to debate among themselves as to which of them was the one about to do this.

(26:23) **(22:31)** **(14:20)**

witnessed and said: Amen, amen I say to you, that one of you will betray me.

22 The disciples began to look at one another perplexed about whom he was speaking.

23 One of his disciples, whom Jesus loved, was reclining on Jesus' bosom;

24 Simon Peter therefore nods to this one and says to him: Say who it is about whom he is speaking.*

25 So he leaning back thus on the breast of Jesus says to him: Lord, who is it?

26 Jesus therefore answers: He is that one to whom I shall dip the morsel and give to him.

Dipping therefore the morsel he takes and gives it to Judas of Simon Iscariot.

27 And after the morsel then did Satan enter into that man. Therefore Jesus says to him: What you do, do quickly.

28 But none of those reclining knew why he said this to him; 29 for some imagined, since Judas had the begging-bag, that Jesus was saying to him: Buy what we need for the feast, or that he was to give something to the poor.

30 Therefore having taken the morsel, that man went out at once. And it was night.

(↓ §335)

§334 Dispute at the Supper (§§278, 281)

MT	LK 22:24-30	MK	JN
(cf. 20:24-27)		**(cf. 10:41)**	

(cf. 20:24-27)

24 And there also took place among them a contention about whom they thought to be the greatest of them.

25 And he said to them: The kings of the nations lord it over them and those in authority over them are called Benefactors.

26 But you yourselves not so, but let the greatest among you become as the junior, and the ruler as the servant.

27 For who is greatest, the one who reclines or the one who serves? Is it not the one who reclines? Yet, I myself am in your midst as the one who serves.

28 And you are the ones who have stayed with me in my trials.

(cf. 19:28)

29 And I bequeath to you, as my Father has bequeathed to me, a Kingdom, 30 so that you will eat and drink at my table in my Kingdom, and you will sit on thrones judging the twelve tribes of Israel.

(↓ §336)

(cf. 10:41)

§335 The New Commandment

MT	LK	MK	JN 13:31-35
			(↑ §333)

31 When therefore he had gone out Jesus says:
Now the Son of Man is glorified, and God is glorified in him.
32 If God is glorified in him, then God will glorify him in him,
and will glorify him at once.
33 Little children, yet a little while I am with you: you will seek
me, and just as I said to the Jews that where I myself am going
you yourselves cannot come, so I say to you now.
34 A new commandment I give you, that you love one another;
just as I have loved you, that you also should love one another.
35 In this will all (men) know that you are my disciples, if you
have love between one another.

§336 Peter's Denials Foretold

MT 26:31-35	LK 22:31-34	MK 14:27-31	JN 13:36-38
(↑ §331)	(↑ §334)	(↑ §331)	

MT: 31 Then Jesus says to them:
You will all be scandalized over me in this night;
for it has been written:
I will strike the shepherd, and the sheep of the flock will be scattered **(Zech. 13:7).**
32 But after I have been raised up, I will go before you into Galilee.

33 And Peter answering said to him: If all shall be scandalized over you, yet will I never be scandalized.

LK: 31 Simon, Simon, behold Satan has begged earnestly for you to sift (you) like wheat.
32 But I asked for you that your faith should not fail; and do you, when you have been converted, confirm your brethren.
33 And he said to him:

Lord with you I am ready to go both to prison and to death.

MK: 27 And Jesus says to them:
You will all be scandalized;

because it has been written:
I will strike the shepherd, and the sheep will be scattered **(Zech. 13:7).**

28 However, after I have been raised up, I will go before you into Galilee.

29 And Peter said to him:
Even if all shall be scandalized, but not I.

JN: 36 Simon Peter says to him: Lord, where are you going off to?
Jesus answered: Where I am going off to, you cannot now follow me, but you will follow later.
37 Peter says to him:
Lord, why can I not follow you now? I will lay down my life for you.

MT 26:31-35
34 Jesus said to him:

Amen I say to you that in this very night
before the cock crows you will thrice deny me.
35 Peter says to him:
Even if I have to die with you, I will not deny you.
And all the disciples said likewise.

(↓ §345)

LK 23:31-34
34 And he said:

I say to you, Peter, to-day

the cock will not crow until you thrice deny knowing me.

MK 14:27-31
30 And Jesus says to him:

Amen I say to you that to-day in this very night
before the cock crows twice you will deny me thrice.
31 But he more emphatically said:
If I have to die together with you, I will not deny you.
And all spoke similarly also.

(↓ §345)

JN 13:36-38
38 Jesus answers: Will you lay down your life for me?
Amen, amen I say to you,

the cock will not crow until you deny me thrice.

(↓ §338)

§337 Jesus' Final Dialogue

MT
(cf. 10:10)

LK 22:35-38
35 And he said to them:
When I sent you without a purse and a wallet and sandals, did you lack anything (cf. 9:3; 10:4)?
And they said: Nothing.
36 And he said to them:
But now he who has a purse let him take it, likewise also the wallet, and he that has not one let him sell his coat and buy a sword.
37 For I say to you that this Scripture must be accomplished in me; namely, And with transgressors was he reckoned; for indeed what (has been written) about me is nearing completion (Is. 53:12).
38 And they said:
Lord, behold two swords here!
And he said to them:
It is enough.

(↓ §345)

MK
(cf. 6:8)

(15:28)

JN

§338 Jesus the Way to the Father

MT   LK   MK

JN 14:1-14
(↑ §336)

1 Let not your heart be troubled; believe in God, and believe in me.
2 In the house of my Father there are many mansions; and if not, would I have told you that I go to prepare a place for you?

MT	LK	MK	JN 14:1-14
			3 And if I go and prepare a place for you, again I come and I will accompany you to myself, so that where I myself am you also may be. 4 And where I am going to, you know the way.
			5 Thomas says to him: Lord, we do not know where you are going to; how do we know the way?
			6 Jesus says to him:
			I myself am the way and the truth and the life; nobody comes to the Father except through me.
			7 If you had known me, then you would surely have known the Father. And from now you do know him and have beheld him.
			8 Philip says to him: Lord, show us the Father, and it is enough for us.
			9 Jesus says to him:
			Have I been with you so long a time and you have not known me, Philip? He who has beheld me has beheld the Father. How say you: Show us the Father? 10 Do you not believe that I am in the Father and the Father is in me? The words which I speak to you I do not speak from myself; but the Father abiding in me does his works.
			11 Believe me, that I am in the Father and the Father in me; and if not, for the very works' sake believe!
			12 Amen, amen, I say to you, he who believes in me, that (man) shall do the works that I do, and greater than these shall he do, because I am going to the Father.
			13 And whatsoever you shall ask the Father in my name, I will do it, so that the Father may be glorified in the Son.
			14* And if you shall ask me anything in my name, I myself will do (it).

§339 Indwelling of Father, Son and Spirit

MT	LK	MK	JN 14:15-24
			15 If you love me, you will keep my commandments.
			16 And I will ask the Father and he will give you another Comforter to be with you for ever, 17 the Spirit of truth, whom the world cannot receive, because it neither beholds nor knows him. But you know him, because he abides with you and will be in you.
			18 I will not leave you orphans, I am coming to you.
			19 Yet a little, and the world no longer beholds me, but you behold me, because I am living and you will be living.
			20 On that day you yourselves will know that I am in my Father and you in me and I in you.
			21 He who has my commandments and keeps them, that is the one who loves me; and he who loves me will be loved by my Father, and I will love him and will manifest myself to him.

MT	LK	MK	JN 14:15-24

22 Judas, not the Iscariot, says to him:
Lord, what has come to pass that you will manifest yourself to us and not the world?
23 Jesus answered and said to him:
If anyone loves me, he will keep my word, and my Father will love him, and will come to him and will make an abode with him.
24 He that does not love me will not keep my words; and the word which you hear is not mine, but the Father's who sent me.

§340 The Spirit of Jesus Gives Peace

MT	LK	MK	JN 14:25-31

25 These things I have spoken to you while abiding with you; 26 but the Comforter, the Holy Spirit, whom the Father will send in my name, he will teach you everything and will remind you of everything that I myself have told you.
27 Peace I leave you, my peace I give you; not as the world gives do I give to you. Let not your heart be troubled, nor let it be cowardly.
28 You heard that I said to you: I am going away and I am coming to you. If you loved me, you would be glad that I am going to the Father, because the Father is greater than I.
29 And now I have told you before it happens, so that when it does happen, you may believe.
30 No longer shall I speak many things with you, for the ruler of the world is coming, and in me he has not anything at all, 31 but that the world may know that I love the Father, and that just as the Father has commanded me, so I do.
Arise, let us go hence.

(cf. 26:30)

§341 The Vine and Its Branches

MT	LK	MK	JN 15:1-17

1 I am the true vine, and my Father is the vine-dresser.
2 Every branch in me not bearing fruit he takes it away, and every one that bears fruit he prunes it so that it may bear more fruit.
3 You are now clean because of the word which I have spoken to you; 4 abide in me and I in you. Just as the branch cannot bear fruit of itself, unless it remain in the vine, so neither you unless you abide in me.
5 I am the vine, you are the branches. He who abides in me and I in him this (one) bears much fruit, because without me you can do nothing.

MT	LK	MK	JN 15:1-17

6 If anyone does not remain in me, he is cast outside like the branch and is dried up, and they gather them up and throw into the fire and they are burnt.

7 If you abide in me and my words abide in you, ask whatever you will and it will be done for you.

8 In this is my Father glorified, that you bear much fruit and you will be my disciples.

9 Just as the Father has loved me, I too have loved you; abide in my love.

10 If you keep my commandments, abide in my love, just as I have kept my Father's commandments and I abide in his love.

11 These things I have spoken to you, that my joy may be in you and your joy may be made complete.

12 This is my commandment that you love one another just as I have loved you.

13 Greater love than this no one has, (than) that he should lay down his life for his friends.

14 You are my friends, if you do what I command you.

15 No longer do I call you slaves, because the slave does not know what his lord is doing; but I have called you friends, because everything that I have heard from my Father, I have made known to you.

16 (It was) not you (who) chose me, but I who chose you, and appointed you to go off and bear fruit and that your fruit should abide, so that whatever you ask the Father in my name he will give it to you.

17 These things I command you, that you love one another.

§342 The World Will Persecute the Disciples

MT	LK	MK	JN 15:18-16:4a

18 If the world hates you, know that it hated me before you.

19 If you were of the world, the world would love its own; but because you are not of the world, but I have chosen you out of this world, for this (reason) the world hates you.

20 Remember the word which I told you: The servant is not greater than his master.

If they persecuted me, they will also persecute you. If they have kept my word they will also keep yours.

21 But all these things they will do to you because of my name, for they do not know him who sent me.

22 If I had not come and spoken to them, they had not had sin. But now they have no excuse about their sin.

23 He who hates me also hates my Father.

24 If I had not done among them the works which no one else has done they had not had sin. But now they have both beheld and

MT	LK	MK	JN 15:18-16:4a

hated both me and my Father. 25 But (it has happened) in order
to fulfil the word which is written in their Law: They hated me
without cause **(Ps. 34 (35):19; Ps. 68 (69):4)**.
26 When the Comforter has come, whom I shall send you from
the Father, the Spirit of truth, who goes forth from the Father, he
will witness about me;
27 And you also bear witness, because you have been with me
from the beginning.
16:1 These things I have spoken to you that you should not be
scandalized.
2 They will put you out of the synagogue; but (the) hour is
coming when everyone who puts you to death will think he is
giving glory to God.
3 And they will do these things because they have not known the
Father or me.
4a But I have spoken these things to you so that when their hour
comes you may remember them that I told you them.

§343 The Benefits of Jesus' Departure

MT	LK	MK	JN 16:4b-33

4b Now I did not tell you these things from the beginning, because
I was with you.
5 But now I go to him who sent me, and none of you asks me:
Where are you going?
6 But because I have spoken these things to you, grief has filled
your heart.
7 But I am telling you the truth, it is for your benefit that I am
going away. If I do not go away, the Comforter will not come to
you; but if I go, I shall send him to you.
8 And when he comes he will prove the world wrong about sin
and about justice, and about judgement;
9 about sin, because they do not believe in me;
10 then about justice - because I go to the Father and you no
longer behold me;
11 and about judgement, because the ruler of this world has been
judged.
12 I have yet many things to say to you, but you cannot bear
them now.
13 But when that one, the Spirit of truth, comes, he will lead you
into the whole truth; for he will not speak from himself, but will
speak whatever he hears, and will announce to you the things
to come.
14 He himself will glorify me, because he will receive from (what
is) mine and will announce to you.
15 Everything that the Father has is mine; that is why I said that

MT	LK	MK	JN 16:4b-33

he receives from (what is) mine and announces to you.

16 A little while, and you behold me no more, and again a little while and you will see me.

17 (Some) of the disciples therefore said to one another: What is this that he is telling us: "A little while and you do not behold me, and again a little while and you will see me"? And "I am going to the Father"?

18 They said therefore: What is this that he is saying. "A little while"? We do not know what he is saying.

19 Jesus knew that they wanted to ask him, and he said to them: You are asking one another about this that I said: "A little while and you do not behold me, and again a little while and you will see me."

20 Amen, amen I say to you, that you yourselves will weep and mourn, but the world will be glad; you will be sad, but your sadness will turn into gladness.

21 When a woman is giving birth, she is sad, because her hour has come; but when the baby is born, she no longer remembers the suffering because of (her) gladness that a man has been born into the world.

22 And you therefore indeed have sadness; but I shall see you again, and your heart shall be gladdened, and your gladness nobody takes from you.

23 And on that day you will not ask me for anything.

Amen amen I say to you, if you ask the Father for anything in my name he will give (it) to you. 24 Until now you have not asked for anything in my name; ask and you shall receive, that your gladness may be filled up.

25 These things I have spoken to you in similes, (the) hour is coming when I will no longer speak to you in similes, but I will openly proclaim to you about the Father.

26 On that day you will ask in my name, and I do not say to you that I shall request the Father about you;

27 for the Father himself loves you, because you have loved me and have believed that I came forth from God.

28 I came forth from the Father and I have come into the world; again I leave the world and go to the Father.

29 His disciples say to him:

See now, in clarity you are speaking and you speak no simile. 30 Now we know that you know all things and have no need that anyone should ask you; because of this, we believe that you came forth from God.

31 Jesus answered them:

Do you believe? 32 Behold (the) hour is coming and has come when each one of you is scattered to his own place and you leave me alone; though I am not alone because the Father is with me.

33 These things I have spoken to you so that in me you may have peace; but be of good heart, I have overcome the world.

MT	LK	MK	JN 17:1-26
			1 Jesus spoke these things and lifting up his eyes to heaven he said:

O Father, the hour has come; glorify thy Son that thy Son may glorify thee, 2 just as thou hast given him authority over all flesh, so that all that thou has given to him, to them he may give eternal life.

3 Now this is eternal life, to know thee, the only true God,and Jesus Christ whom thou has sent.

4 I have glorified thee upon the earth, having accomplished the work which thou hast given me to do; 5 and now glorify thou me, O Father, with thyself with the glory which I had with thee before the world came to be.

6 I manifested thy name to the men whom thou gavest me out of the world. Thine they were and thou gavest them to me, and they have kept thy word.

7 Now they know that all things which thou has given to me are from thee.

8 Because I have given to them the words that thou gavest to me, and they accepted them and have truly known that I came forth from thee, and they believed that thou has sent me.

9 About them I am asking; I do not ask about the world, but about those whom thou hast given to me, because they are thine, 10 and all that is mine is thine, and thine is mine, and I have been glorified in them.

11 And I am no longer in the world, but they are in the world, and I am coming to thee. O Holy Father, keep them in thy name, whom thou hast given to me that they may be one, just as we (are).

12 When I was with them, in thy name I kept those whom thou hast given to me, and I guarded (them) and none of them was lost save the son of perdition, so that the Scripture should be fulfilled.

13 But now I am coming to thee, and I am speaking these things in the world that they may have my own joy fulfilled in them.

14 I have given thy word to them, and the world hated them, because they are not from the world, just as I am not from the world.

15 I do not ask that thou shouldst take them out of the world, but that thou shouldst protect them from the Evil One. 16 They are not from the world, just as I am not from the world.

17 Sanctify them in the truth; thy word is truth.

18 Just as thou didst send me into the world, I too have sent them into the world, 19 and on behalf of them I sanctify myself, so that they too may be sanctified in truth.

20 And not for these only do I ask, but also for those who will believe in me through their word, 21 that they may all be one, just as thou, Father, in me and I in thee, that they too may be one in us, that the world may believe that thou hast sent me.

22 And I have given to them the glory which thou hast given to me, that they may be one, just as we are one.

MT	LK	MK	JN 17:1-26
			23 I in them and thou in me, that they may be perfected into one, that the world may know that thou didst send me and hast loved them just as thou didst love me.
			24 Father, whom thou hast given me I will that where I am they also may be with me, that they may behold the glory that is mine, which thou hast given to me because thou didst love me before the foundation of the world.
			25 O just Father, though the world did not know thee yet I knew thee, and these have known that thou didst send me.
			26 And I have made known thy name to them, and I will make (it) known, so that the love with which thou didst love me may be in them and I in them.

§345 Jesus at Gethsemane

MT 26:36-46 (↑§336)	LK 22:39-46 (↑§337)	MK 14:32-42 (↑§336)	JN 18:1
36 Then Jesus comes with them	39 And going out he went according to his custom to the Mount of Olives; and his disciples also followed him.	32 And they come	1 Having said these things Jesus went out with his disciples across the wadi Kidron,
to a property called Gethsemani,	40 And coming upon the place,	to a property whose name was Gethsemani,	where there was a garden, into which he and his disciples entered.
and he says to the disciples: Sit here while I go off there and pray. 37 And taking along Peter and the two sons of Zebedee, he began to grow sad and dismayed.	he said to them: Pray not to enter into temptation.	and he says to his disciples: Sit here while I pray. 33 And he takes Peter and James and John along with him, and he began to be distressed and dismayed.	
38 Then he says to them: My soul is very sad, unto death; stay here and watch with me. 39 And going forward a little,	41 And he was withdrawn from them about a stones' throw and kneeling he prayed, 42 saying:	34 And he says to them: My soul is very sad, unto death; stay here and watch. 35 And going forward a little,	
he fell on his face praying and saying:		he fell on the ground and he prayed that if it were possible the hour might pass away from him, 36 and he said:	
My Father, if it is possible, let this cup pass away from me; yet not as I will, but as thou.	Father if thou wilt, remove this cup from me; yet not my will but thine be done. 43* Now an angel from heaven appeared to him strengthening him; 44* And being in an agony he prayed more earnestly. And his sweat became like drops of blood falling down on the ground.	Abba, Father, all things are possible to thee; remove this cup from me; but not what I will, but what thou.	

MT 26:36-46

40 And he comes to the disciples and finds them sleeping,
and he says to Peter:
So you were not able to watch one hour with me?
41 Watch and pray, that you do not enter into temptation; for the spirit is eager, but the flesh is weak.
42 Again a second time going off he prayed saying:
My Father, if this cannot pass away except I drink it, let thy will be done.
43 And coming again he found them sleeping, for their eyes were weighed down.

44 And leaving them again going off he prayed a third time, again saying the same thing.
45 Then he comes to the disciples and says to them:
Sleep on now and rest;
Behold, the hour is at hand, and the Son of Man is betrayed into sinners' hands.
46 Arise, let us go; behold, my betrayer is at hand.

LK 22:39-46

45 And rising from the prayer, coming to the disciples he found them falling asleep from grief.
46 And he said to them:
Why are you sleeping?

Get up and pray, that you do not enter into temptation.

(cf. 22:42)

MK 14:32-42

37 And he comes and he finds them sleeping,
and he says to Peter:
Simon, are you sleeping? Were you not able to watch one hour?
38 Watch and pray, that you do not come into temptation; for the spirit is eager, but the flesh is weak.
39 And again going off he prayed saying the same thing.

40 And again coming he found them sleeping, for their eyes were becoming heavy, and they did not know what to answer him.

41 And he come the third time and says to them:
Sleep on now and rest; it is over.
The hour has come. Behold, the Son of Man is betrayed into the hands of sinners.
42 Arise, let us go; behold, my betrayer is at hand.

JN 18:1

§346 Jesus Is Arrested

MT 26:47-56

47 And while he was still speaking,

behold Judas, one of the Twelve, came.
and with him a large crowd with swords and staves from the high-priests and elders of the people.

48 Now his betrayer had given them

LK 22:47-53

47 While he was still speaking,

behold a crowd, and the one called Judas, one of the Twelve,
came at their head

MK 14:43-52

43 And at once while he was still speaking,
Judas, one of the Twelve, arrives,

and with him a crowd with swords and staves, from the high-priests and the scribes and the elders.

44 Now his betrayer had given them

JN 18:2-11

2 And Judas, who betrayed him, also knew the place because very often Jesus had assembled there with his disciples.

3 Judas therefore, taking the troop

and attendants from the high-priests and from the Pharisees, comes there with lanterns and torches and weapons.

MT 26:47-56	LK 22:47-53	MK 14:43-52	JN 18:2-11
a sign, saying: Whomever I kiss he is the one; seize him.		a signal, saying: Whomever I kiss, he is the one, seize and lead him away securely.	
49 And at once coming up to Jesus he said: Hail, Rabbi, and he kissed him.	and drew near to Jesus to kiss him.	45 And at once coming, coming up to him he says: Rabbi, and he kissed him.	
50 And Jesus said to him: Comrade, for what are you here?	48 And Jesus said to him: Judas, do you betray the Son of Man with a kiss?		
			4 Jesus therefore knowing all things about to come upon him, went forth and says to them: Whom are you seeking?
			5 They answered him: Jesus the Nazarene.
			He says to them: I am he.
			Now Judas his betrayer also stood with them.
			6 When therefore he said to them: I am he, they went backwards and fell on the ground.
			7 Again therefore he questioned them: Whom are you seeking?
			And they said: Jesus the Nazarene.
			8 Jesus answered:
			I tell you that I am he; if therefore you seek me, let these go away.
			9 —In order to fulfill the word that he spoke: Those whom you have given me, I have not lost any one of them (Jn. 6:39).
Then coming up they laid hands upon Jesus and seized him.		46 And they laid hands upon him and seized him.	
	49 And when those around him saw what was about to occur they said: Lord, shall we strike with the sword?		
51 And behold, one of those with Jesus, stretching out his hand, drew out his sword,	50 And a certain one of them	47 And a certain one of the bystanders drawing the sword	10 Then Simon Peter having a sword drew it
and striking the servant of the high-priest,	struck the servant of the high-priest	hit the servant of the high-priest	and hit the high-priest's servant
severed his ear.	and severed his right ear.	and severed his ear.	and cut off his right ear and the servant's name was Malchus.
52 Then Jesus says to him: Return your sword to its place; for all who take the sword will perish by the sword.	51 And Jesus answering said: Do you take it even as far as this?*		11 Therefore Jesus said to Peter: Put the sword into its sheath;
53 Or do you imagine that I am not able to appeal to my Father and he			

MT 26:47-56	LK 22:47-53	MK 14:43-52	JN 18:2-11
will put now at my disposal more than twelve legions of angels? 54 How then would the Writings, that so it has to happen, be fulfilled?			the cup which the Father has given me, shall I not drink it?
55 In that hour Jesus said to the crowds:	And touching the ear he healed it. 52 And Jesus said to the high-priests and police of the temple and elders coming out against him:	48 And Jesus answering said to them:	
Have you come out as if against a robber, with swords and staves to apprehend me? Day by day I used to sit among you in the Temple teaching, and you did not seize me.	Have you come out as if against a robber, with swords and staves? 53 Day by day when I was with you in the Temple, you did not stretch out your hands against me. But this is your hour and the power of darkness.	Have you come out as if against a robber, with swords and staves to apprehend me? 49 Day by day I was among you in the Temple teaching and you did not seize me,—	
56 Now all this has happened in order to fulfil the Writings of the Prophets. Then all the disciples leaving him fled.		but that the Writings might be fulfilled.	
(↓ §350)		50 And leaving him they all fled.	
		51 And a certain young man was following him, wearing a sheet over his nakedness, and they seize him. 52 But he left the sheet and fled naked from them.	
		(↓ §350)	

§347 Peter Follows Jesus

MT	LK 22:54	MK	JN 18:12-16
(26:50)	54 And taking hold of him,	(14:46)	12 The troop therefore and the tribune and the attendants of the Jews took hold of Jesus and bound him,
(26:57)	they led (him) and brought him into the house of the high-priest;	(14:53)	13 and led (him) to Annas first, for he was brother-in-law of Caiaphas, who was high-priest of that year. 14 Now Caiaphas was the one who had counseled the Jews that it was expedient that one man should die for the people.
(26:58)	and Peter followed at a distance.	(14:54)	15 Now Simon Peter followed Jesus, and the other disciple. And that disciple was known to the high-priest, and entered together with Jesus into the hall of the high-priest; 16 but Peter stood without the gate. Then the other disciple, the one known to the high-priest, went out and spoke to the portress; and he brought Peter in.

MT 26:69-70	LK 22:55-57	MK 14:66-68a	JN 18:17-18
69 Now Peter was sitting without in the courtyard,	55 And when they had lit a fire in the middle of the courtyard and were sitting around it, Peter was sitting in their midst.	*66 And while Peter was below in the courtyard,*	**(cf. 18:18)**
and a servant-girl came up to him, saying:	56 And a certain servant-girl seeing him sitting by the fire, and gazing at him, said:	*one of the servant-girls of the high-priests comes, 67 and seeing Peter warming himself, looking at him, says:*	17 So the servant-girl, the portress, says to Peter:
You too were with Jesus the Galilean.	This one too was with him.	*You too were with Jesus the Nazarene.*	Are not you too of the disciples of this man? He says:
70 But he denied in front of all saying:	57 But he denied, saying:	*68a But he denied, saying:*	
I do not know what you are saying.	I do not know him, O woman.	*Neither do I know nor do I understand what you are saying.*	I am not.
	(↓ §351)		18 And the slaves and the attendants were there, and had made a charcoal-fire, because it was cold and they were warming themselves; and Peter was also present with them and warming himself.

§349 Annas Questions Jesus

MT	LK	MK	JN 18:19-23
			19 The high-priest therefore questioned Jesus about his disciples and about his teaching.
			20 Jesus answered him: I have spoken openly to the world; I taught always in a synagogue and in the Temple, where all the Jews foregather, and I have spoken nothing in secret. 21 Why do you ask me? Ask those who have heard what I said to them. Behold, these people know what I said.
			22 And when he said these things one of the attendants standing by gave Jesus a blow, saying: Is this how you answer the high-priest?
			23 Jesus answered him: If I have spoken wrongly, witness concerning the wrong; but if well, why do you beat me?

§350 Jesus before Caiaphas

MT 26:57-58
(↑ §346)

57 And those who had seized Jesus led (him) away to Caiaphas the high-priest, where the Scribes and the elders were gathered together.
58 Now Peter was following him from a distance as far as the courtyard of the high-priest, and entering within he was sitting with the attendants to see the end.

(↓ §352)

LK 22:54-55

54 And taking hold of him they led (him) and brought him into the house of the high-priest;

and Peter followed at a distance.

55 And when they had lit a fire in the middle of the courtyard and were sitting round it, Peter was sitting in their midst.

MK 14:53-54
(↑ §346)

53 And they led Jesus away to the high-priest, and all the high-priests and the elders and scribes are gathered together.
54 And Peter followed him from a distance as far as within into the courtyard of the high-priest, and he was sitting together with the attendants and warming himself at the glow.

(↓ §352)

JN 18:24

24 Annas therefore sent him bound to Caiaphas the high-priest.

(cf. 18:15-16)

(cf. 18:18)

§351 Peter's Second and Third Denials (Lk, Jn) (§354)

MT 26:71-75

71 And when he had gone out to the gate-porch, another (girl) saw him and says to those there:

This (man) was with Jesus the Nazarene.
72 And again he denied with an oath: I know not the man.
73 But a little after those present coming up said to Peter:

Truly, you too are of them, for even your speech makes you conspicuous.
74 Then he began to curse and to swear: I know not the man.

And at once a cock crew.

75 And Peter remembered the word Jesus had spoken:
Before the cock crows you will thrice deny me.
And going forth outside he wept

LK 22:58-62
(↑ §348)

58 And after a short while, another (man) seeing him said:

You too are of them.

But Peter said:
O man, I am not.
59 And about an hour intervening, a certain other man asserted, saying:

In truth this one too was with him, for he too is a Galilean.

60 But Peter said: O man, I know not what you are saying.

And immediately while he was yet speaking a cock crew.
61 And the Lord turning, looked at Peter.
and Peter recalled the word of the Lord, how he had said to him:
Before the cock crows today, you will thrice deny me.
62 And going forth outside he wept

MK 14:68b-72

68b And he went out to the forecourt and a cock crowed
69 and the girl seeing him began to say again to those present:
This (man) is one of them.

70 But he again denied.

And after a little again those standing there began to say to Peter:

Truly you are of them.
For you also are a Galilean.

71 But he began to curse away and to swear: I know not this man whom you speak of.
72 And at once a cock crew a second time.

and Peter recollected the word how Jesus had said to him;
Before the cock crows twice you will deny me thrice.
And he began to weep.

JN 18:25-27

25 And Simon Peter was present and warming himself. They said therefore to him:

Surely you too are of his disciples?

He denied and said:
I am not.

26 One of the slaves of the high-priest, being a relative of him whose ear Peter had severed, says:

Did I not see you in the garden with him?
27 Again then Peter denied,

and at once a cock crew.
(↓ §355)

257

MT 26:71-75
bitterly.

LK 22:58-62
bitterly.
(↓ §353)

MK 14:68b-72

JN 18:25-27

§352 Jesus Found Guilty (§355)

MT 26:59-66 (↑ §350)	LK 22:66-71	MK 14:55-64 (↑ §350)	JN
59 And the high-priests and the whole Sanhedrin sought false witness against Jesus how to put him to death.	66 *And when day came, the senate of the people, both high-priests, and Scribes, assembled and led him away into their Sanhedrin,*	55 And the high-priests and the whole Sanhedrin sought witness against Jesus to put him to death,	
60 and they did not find (any), many false witnesses coming forward.		and were not finding (any). 56 For many bore false witness against him, and their witnessings were not in agreement.	
But later two coming forward, 61 said:		57 But some rising bore false witness against him, saying:	
This man said: I can destroy the Holy Place of God and after three days build it.		58 We heard him say: I will destroy this Holy Place that is built by hands and after three days I will build another not made by hands. 59 And even so their witness was not in agreement.	
62 And the high-priest rising said to him:		60 And the high-priest rising in the midst questioned Jesus, saying:	
Do you answer nothing? What are these men witnessing against you? 63 But Jesus was silent,		Do you not answer anything? What are these men witnessing against you? 61 But he was silent, and did not answer anything.	
And the high-priest said to him:	67 *saying:*	Again the high-priest questioned him and says to him:	
I adjure you by the Living God that you tell us if you are the Christ the Son of God?	*If you are the Christ, tell us.*	Are you the Christ the Son of the Blessed?	
	And he said to them: If I were to tell you, you would not believe. 68 And if I should question you, you would not answer me nor let me go. 69 But from now the Son of Man will be sitting on the right hand of the power of God **(Dan. 7:13).** *70 And they all said: You are then the Son of God?*		
64 Jesus says to him: You have said it.	*And he said to them: You yourselves say that I am.* **(22:69)**	62 And Jesus said to him: I am.	
However, I say to you, from now you will see the Son of Man sitting on the right hand of		And you will see the Son of Man sitting on the right hand of the Power, and coming with	

258

MT 26:59-66	LK 22:66-71	MK 14:55-64	JN
the Power, and coming on the clouds of heaven **(Dan. 7:13)**. 65. Then the high-priest tore his robes, saying: He has blasphemed; what further need have we of witnesses: See now, you have heard the blasphemy; 66 What do you think? And they answering, said: He is guilty of death.	*71 And they said:* *What further need have we of witness? For we ourselves have heard from his own mouth.*	the clouds of heaven **(Dn. 7:13)**. 63 And the high-priest tearing his garments says: What further need have we of witnesses? 64 You have heard the blasphemy; What does it seem to you? And they all condemned him to be guilty of death.	

§353 Jesus Is Mocked

MT 26:67-68	LK 22:63-65 (↑ §351)	MK 14:65	JN
67 Then they spat in his face and slapped him and some hit him, 68 saying: Prophesy to us, O Christ, who is it who is striking you?	63 And the men who held him, mocked him, beating him, 64 and covering him up, they questioned (him) saying: Prophesy, who is it who is striking you? 65 And many other things blaspheming they said to him: (↓ §355)	65 And some began to spit on him and to cover up his face and to slap him and to say to him: Prophesy; and the attendants received him with blows.	

§354 Peter's Three Denials (Mt, Mk) (§§348, 351)

MT 26:69-75	LK 22:55-62	MK 14:66-72	JN 18:17, 25-27
69 Now Peter was sitting without in the courtyard; and a servant-girl came up to him, saying, You too were with Jesus the Galilean. 70 But he denied in front of all, saying: I do not know what you are saying.	*55 And when they had lit a fire in the middle of the courtyard and were sitting round it, Peter was sitting in their midst.* *56 And a certain servant-girl seeing him sitting by the fire, and gazing at him, said:* *This one too was with him.* *57 But he denied, saying:* *I do not know him, O woman.*	66 And while Peter was below in the courtyard, one of the servant-girls of the high-priest comes, 67 and seeing Peter warming himself, looking at him, says, You too were with Jesus the Nazarene. 68 But he denied, saying: Neither do I know, nor do I understand, what you are saying.	*17 So the servant-girl, the portress says to Peter:* *Are not you too one of the disciples of this man?* *He says:* *I am not.*

259

MT 26:69-75	LK 22:55-62	MK 14:66-72	JN 18:17, 25-27
71 And when he had gone out to the gate-porch, another (girl) saw him, and says to those there: He was with Jesus the Nazarene. 72 And again he denied with an oath: 'I know not the man.' 73 And a little after, those present coming up said to Peter: Truly, you too are of them, for even your speech makes you conspicuous. 74 Then he began to curse and to swear, I know not the man. And at once a cock crew.	*58 And after a short while, another (man) seeing him said: You too are of them. But Peter said: O man, I am not. 59 And about an hour intervening, a certain other man asserted, saying: In truth, this one too was with him, for he too is a Galilean. 60 But Peter said: O man, I know not what you are saying. And immediately, while he was yet speaking, a cock crew.*	And he went out outside to the forecourt, and a cock crew. 69 And the servant-girl seeing him began to say again to those present: He is one of them. 70 But he again denied. And a little after those standing there began to say to Peter: Truly, you are of them, for you too are a Galilean. 71 But he began to curse away and to swear: I know not this man, whom you speak of. 72 And at once a cock crew the second time.	*25 And Simon Peter was present and warming himself. 25b They said therefore to him: Surely you too are of his disciples? He denied and said: I am not. 26 One of the slaves of the high-priest, being a relative of him whose ear Peter had severed, says: Did I not see you in the garden with him? 27 Again then Peter denied, and at once a cock crew.*
75 And Peter remembered the word Jesus had spoken: Before the cock crows, you will thrice deny me. And going forth outside he wept bitterly.	*61 And the Lord turning looked at Peter, and Peter recalled the word of the Lord, how he had said to him: Before the cock crows today, you will thrice deny me. 62 And going out he wept bitterly.*	And Peter recollected the word, how Jesus said to him: Before the cock crows twice, you will deny me thrice. And he began to weep.	

§355 The Morning Council (§352)

MT 27:1-2	LK 22:66-23:1	MK 15:1	JN 18:28
	(↑ §353)		(↑ §351)
1 And when dawn came, all the high-priests and the elders of the people held a consultation against Jesus, so as to put him to death. **(cf. 26:59f)**	66 And when day came, the senate of the people, both high-priests and Scribes assembled, and led him away into their Sanhedrin, 67 saying: If you are the Christ, tell us. And he said to them: If I were to tell you you would not believe. 68 And if I should question you, you would not answer me nor let me go. 69 But from now the Son of Man will be sitting on the right hand of	1a And at once at dawn having had a consultation the high-priests with the elders and Scribes and the whole Sanhedrin, **(cf. 14:55f)**	
(cf. 26:64)		**(cf. 14:62)**	

MT 27:1-2

LK 22:66-23:1
the Power of God.
70 And they all said:
You are then the Son of God?
And he said to them:
You yourselves say that I am.
71 And they said: What further need
have we of witness? For we ourselves
have heard from his mouth.
23:1 And the whole body of them
rising up, led him off to Pilate.

(↓ §357)

MK 15:1

JN 18:28

2 And having bound him they led
him away and handed him over to
Pontius Pilate the governor.

1b having bound Jesus, led (him)
away and handed (him) over to
Pilate.

(↓ §357)

28 Then they lead Jesus from
Caiaphas to the Praetorium;

and it was early morning; and they
themselves did not enter into the
Praetorium; lest they should be
defiled, so that they might eat the
Passover.

(↓ §357)

§356 The Suicide of Judas

MT 27:3-10
3 Then Judas who betrayed him seeing that he was
condemned, moved by remorse returned the thirty silver
pieces to the high-priests and elders. 4 saying: I have
sinned betraying innocent blood.
But they said: What is that to us? Look you to it.
5 And throwing the pieces into the holy place, he
withdrew, and going off strangled himself.
6 But the high-priests taking the pieces said: It is not
lawful to put them into the temple-treasure, because they
are the price of blood.
7 And taking counsel they bought with them the Potter's
Field as a burial-place for strangers.
8 Wherefore that field has been called the Field of Blood
even to this day.
9 Then was fulfilled the saying spoken by the prophet
Jeremiah:
And they took the thirty pieces of silver,
the price of him who had been priced,
whom they priced from the sons of Israel;
10 and they gave them for the Potter's Field,
as the Lord instructed me **(Jer. 32:6-9; Zech. 11:12-13)**.

LK   MK   JN

AC 1:15-20
*15 And in those days Peter rising up in the midst of the
brethren said—now there was a crowd of persons together
(of) about one hundred and twenty—:*
*16 Men, brethren, the Scripture had to be fulfilled which
the Holy Spirit foretold through the mouth of David
about Judas who became the leader of those who seized
Jesus;*
*17 for he had been numbered among us and had received
the lot of this ministry;*
*18 who then indeed acquired a field from the wages of
unrighteousness, and falling headlong burst open in the
middle, and all his bowels were poured out.*
*19 And it became known to all who dwelt in Jerusalem,
so that that field was called in their own language,
Hakeldamak that is, Field of Blood.*
20 For it has been written in the Book of Psalms:
*Let his dwelling become derelict,
and let no one dwell in it* **(Ps. 68[69]:25)**;
and, His overseership let another receive **(Ps. 108[109]:8)**.

§357 Jesus before Pilate

MT 27:11-14	LK 23:2-5	MK 15:2-5	JN 18:29-38
	(↑ §355)	(↑ §355)	(↑ §355)
11 Now Jesus stood before the governor.			29 Pilate therefore went outside to them, and says: What accusation do you bring against this man?
	2 And they began to accuse him, saying: We have found this man perverting our race, and forbidding to pay tribute to Caesar, and saying that he is Christ a king.		30 They answered and said to him: If this man were not an evil-doer, we would not have handed him over to you.
			31 Pilate therefore said to them: Take him yourselves and judge him according to your law: Then the Jews said to him: It is not lawful for us to kill anyone;
			32 so that the word of Jesus might be fulfilled which he had said signifying by what sort of death he was to die.
And the governor questioned him saying:	3 And Pilate questioned him saying:	2 And Pilate questioned him:	33 He therefore again entered into the Praetorium, and summoned Jesus and said to him:
Are you the King of the Jews? And Jesus said to him.	Are you the King of the Jews? And answering he said to him:	Are you the King of the Jews? And answering he said to him:	Are you the King of the Jews:
			34 Jesus answered: Do you say this of yourself or do others say it to you about me?
			35 Pilate answered: Am I a Jew? Your own race and the high-priests have handed you to me; what have you done?
			36 Jesus answered: My Kingdom is not of this world; if my Kingdom was of this world, my attendants would have fought that I should not be handed over to the Jews. But now my Kingdom is not from here.
			37 Then Pilate said to him: Are you not then a king? Jesus answered:
You say (it).	You say (it).	You say (it).	You say that I am a king. For this was I born and for this I have come into the world, to bear witness to the truth. Everyone who is of the truth hears my voice.
			38 Pilate then says to him: What is truth?
12 And while he was being accused by the high-priests and elders, he answered nothing.		3 And the high-priests accused him strongly.	

MT 27:11-14

13 Then Pilate says to him:

Do you not hear how many things they testify against you?
14 And he did not answer, not so much as one word, so that the governor was much amazed.

(↓ §360)

LK 23:2-5

4 And Pilate said to the high-priests and the crowds: I find no guilt in this man.
5 But they insisted, saying: He disturbs the people, teaching throughout all Judea, and beginning from Galilee to here.

MK 15:2-5

4 And Pilate again questioned him saying:
Do you not answer anything? See, how many things they accuse you of.
5 And Jesus did not further answer anything, so that Pilate was amazed.

(↓ §360)

JN 18:29-38

And saying this he again went out to the Jews and says to them: I find no guilt at all in him.

(↓ §360)

§358 Jesus before Herod

MT

(cf. 14:1-2)

LK 23:6-12

6 And when Pilate heard, he inquired if the man was a Galilean,
7 and discovering that he was from Herod's jurisdiction, he sent him up to Herod, who was also in Jerusalem in those days.
8 And Herod seeing Jesus was exceedingly pleased; because for a long time he had been wanting to see him because of repeatedly hearing about him, and he was hoping to see some sign accomplished by him.
9 And he questioned him at length; but he answered him nothing.
10 And the high-priests and the Scribes were there accusing him violently.
11 And Herod with his soldiers despised him, and mocking and dressing him up in splendid clothing sent him back to Pilate.
12 And Herod and Pilate became friends with each other on that day; for they had formerly been at enmity with one another.

MK

JN

§359 Pilate Declares Jesus Innocent

MT

LK 23:13-16

13 And Pilate calling together the high-priests and the leaders and the people, 14 said to them:
You have brought this man to me as one who perverts the people, and behold, I examining (him) before you have found no guilt at all in this man, with respect to the things you accuse him of;
15 nor Herod either, for he sent him back to us. And, behold,

MK

JN

263

MT	LK 23:13-16	MK	JN
	nothing worthy of death has been done by him; 16 I will punish him therefore and let him go.		

§360 Jesus or Barabbas?

MT 27:15-23	LK 23:17-23	MK 15:6-14	JN 18:39-40
(↑ §357)		(↑ §357)	(↑ §357)
15 Now at the Festival the governor was accustomed to release for the crowd one prisoner whom they wanted.	17* Now at the Festival he was under constraint to release for them one (man).	6 Now at the Festival he used to release for them one prisoner, whom they demanded.	39 You have a custom that I should free someone at the Passover.
16 And he had then an important prisoner called Barabbas.		7 And there was the one called Barabbas who had been imprisoned with the rioters, who in the riot had committed murder.	
17 When therefore they had assembled,	(cf. 23:18-19)	8 And the crowd going up began to ask him (to do) for them as he used to do.	
Pilate said to them: Whom do you want me to release to you, Barabbas, or Jesus who is called Christ?		9 And Pilate answered them saying: Do you want me to release to you the King of the Jews?	Do you desire me to release to you the King of the Jews?
18 For he perceived that they handed him over through envy.		10 For he knew that the high-priests had handed him over through envy.	
19 Now while he was sitting on the judgement seat his wife sent to him, saying: Have nothing to do with that just man; for I have suffered greatly to-day in a dream because of him.			(cf. 19:13)
20 Now the high-priests and the elders persuaded the crowds to ask for Barabbas and to destroy Jesus.		11 Now the high-priests stirred up the crowd for him rather to release for them Barabbas.	
21 And the governor answering said to them: Which of the two do you want me to release for you? And they said:			
Barabbas.	18 And they shouted out all together, saying: Away with this man, and release for us Barabbas:		40 Therefore they shouted again, saying: Not this man, but Barabbas.
	19 He was one who had been thrown into prison for some riot that took place in the city and for murder.		Now Barabbas was a robber.
22 Pilate says to them:	20 And again Pilate addressed them,	12 And Pilate again answering said to

MT 27:15-23	LK 23:17-23	MK 15:6-14	JN 18:39-40
What then shall I do with Jesus, who is called Christ?	wanting to release Jesus.	them: What then do you wish me to do with (him) whom you call the King of Jews?	
They all say: Let him be crucified.	21 And they began to call out, saying: Crucify, crucify him.	13 And they again shouted out: Crucify him.	
23 And he said: But what evil has he done?	22 And a third time he said to them: But what evil has this man done? I have found no reason for death in him; therefore I will punish him and release him.	14 And Pilate said to them: But what evil has he done?	
But they shouted the more, saying: Let him be crucified.	23 But they insisted with loud cries, demanding that he be crucified; and their voices prevailed, and those of the high-priests.*	But they shouted the more: Crucify him.	**(cf. 19:15)**
(↓ §362)	(↓ §362)	(↓ §362)	

§361 "Behold the Man!" (§363)

MT 27:27-30	LK	MK 15:16-18	JN 19:1-15
27 Then the soldiers of the governor, taking Jesus into the Praetorium, gathered together against him the whole maniple. 28 And stripping him they placed around him a scarlet cloak 29 and plaiting a crown of thorns they set it on his head, and a reed in his right hand, and genuflecting in front of him, they mocked him, saying: Hail, king of the Jews. 30 And spitting on him they took the reed and struck at his head.		*16 Then the soldiers led him away inside the courtyard, that is, the Praetorium, and call together the whole maniple. 17 And they put on him purple and plaiting a thorny crown they set it on him,* *and they began to salute him: Hail, king of the Jews. 18 And they struck his head with a reed and spat at him.*	1 Then Pilate took and scourged Jesus. 2 And the soldiers plaited a crown of thorns and put it on his head, and they threw around him a purple garment, 3 And they came to him and said: Hail, O king of the Jews; and they gave him blows. 4 And Pilate went out again and says to them: See, I bring him out to you, that you may know that I find no wrong in him. 5 Jesus therefore went outside, wearing the crown of thorns and the purple garment. And he says to them: Behold the Man. 6 When therefore the high-priests and the attendants saw him, they shouted, saying: Crucify, crucify. Pilate says to them: Take him yourselves and crucify him, for I find no wrong in him. 7 The Jews answered him: We have a law, and according to the law he ought to die, because

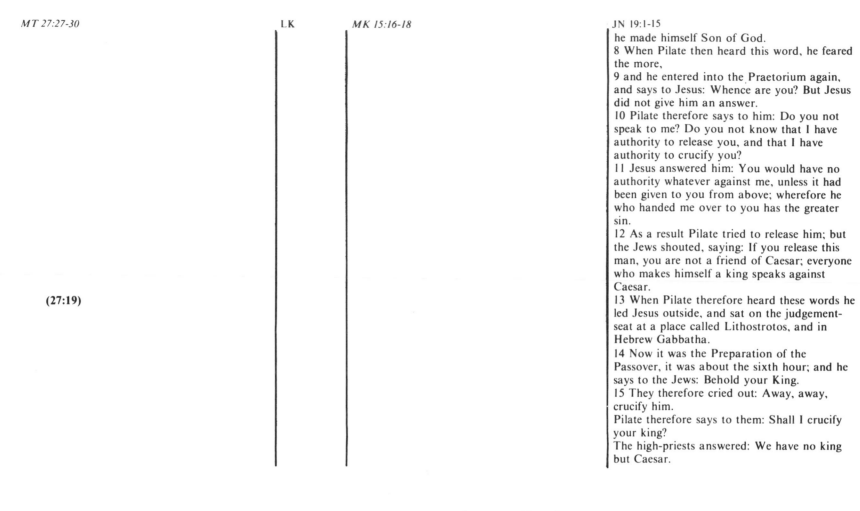

MT 27:27-30

LK

MK 15:16-18

JN 19:1-15

he made himself Son of God.
8 When Pilate then heard this word, he feared the more,
9 and he entered into the Praetorium again, and says to Jesus: Whence are you? But Jesus did not give him an answer.
10 Pilate therefore says to him: Do you not speak to me? Do you not know that I have authority to release you, and that I have authority to crucify you?
11 Jesus answered him: You would have no authority whatever against me, unless it had been given to you from above; wherefore he who handed me over to you has the greater sin.
12 As a result Pilate tried to release him; but the Jews shouted, saying: If you release this man, you are not a friend of Caesar; everyone who makes himself a king speaks against Caesar.
13 When Pilate therefore heard these words he led Jesus outside, and sat on the judgement-seat at a place called Lithostrotos, and in Hebrew Gabbatha.
14 Now it was the Preparation of the Passover, it was about the sixth hour; and he says to the Jews: Behold your King.
15 They therefore cried out: Away, away, crucify him.
Pilate therefore says to them: Shall I crucify your king?
The high-priests answered: We have no king but Caesar.

(27:19)

§362 Pilate Sentences Jesus to Death

MT 27:24-26

(↑ §360)

24 Then Pilate seeing that nothing availed but rather an uproar was occurring, taking water washed his hands in front of the crowd, saying: I am innocent of the blood of this just one; look you to it.
25 And the whole people answered,

LK 23:24-25

(↑ §360)

24 And Pilate judged that their demand should be granted;

MK 15:15

(↑ §360)

15 And Pilate deciding to satisfy the crowd,

JN 19:16a

MT 27:24-26
saying:
His blood (is) upon us and upon our
children.
26 Then he released for them
Barabbas,

but handed over Jesus, after
scourging, to be crucified.

LK 23:24-25

25 and he released the one who for
riot and murder had been thrown
into prison, whom they demanded,
but handed over Jesus to their will.
(↓ §364)

MK 15:15

released for them Barabbas,

and handed over Jesus, after
scourging, to be crucified.

JN 19:16a

16a Then he handed him over to
them to be crucified.
(↓ §364)

§363 The Soldiers Mock Jesus (§361)

MT 27:27-31a
27 Then the soldiers of the governor, taking
Jesus into the Praetorium,
gathered together against him the whole
maniple.
28 And stripping him, they placed around him
a scarlet cloak,
29 and plaiting a crown of thorns they set it
on his head,
and a reed in his right hand and genuflecting
in front of him
they mocked him, saying:
Hail, king of the Jews;
30 and spitting on him they took the reed and
struck at his head.

31 And when they had mocked him, they took
the cloak off him, and put his own garments
on him.

LK

MK 15:16-20a
16 Then the soldiers led him away inside the
courtyard, that is the Praetorium,
and call together the whole maniple

17 And they put purple on him

and plaiting a thorny crown they set it on him,

18 and they began to salute him:
Hail, O king of the Jews;
19 and they struck his head with a reed and
spat at him, and kneeling they worshipped
him.
20a And when they had mocked him, they
took the purple off him, and put his own
garments on him.

JN 19:2-3

2 And the soldiers plaited a crown of thorns
and put it on his head,
and they threw around him a purple garment.

3 And they came to him and said:
Hail, O king of the Jews;
and they gave him blows.

§364 The Way to Golgotha

MT 27:31b-32

And they led him away for
crucifying.

32 And going out they found a man,
a Cyrenian, Simon by name;

LK 23:26-32
(↑ §362)
26 And as they led him away,

seizing a certain Simon, a Cyrenian,
coming from the country,

MK 15:20b-21

20b And they led him out to crucify
him.

21 And they force a certain passer-by
Simon, a Cyrenian, coming from the

JN 19:16b-17a
(↑ §362)
16b They therefore took Jesus along,
17a and carrying his own cross, he
went out

MT 27:31b-32	LK 23:26-32	MK 15:20b-21	JN 19:16b-17a
		country, the father of Alexander and Rufus,	
him they forced to take up his cross.	they imposed on him the cross to carry behind Jesus. 27 And a great multitude of the people followed him and women who mourned and lamented him. 28 And turning to them Jesus said: Daughters of Jerusalem, weep not for me; rather weep for yourselves and for your children. 29 For behold the days are coming in which they will say: Blessed are the childless and the wombs that have not borne, and the breasts that did not give suck. 30 Then they will begin to say to the mountains, Fall upon us, and to the hills, Cover us. 31 Because if in the green wood they do these things, what will happen in the dry? 32 And also two other criminals were led with him to be executed.	to take up his cross.	

§365 The Crucifixion

MT 27:33-38	LK 23:33-34	MK 15:22-28	JN 19:17b-24
33 And coming to a place called Golgotha, which is called Place of a Skull, 34 they gave him wine mixed with gall to drink; and tasting it he would not drink. 35 And having crucified him,	33 And when they came upon the place named Skull, there they crucified him,	22 And they bring him to the place of Golgotha, which is translated Place of a Skull, 23 and they gave him wine spiced with myrrh; but he did not take it. 24 And they crucify him,	17b to the (place) called Place of a Skull, which in Hebrew is called Golgotha, 18 where they crucified him, and with him two others on either side and Jesus in the middle.
they divided his garments, casting lots. 36 And sitting down they guarded him there. **(27:45)**	*34b And dividing his garments they cast lots.* **(23:44)**	and divide his garments, casting lots upon them who should take what. 25 And it was the third hour and they crucified him.	**(19:23f)**
37 And they put up over his head his indictment written:	**(23:38)**	26 And the inscription of his indictment had been inscribed:	19 And Pilate also wrote a title and put it on the cross: and it was written:

MT 27:33-38	LK 23:33-34	MK 15:22-28	JN 19:17b-24
This is Jesus the King of the Jews.		The King of the Jews.	Jesus the Nazarene, the King of the Jews. 20 Many therefore of the Jews read this title, because the place where Jesus was crucified was near the city, and it was written in Hebrew, Latin and Greek. 21 Therefore the high-priests of the Jews said to Pilate: Do not write 'The King of the Jews', but that 'The man said, I am the King of the Jews.' 22 Pilate replied: What I have written, I have written.
38 Then two robbers are crucified with him, one on the right and one on the left.	and the criminals, one on the right and one on the left.	27 And with him they crucify two robbers, one on his right and one on his left. 28* And the Scripture was fulfilled which says: And with the wicked was he reckoned (Is. 53:12).	(19:18)
(27:35)	34* And Jesus said: Father, forgive them, for they know not what they do. And dividing his garments they cast lots.	(15:24)	23 The soldiers therefore when they had crucified Jesus, took his garments and made four parts, a part to each soldier, and the tunic. Now the tunic was seamless woven throughout from the top. 24 They said therefore to one another: Let us not tear it, but let us cast lots for it, whose it shall be. That the Scripture might be fulfilled that says: They divided my garments among them And over my vesture they cast lots. (Ps. 21 (22):18). The soldiers therefore did these things.

§366 The Spectators of His Agony

MT 27:39-43	LK 23:35-38	MK 15:29-32a	JN 19:25-27
	35 And the people stood gazing:		25 And by the cross of Jesus stood his mother, and his mother's sister,

MT 27:39-43   LK 23:35-38   MK 15:29-32a   JN 19:25-27

Mary the (wife) of Clopas, and Mary
the Magdalene,
26 Jesus therefore, seeing his mother
and the disciple whom Jesus loved
standing by, says to his mother:
Woman, See, your son.
27 Then he says to the disciple:
See, your mother.
And from that hour the disciple took
her unto his own.

39 And the passers-by blasphemed
him, wagging their heads 40 and
saying:
You who destroy the Holy Place and
build it in three days, save yourself; if
you are the Son of God, just come
down from the cross.
41 Likewise also the high-priests
mocking, together with the Scribes
and elders, said:
42 Others he saved, himself he cannot
save;
if he is King of Israel,

let him now come down from the
cross, and we will believe in him.
43 He trusted in God, let him now
rescue him if he wants him; for he
said: I am Son of God.

but the high-priests also scoffed,
saying:

Others he saved, let him save himself,

if he himself is the Christ of God, the
Chosen One.

29 And the passers-by blasphemed
him, wagging their heads, and saying:

Vah! You who destroy the Holy
Place and build it in three days, 30
save yourself, coming down from the
cross.
31 Likewise also the high-priests
mocking, together with the Scribes,
said to one another:
Others he saved, himself he cannot
save;
let the Christ, 32a the King of Israel,

now come down from the cross that
we may see, and believe.

36 And the soldiers also mocked him,
coming up, presenting him vinegar,
37 and saying: If you are the King of
the Jews, save yourself.
38 For there was indeed the
inscription written over him: This is
the King of the Jews.

(27:37)   (15:26)   (19:19)

§367 The Two Thieves

MT 27:44   LK 23:39-43   MK 15:32b   JN

44 And the robbers crucified together with him
reviled him in the same way.

39 And one of the hanging criminals was
blaspheming him: Are you not the Christ?
Save yourself and us.
40 And the other answering, rebuking him,
said: Do you then not fear God, because you
are in the same judgement? 41 And we indeed

32b And those crucified together with him,
reviled him.

MT 27:44

LK 23:39-43
justly, for we are receiving back things worthy of what we did. But this one has done nothing amiss.
42 And he said: Jesus, remember me when you come into your Kingdom.
43 And he said to him:
Amen I say to you, to-day you shall be with me in Paradise.

MK 15:32b

JN

§368 The Death of Jesus

MT 27:45-53

45 And from the sixth hour, darkness came over the whole earth until the ninth hour.

(27:51)

46 And about the ninth hour Jesus cried out with a loud voice saying:
Eli, Eli, lema sabachthani,
that is,
O my God, O my God, why hast thou forsaken me? **(Ps. 21[22]:2)**.
47 And when some of those standing there heard, they said: He is calling Elijah.

48 And one of them at once running and taking a sponge, soaking it with vinegar, and putting it round a reed, gave him to drink. 49 But the rest said:
Leave it, let us see if Elijah comes saving him.

50 And Jesus, again exclaiming with a great cry,

LK 23:44-46

44 And it was now about the sixth hour, and darkness came over the whole earth until the ninth hour,
45 the sun failing.
And the veil of the Holy Place was rent down the middle.

46 And Jesus, calling with a great cry, said:
Father, into thy hands I commend

MK 15:33-38

33 And the sixth hour coming, darkness came over the whole earth until the ninth hour.

(15:38)

34 And at the ninth hour Jesus cried with a loud voice:
Eloi, Eloi, lema sabachthani,
which is translated:
O my God, O my God, wherefore hast thou forsaken me?
35 And when some of the by-standers had heard, they said: 'See, he is calling Elijah.

36 And someone running and filling a sponge with vinegar, putting it round a reed, gave him to drink, saying:

Leave it, let us see if Elijah comes to take him down.

37 And Jesus, letting out a great cry,

JN 19:28-30

(↑ §366)

28 After this, Jesus, knowing that everything had now been accomplished, in order that the Scripture might be fulfilled, says: I thirst.
29 A vessel full of vinegar stood there. Putting therefore a sponge full of vinegar round a hyssop, they presented it to his mouth.

30 When therefore Jesus had received the vinegar, he said: It has been accomplished.
And bowing his head

MT 27:45-53	LK 23:44-46	MK 15:33-38	JN 19:28-30
released the spirit.	my spirit. And saying this he expired.	expired.	he handed over (his) spirit.
51 And behold the veil of the Holy Place was rent in two from top to bottom, and the earth quaked, and the rocks were split, 52 and the tombs were opened, and many bodies of the saints laid to rest were raised; 53 and going out of the tombs after his resurrection entered into the holy city, and appeared to many.	**(23:45)**	38 And the veil of the Holy Place was rent in two from top to bottom.	(↓§371)

§369 The Centurion's Witness

MT 27:54	LK 23:47	MK 15:39	JN
54 And the centurion and those with him guarding Jesus, seeing the earth-quake and the happenings, were exceedingly afraid, saying: Truly this was the Son of God.	47 And the centurion, seeing what had happened, glorified God saying: Indeed, this man was just.	39 And the centurion who had stood by opposite him, seeing that he had expired crying out in this way, said: Truly this man was the Son of God.	

§370 Other Witnesses of Jesus' Death

MT 27:55-56	LK 23:48-49	MK 15:40-41	JN
	48 And all the crowds that were present together at this spectacle, beholding the events, returned beating their breasts.		
55 And there were many women there beholding from afar, who had followed Jesus from Galilee, ministering to him,	49 And all his acquaintance stood far off, and the women who had accompanied him from Galilee, watching these things.	40 And there were also women beholding from afar,	
56 among whom were Mary the Magdalene, and Mary the mother of James and Joseph and the mother of the sons of Zebedee.	**(cf. 23:55)** (↓§372)	among whom were both Mary the Magdalene and Mary the mother of James the Little and Joses, and Salome, 41 who, when he was in Galilee, had followed him and ministered to him, and many other (women) who had come up with him to Jerusalem.	**(cf.19:25)**
(↓§372)		(↓§372)	

MT	LK	MK	JN 19:31-37
			(↑ §368)

31 The Jews therefore, since it was the Preparation, in order that
the bodies should not remain on the cross on the Sabbath—for
that Sabbath was a great day—asked Pilate that their legs might
be broken and that they might be taken away.
32 The soldiers therefore came, and they broke the legs of the first
and of the other crucified together with him;
33 but coming up to Jesus, when they saw that he had already
died, they did not break his legs;
34 but one of the soldiers pierced his side with a lance, and at
once blood and water came out.
35 And he who saw it has borne witness, and his witness is true,
and he knows that he speaks truly, so that you too may believe.
36 For these things happened that the Scripture might be fulfilled:
Not a bone of him shall be broken (**Ex. 12:46; Ps. 33[34]:20**).
37 And again another Scripture says:
They shall look upon him whom they pierced (**Zech. 12:10**).

§372 The Burial of Jesus

MT 27:57-60	LK 23:50-54	MK 15:42-46	JN 19:38-42
(↑ §370)	(↑ §370)	(↑ §370)	
57 And evening coming,	50 And behold	42 And evening now coming, since it was the Preparation—that is, the day before the Sabbath—	38 After these things,
there came a rich man, from Arimathea, of the name of Joseph,	a man by name Joseph, being a Councillor, a good and just man - 51 he himself had not assented to their plan and deed, - from Arimathea, a city of the Jews,	43 Joseph coming, who was from Arimathea, a respected Councillor,	Joseph from Arimathea asked Pilate,
who had also himself become a disciple of Jesus; 58 he, going up to Pilate, asked for the body of Jesus.	who was awaiting the Kingdom of God, 52 he, going up to Pilate, asked for the body of Jesus.	who was also himself awaiting the Kingdom of God, taking courage came in to Pilate and asked for the body of Jesus. 44 Now Pilate wondered if he had already died, and summoning the centurion, questioned him if he was already dead.	being a disciple of Jesus, but secretly out of fear of the Jews, (permission) to take away the body of Jesus;
Then Pilate ordered the body to be given up.		45 And learning from the centurion he granted the body to Joseph.	and Pilate gave permission.
			He therefore came and took away his body. 39 And Nicodemus also came, the one who first came to him by night, bringing a mixture of myrrh and aloes, about a hundred pounds' weight.

MT 27:57-60	LK 23:50-54	MK 15:42-46	JN 19:38-42
59 And taking the body, Joseph wrapped it in a new linen shroud,	53 And taking it down he wrapped it in a linen shroud,	46 And having bought a linen shroud, taking it down he wrapped it up in the linen shroud,	40 He therefore took the body of Jesus and bound it by bandages together with the spices, as is the custom of the Jews to bury. 41 Now there was a garden at the place where he was crucified, and in the garden a new tomb, in which so far no one had been laid.
60 and laid it in his new tomb which he had hewn in the rock;	and laid it in a hewn out monument in which no one had as yet been laid to rest.	and laid it down in a tomb that had been hewn out of the rock,	42 There then because of the Preparation of the Jews, since the tomb was near, they laid Jesus.
and rolling a great stone in front of the entrance of the tomb he went away.		and he rolled in front a stone at the entrance of the tomb.	(↓§375)
	54 And it was the Preparation and the Sabbath was drawing on.		

§373 The Women Take Note of the Tomb

MT 27:61	LK 23:55-56	MK 15:47-16:1	JN
61 And Mary the Magdalene was there, and the other Mary, sitting over against the tomb.	55 And the women who had followed after, who had come up together from Galilee with him, beheld the tomb and how the body was laid.	47 And Mary the Magdalene and Mary of Joses beheld where he had been laid.	
	56 And returning they prepared spices and oils. And on the Sabbath they rested according to the commandment.	16:1 And, the Sabbath intervening, Mary the Magdalene, and Mary of James and Salome, bought spices, so that they might come and anoint him.	
	(↓§375)	(↓§375)	

§374 The Guard at the Tomb

MT 27:62-66	LK	MK	JN
62 And the next day, (which is after the Preparation), the high-priests and the Pharisees assembled before Pilate, 63 saying: Sir, we have remembered that this deceiver said when still living: After three days I am being raised. 64 Therefore order the tomb to be secured until the third day, lest perhaps his disciples come and steal him, and say to the people: He has been raised from the dead, and the last deceit shall be worse than the first. 65 Pilate said to them: You have a guard; go and secure it as you can. 66 And they went and made the tomb secure, sealing the stone with the guard.			

MT 28:1-8

1 And after the Sabbath, in the dawn on the first (day) of the week, Mary the Magdalene and the other Mary came to look at the burial place.
2 And behold a great earth-quake had occurred; for an angel of the Lord had come down from heaven and approached and rolled away the stone from the entrance and sat upon it.
3 And his appearance was like lightning and his vesture white as snow.
4 And the guards were seized with fear of him and became like dead men.

5 And the angel answering said to the women:
Do not let yourselves be frightened.
For I know that you seek Jesus, who has been crucified,
6 He is not here; for he is risen just as he said.
Come, see the place where the Lord was laid.

7 And go quickly and tell his disciples

LK 24:1-11
(↑ §373)

1 And on the first (day) of the week, exceedingly early, they came to the tomb carrying the spices which they had prepared.

2 And they found the stone rolled away from the sepulchre.

3 And entering in they did not find the body of the Lord Jesus.
4 Now it happened that while they were nonplussed by it,
behold, two men stood by them in dazzling array. 5 And as they were frightened and bowing their faces to the ground,
they said to them:

Why do you seek him who is living among the dead?
6 He is not here, but is risen.*

Remember how he spoke to you while he was still in Galilee, 7 saying that the Son of Man had to be betrayed into the hands of men, sinners, and to be crucified and to be raised up on the third day.
8 And they remembered his words.

MK 16:2-8
(↑ §373)

2 And very early on the first (day) of the week, they come to the sepulchre, the sun having risen.

3 And they said to one another: Who will roll away the stone from the entrance of the sepulchre?
4 And looking up they observe that the stone has been rolled away; for it was exceedingly large.
5 And entering into the sepulchre

they saw a young man seated on the right hand side wearing a white robe, and they were struck with awe.

6 And he says to them:

Do not stay awestruck!
You seek Jesus the Nazarene who has been crucified.
He is risen, he is not here.

See the place where they put him.

7 But go off and tell his disciples and Peter

JN 20:1
(↑ §372)

1 And on the first (day) of the week, Mary the Magdalene comes early while it was still dark to the sepulchre.

and she sees that the stone has been removed from the sepulchre.

MT 21:1-8	LK 24:1-11	MK 16:2-8	JN 20:1
that he is risen from the dead, and behold he goes before you into Galilee; there you will see him. Behold, I have told you. 8 And quickly going away from the sepulchre, with fear and great joy, they ran to announce to his disciples. (↓ §377)	 9 And returning from the sepulchre, they announced all these things to the Eleven and all the others. 10 And they were* Mary the Magdalene and Joanna and Mary of James, and the others with them were saying these things to the apostles. 11 And these words seemed to them like nonsense, and they disbelieved them.	that he goes before you into Galilee; there you will see him just as he told you. 8 And coming out they fled from the sepulchre, for trembling possessed them and amazement; and they said nothing to anyone, for they were afraid. (↓ §383)	

§376 Peter and John Run to the Tomb

MT	LK 24:12	MK	JN 20:2-10
	   12* And Peter getting up ran to the tomb, and stooping he sees the bandages alone; and he went away to his own place amazed at what had happened. (↓ §380)		2 She runs therefore and comes to Simon Peter and to the other disciple whom Jesus loved, and says to them: They have taken away the Lord from the tomb, and we know not where they have put him. 3 Peter therefore went out, and the other disciple, and came to the tomb. 4 And the two disciples ran together, and the other disciple ran ahead faster than Peter and came first to the tomb, 5 And stooping he sees the bandages lying, but did not however go in. 6 And then comes Simon Peter following him and entered into the tomb; and he beholds the bandages lying, 7 and the sweat-cloth which was over his head, not lying with the bandages, but apart having been folded up into one place. 8 Then therefore the other disciple, who came first to the tomb, also entered, and saw and believed. 9 For not yet did they understand the Scripture that he had to rise up from the dead. 10 The disciples went off again therefore to their place. (↓ §389)

IX. The Post-Resurrection Appearances of Jesus
§§ 377-396

MT 28:9-10	LK	MK	JN
(↑ §375)			

9 Now while they were going to announce to his disciples,* behold Jesus met them, saying: Hail.
And coming up they took hold of his feet and worshipped him.
10 Then Jesus says to them:
Do not be afraid. Go off, inform my brothers, that they go away into Galilee; and there they will see me.

§378 The Story of the Guards

MT 28:11-15	LK	MK	JN

11 And while they were going, behold some of the guard came into the city and informed the high-priests of all that had happened.
12 And assembling together with the Elders they made a plan and gave a lot of money to the soldiers,
13 saying: Say that his disciples came by night and stole him away, while we were asleep.
14 And if this should come to the ears of the governor, we will persuade him and we will cause you to be without anxiety.
15 And they took the money, and did as they were instructed. And this report was spread among the Jews down to the present day.

§379 Jesus Appears to the Eleven

MT 28:16-20	LK	MK	JN
16 And the Eleven disciples went to Galilee to the mountain where Jesus had appointed them; 17 and seeing him they worshipped him, but some doubted.		(16: 14)	
18 And Jesus coming up spoke to them, saying: All authority has been given to me in heaven and on the earth.			
19 Go therefore, make all nations disciples, baptizing them into the name of the Father and of the Son and of the Holy Spirit, 20 teaching them to observe all whatsoever I have commanded you. And behold I myself am with you all the days until the completion of the Age.		(16: 15)	

MT   LK 24:13-35   MK   JN

(↑ §376)

13 And behold two of them on that very day were going to a
village sixty stadia distant from Jerusalem, Emmaus by name, 14
and they were talking to one another about all these things that
had come to pass.
15 And it happened while they were talking and discussing that
Jesus himself drew near and journeyed with them; 16 but their
eyes were held so that they did not recognize him.
17 And he said to them:
What are these words that you are exchanging with one another
as you walk?
And they stood dejected.
18 And one of them, Cleopas by name, answering said to him:
Are you the only visitor to Jerusalem that does not know what
happened there during these days?
19 And he said to them:
What things?
And they said: What happened to Jesus the Nazarene, who was a
man, a prophet, powerful in word and deed before God and all
the people, 20 how our high-priests and rulers delivered him up to
judgement of death and crucified him.
21 But we were hoping that he was going to be the one to redeem
Israel; but in addition to all these things, it is now the third day
since these things happened.
22 And moreover some women of ours astonished us, being at the
tomb early in the morning, 23 and not finding his body, came
saying that they had also seen a vision of angels, who say that he
is living.
24 And some of those with us went off to the tomb, and found it
just as indeed the women had said, but him they did not see.
25 And he said to them:
O stupid and slow of heart to believe in all that the prophets said!
26 Surely the Christ had to suffer these things and to enter into
his glory?
27 And beginning from Moses and from all the prophets he
explained to them the things about him in all the Scriptures.
28 And they drew near to the village where they were going, and
he made as if he was going further. 29 And they urged him,
saying: Remain with us, because evening is near and the day has
already declined. And he went in to remain with them.
30 And it came to pass that when he was at table with them,
taking bread he blessed and broke and handed to them;
31 and their eyes were opened up, and they recognized him; and
he became invisible to them.
32 And they said to one another: Was not our heart burning with
us as he spoke to us on the way, as he opened up the Scriptures to
us?
33 And arising in that hour they returned to Jerusalem, and found

MT   LK 24:13-35   MK   JN

the Eleven and those with them assembled,
34 saying, The Lord is really risen and has appeared to Simon.
35 And they related the events on the way and how he was known
by them in the breaking of the bread.

§381 Jesus Appears to the Eleven

MT   LK 24:36-49   MK   JN

36 And while they were saying these things, he stood in their
midst and says to them: Peace to you.* 37 But frightened and
being terrified they thought they saw a spirit.
38 And he said to them:
Why are you upset? And why do thoughts arise in your heart? 39
See my hands, and my feet, that I am myself. Touch me, and see
that a spirit does not have flesh and bones as you behold me to
have.
40*And saying this he showed them his hands and feet.
41 And while they were still disbelieving from joy, and wondering,
he said to them:
Have you anything here to eat?
42 And they handed him a piece of baked fish. 43 And he took
and ate it in their presence.
44 And he said to them:
These words of mine which I have spoken to you while I was still
with you, (mean) that there had to be fulfilment of everything
written about me in the Law of Moses and the Prophets and the
Psalms.
45 Then he opened up their mind to understand the Scriptures,
46 and he said to them:
Thus it has been written that the Christ will suffer and be raised
from the dead on the third day, 47 and that in his name
repentance unto forgiveness of sins will be preached to all the
nations - beginning from Jerusalem. 48 You are witnesses of these
things.
49 And behold I am sending upon you the Promise of my Father. And
do you yourselves stay in the city until you are clothed with power
from on high.

§382 The Ascension

MT   LK 24:50-53   MK   JN

| 50 And he led them out as far as Bethany, and lifting up his hands |

MT	LK 24:50-53	MK	JN
	he blessed them. 51 And it happened that while he was blessing them he departed from them and was carried up into heaven.* 52 And they worshipped him* and returned to Jerusalem with great joy, 53 and they were continually in the Temple blessing God.		

The Long Ending of Mark (16:9-20)

§383 Jesus Appears to Mary Magdalene

MT	LK	MK 16:9-11	JN
		(↑ §375)	
(cf. 28:1)	(cf. 24:1)	9 And rising early on the first day of the week	(cf. 20:1)
	(cf. 8:2)	he appeared first to Mary the Magdalene, from whom he had cast out seven demons.	(cf. 20:11-18)
(cf. 28: 10)	(cf. 24:9-10)	10 She going reported to those who had been with him, as they mourned and wept.	(cf. 20:18)
	(cf. 24:11)	11 And when they heard that he was alive, and had been seen by her, they disbelieved.	

§384 Jesus Appears to Two Disciples

MT	LK	MK 16:12-13	JN
	(cf. 24:13-35)	12 And after these things, he was seen by two of them, as they were going into the country.	
(cf. 28:17)	(cf. 24:37)	13 And these going off, announced to the rest; and they did not believe them either.	

§385 Jesus Appears to the Eleven (§381)

MT	LK	MK 16:14	JN
(cf. 28:17)	(cf. 24:38f)	14 And later, while they were reclining he appeared to the Eleven, and reproached their unbelief and hardness of heart, because they did not believe those who had seen him after he had been raised up.	(cf. 20:24-29)

§386 Commissioning of the Eleven

MT	LK	MK 16;15-16	JN
(cf. 28:16-20)	(cf. 24:44-49)	15 And he said to them: Go into the entire world and preach the Gospel to every creature. 16 He who believes and is baptized will be saved; but he who disbelieves will be condemned.	(cf. 20:19-23)

§387 Believers Will Work Signs

MT	LK	MK 16:17-18	JN
(cf. 14:14)		17 And these signs will accompany those who believe: In my Name they will cast out demons (**Ac. 2:38; 16:31, 33**); they will speak with new tongues (**Ac. 2:4, 11; 8:7; 16:18;**); 18 and in their hands they will pick up serpents(**Ac. 28:3-6**); and if they drink something deadly, it wil not hurt them at all (**cf. Lk. 10:19**); and they will lay hands on the sick and they will get well (**Ac. 4:30; 5:16; Mk. 6:13**).	

§388 Christ's Ascension

MT	LK	MK 16:19-20	JN
	(cf. 24:50-53)	19 The Lord Jesus therefore, after speaking to them, was raised up into heaven and took his seat at the right hand of God (**Ac. 1:9-11**). 20 And they going out preached everywhere, the Lord working with (them) and confirming the word through the accompanying signs.	

§389 Jesus Appears to Mary Magdalene

MT	LK	MK	JN 20:11-18
			(↑ §376)
			11 Now Mary was standing by the tomb outside weeping. While therefore she was weeping she stooped to peer into the tomb, 12 and she beholds two angels in white, one seated at the head and one at the feet, where the body of Jesus had been lying. 13 And they say to her: Woman, why are you weeping? She says to them: Because they have taken away my Lord, and I know not where they have put him. 14 Having said this, she turned round and beholds Jesus standing,

MT	LK	MK	JN 20:11-18

though she did not know that it was Jesus.

15 Jesus says to her:
Woman, why are you weeping? Whom do you seek?
She, thinking that he was the gardener, says to him:
Sir, if you have carried him off, tell me where you have put him,
and I will remove him.
16 Jesus says to her: Mary.
Turning she says to him in Hebrew: Rabbouni—which means
Teacher.
17 Jesus says to her:
Do not touch me, for not yet have I gone up to my Father.
But go to my brothers and say to them:
I am going up to my Father and your Father and my God and
your God.
18 Mary Magdalene comes and announces to the disciples: I have
beheld the Lord; and (that) he said these things to her.

§390 Jesus Appears to the Eleven

MT	LK (cf. 24:36)	MK	JN 20:19-25

19 Now when it was evening on that day, the first (day) of the
week, and when the doors had been locked where the disciples
were, for fear of the Jews, Jesus came and stood in the midst and
says to them:
Peace (be) to you.
20 And having said this he showed them (his) hands and side. The
disciples therefore seeing the Lord were glad.
21 Jesus therefore again says to them:
Peace (be) to you; just as the Father has sent me, so do I send
you.
22 And having said this he breathed on them and says:
Receive the Holy Spirit; 23 if you forgive the sins of any, they are
forgiven them, if you hold (those) of any, they remain held.
24 Now Thomas, one of the Twelve, the one called Didymus, was
not with them when Jesus came.
25 The other disciples were therefore telling him: We have beheld
the Lord.
And he said to them: Unless I see in his hands the mark of the
nails and put my finger into the mark of the nails and put my
hand into his side I shall not believe.

MT	LK	MK	JN 20:26-29

26 And after eight days, his disciples were again indoors and
Thomas with them. Jesus comes, the doors being shut, and stood
in the midst and said:
Peace (be) to you.
27 Then he says to Thomas:
Bring your finger here and see my hands, and bring your hand
and put (it) into my side, and be not faithless but faithful.
28 Thomas answered and said to him: My Lord and my God.
29 Jesus says to him:
Because you have beheld me you have believed; blessed are they
that have not seen and have believed.

§392 First Conclusion of John's Gospel

MT	LK	MK	JN 20:30-31

30 So then many others signs too did Jesus in the presence of his
disciples, which are not written in this book;
31 but these have been written that you may believe that Jesus is
the Christ the Son of God, and that believing you may have life in
his name.

§393 The Second Miraculous Catch (cf. §§40, 47)

MT	LK	MK	JN 21:1-14

1 After these things Jesus manifested himself again to the
disciples on the Sea of Tiberias; and he manifested (himself) thus.
2 There were together Simon Peter and Thomas, the one called
Didymus, and Nathanael, the one from Cana of Galilee, and the
(sons) of Zebedee, and two more of his disciples.
3 Simon Peter says to them: I am going off to fish.
They say to him: We too are coming with you.
They went out and embarked on the boat, and on that night they
caught nothing.
4 But when morning had already come Jesus stood on the shore;
but the disciples however did not know that it was Jesus.
5 Jesus then says to them:
Children you haven't anything to eat, have you?
They answered him: No.
6 And he said to them:
Cast the net on the right side of the boat, and you will find.
They cast therefore, and they were no longer able to haul it from
the multitude of the fishes.
7 Therefore that disciple, whom Jesus loved, said to Peter: It is

| MT | LK | MK | JN 21:1-14 |

the Lord.
Simon Peter, therefore, hearing that it was the Lord, fastened on (his) outer garment, for he was stripped, and threw himself into the sea.
8 But the other disciples came in the boat, for they were not far from the land but about two hundred cubits off, dragging the net with the fishes.
9 When therefore they went up on to the land, they see a charcoal fire lit and lying on it food and bread.
10 Jesus says to them:
Bring (some) of the food which you have just caught.
11 Simon Peter therefore went aboard and hauled the net on to the land full of great fishes, one hundred and fifty-three; and though they were so many the net was not torn.
12 Jesus says to them:
Come, break your fast.
Now none of the disciples dared to question him: Who are you?, knowing that it was the Lord.
13 Jesus comes and takes the bread and gives it to them, and the cooked (fish) likewise.
14 This was now the third time that Jesus was manifested to the disciples, after being raised from the dead.

§394 Jesus and Peter

| MT | LK | MK | JN 21:15-19 |

15 Now when they had breakfasted, Jesus says to Simon Peter:
Simon (son) of John, do you love me more than these?
He says to him: Yes, Lord, you know that I am fond of you.
He says to him:
Feed my lambs.
16 He says to him again a second time:
Simon (son) of John, do you love me?
He says to him: Yes, Lord, you know that I am fond of you.
He says to him:
Shepherd my sheep.
17 He says to him the third time:
Simon (son) of John, are you fond of me?
Peter was grieved because he said to him for the third time: Are you fond of me?, and says to him:
Lord, you know all things; you know that I am fond of you.
Jesus says to him:
Feed my sheep.
18 Amen amen I say to you, when you were younger, you girded yourself and walked where you wished; but when you are grown old, you will stretch out your hands and another will gird you,

MT	LK	MK	JN 21:15-19

and will bring you where you do not wish.
19 Now he said this signifying by what kind of death he would glorify God. And having said this, he says to him:
Follow me.

§395 Jesus, Peter, and John

MT	LK	MK	JN 21:20-23

20 Peter turning round sees the disciple, whom Jesus loved, following, who also at the supper reclined upon his breast, and said: Lord, who is it who is going to betray you? **(cf. 13:23-25)**.
21 Peter therefore seeing this (disciple) says to Jesus:
Lord, what about him?
22 Jesus says to him:
If I wish him to abide until I come, what (is it) to you? Do you follow me.
23 Therefore this is the word that went forth to the brothers, that that disciple would not die.
But Jesus did not say to him 'He will not die', but 'If I wish him to abide until I come, what (is it) to you?'

§396 Second Conclusion of John's Gospel

MT	LK	MK	JN 21:24-25

24 It is this disciple who is witnessing about these things and who has written these things, and we know that his witness is true.
25 Now there are also many other things which Jesus did, which if they were written one by one, I do not think the world itself would have room for the books that would be written.

A Select List of Major Alternative Readings

The following list is not intended to be exhaustive. On the contrary, it contains only a select list of major variants, the majority of which concern those passages in the Synoptic Gospels where there is either an important variant, or where some assimilation or harmonizaton may be suspected or where a number of ancient authorities omit the word or passage or verse in question.

An asterisk (*) in the text following a word or a phrase or a verse number indicates that an alternative will be found in this list, in which the reference is always to the section number in which the variant is to be found. Also in one or two passages of special interest brackets ([ ]) have been used to indicate additions, which, though having but little textual support, yet have had an important role in later theological tradition.

MAW = Many Ancient Witnesses;
SAW = Some Ancient Witnesses.

For lists of manuscripts supporting variants, the reader is referred to the standard works that list them.

§3	JN 1:18	SAW read: 'only-begotten Son'
§5	MT 1:25	SAW omit: 'first-born'
§25	JN 1:28	SAW read: 'Bethabara'
§32	JN 3:25	SAW read: 'a Jew'
§39 (41)	MK 1:14	SAW omit: 'of the Kingdom'
§42	MK 1:27	SAW read: 'a new teaching with authority'
§46	LK 4:44	SAW read: 'of Galilee'
§49	JN 5:1	SAW read: '*the* feast'
§49	JN 5:2	SAW read: 'Bethsaida'
§49	JN 5:3b	SAW omit: 'waiting for the stirring of the waters'
§49	JN 5:4	Most AW omit this verse as being an ancient gloss
§52 (115)	MK 2:17	SAW omit: 'to repentance'
§54 (135)	LK 6:1	MAW omit: 'Second-first'
§55 (136, 244)	LK 6:10	MAW omit: 'in anger'
§58 (56, 123)	MK 3:14	SAW omit: 'whom also he named apostles'
§64	MT 5:22:	MAW omit: 'without reason'
§71 (69)	MT 5:44	SAW omit: 'Bless those who curse you, do good to those who hate you'
§80 (228)	MT 6:27	The Gk word rendered 'span' usually means 'maturity'
§99 (108, 142)	MK 3:32	SAW omit: 'and your sisters'
§113	MT 8:28 =	There is considerable confusion and/or harmonization in the MSS
	LK 8:26 =	forms between 'Gadarenes', 'Gerasenes,' and 'Gergesenes'
	MK 5:1	
§115 (52)	MT 9:13	SAW omit: 'to repentance'
§119 (98, 138)	MT 9:34	SAW omit this verse
§120 (38, 157)	MK 6:3	SAW omit: 'Joses'
§123 (56, 58)	MT 10:3	SAW read: "Lebbaios'
§131 (94)	*MT 11:19*	SAW read: 'children'
§142 (99, 108)	MT 12:47	SAW omit this verse
§151 (107)	MT 13:35	SAW omit: 'of the world'
§157 (38, 120)	MT 13:55	SAW read: 'Joses'
§164	JN 6:23	There is a considerable number of minor variants possible here.

§166	JN 6:69	SAW read: 'The Christ'
§167	MK 7:3	SAW read: 'up to the elbow'
§167	MK 7:4	SAW omit: 'and beds'
§171 (234)	MT 16:2b-3	SAW omit these verses
§180	MK 9:19	MAW omit: 'and perverted'
§180	MK 9:24	SAW omit: 'with tears'
§180	MT 17:21	SAW omit this verse
§180	MK 9:29	SAW omit: 'and fasting'
§185	MK 9:44, 46	SAW omit these verses
§185	MK 9:45	SAW omit: 'of unquenchable fire'
§186 (61, 250)	MK 9:49	MAW omit: 'and every offering . . . salt'
§187 (283)	MT 18:11	MAW omit this verse
§196	JN 7:53-8:11	MAW omit pericope or place it elsewhere
§198	JN 8:25	This verse may also be rendered *either*
		'Why should I speak to you at all ?'
		or 'What I have told you from the outset'
§200	JN 9:38-39a	SAW omit this passage
§202	LK 9:54	SAW omit: 'as Elijah also did'
§202	LK 9:55b-56	SAW omit everything from 'he said . . . to save' inclusive
§204	LK 10:1	SAW read: 'seventy'
§206	LK 10:17	SAW read: 'seventy'
§207	LK 10:22a	SAW omit: 'And turning. . .said' inclusive
§211	LK 10:41b-42a	SAW omit: 'you worry. . .one thing' inclusive
§211	LK 10:42a	SAW read instead: 'Of few things is their need, or of one'
§212	LK 11:2-4	MAW omit all the words in brackets
§214 (83)	LK 11:11b-12a	SAW omit: 'bread . . . .or again' inclusive
§228 (80)	LK 12:25	See note on MT 6:27 at §80
§244 (136)	LK 14:5	SAW read: 'son' instead of 'ass'
§267 (314)	LK 17:36	SAW omit this verse
§277	MT 19:16	SAW read: 'Good teacher'
§277	MT 19:17	SAW read: 'God is the Good'
§278	MK 10:24	SAW omit: 'for those who trust in riches'
§278	MT 19:29=MK 10:29	SAW omit: 'or wife'
§279	MT 20:16	SAW omit: 'For many . . . chosen'
§284 (318)	LK 19:25	SAW omit this verse
§286	JN 12:1	SAW omit: 'the one who died'
§295 (75)	MK 11:26	SAW omit this verse
§297	MT 21:29-30	The manuscript tradition in these verses remains confused
§298	MT 21:44	SAW omit this verse
§304 (221)	MT 23:4	SAW omit: 'hard to carry'
§304 (221)	MT 23:13	SAW omit this verse (also omitted by UBS 3rd ed. and N-A 26th ed.)
§304	MT 23:14	This verse is denoted '23:13' by UBS 3rd ed. and N-A 26th ed.
§305 (243)	MT 23:38	SAW omit: 'desolate'

§312	MT 24:31	SAW omit: 'and sound'
§331	LK 22:19b-20	SAW omit these verses
§331	MT 26:28	SAW omit: 'new'
§331	MK 14:22	SAW omit: 'eat'
§333	JN 13:24b	SAW omit: 'say. . .speaking' the second half of this verse
§338	JN 14:14	SAW omit this verse
§345	LK 22:43-44	SAW omit these verses
§346	LK 22:51	This verse also may be rendered: 'Stop, let them be!'
§360	LK 23:17	SAW omit this verse
§360	LK 23:23	SAW omit: 'those of the high-priests'
§365	LK 23:34	SAW omit this verse
§365	MK 15:28	SAW omit this verse
§375	LK 24:6	SAW omit: 'He. . .risen'
§375	LK 24:10	SAW omit: 'And they were'
§376	LK 24:12	SAW omit this verse
§377	MT 28:9a	SAW omit: 'Now. . .disciples' inclusive
§381	LK 24:36b	SAW omit: 'and says to them: Peace to you'
§381	LK 24:40	SAW omit this verse
§382	LK 24:51b	SAW omit: 'and was carried up into heaven'
§382	LK 24:52	SAW omit: 'and they worshipped him'
§383-388	MK 16:9-20	These verses are omitted by about one half of the best manuscripts while being retained by the other half. The Catholic Church and the Eastern Churches, however, accept them as belonging to the Canon of Scripture.

List of Texts Explicitly Cited as Scripture

§§	MT	O.T. REF.	LK	O.T. REF.	MK	O.T. REF.	JN	O.T. REF.
5	1:23	Is. 7:14; 8:8						
6	2:6	Mic. 5:2; 2 Sam. 5:2						
7	2:15	Hos. 11:1						
7	2:18	Jer. 31:15						
14			2:23	Ex. 13:2, 12, 15				
14			2:24	Lv. 12:8				
17					1:2	Mal. 3:1		
17	3:3	Is. 40:3; Ex. 23:20	3:4	Is. 40:3-5; Ex. 23:20	1:3	Is. 40:3; Ex. 23:20		
24	4:4	Dt. 8:3	4:4	Dt. 8:3				
24	4:6	Ps. 90[91]:11-12	4:10-11	Ps. 90[91]:11-12				
24	4:7	Dt. 6:16	4:12	Dt. 6:16				
24	4:10	Dt. 6:13	4:8	Dt. 6:13				
30							2:17	Ps. 69[70]:9
38			4:18-19	Lev. 25:10-13; Is. 61:1-2				
39	4:15-16	Is. 9:1-2						
54			6:3-4	1 Sam. 21:1-6	2:25-26	1 Sam. 21:1-6		
64	5:21	Ex. 20:13; Dt. 5:17						
66	5:27	Ex. 20:14; Dt. 5:18						
67	5:31	Dt. 24:1						
68	5:33	Lv. 19:12; Nu. 30:2; Dt. 23:21						
69	5:38	Ex. 21:24; Lv. 24:20; Dt. 19:21						
71	5:43	Lv. 19:18						
94			7:27	Mal. 3:1; Ex. 23:20				
110	8:17	Is. 53:4						
115	9:13	Hos. 6:6						
131	11:10	Mal. 3:1; Ex. 23:20						
135	12:7	Hos. 6:6						
137	12:18-21	Is. 42:1-4						
145	13:14-15	Is. 6:9-10						

§§	MT	O.T. REF.	LK	O.T. REF.	MK	O.T. REF.	JN	O.T. REF.
151	13:35	Ps. 77[78]:2						
164							6:31	Ps. 77[78]:24; Ex. 16:4
165							6:45	Is. 54:13
167	15:4	Ex. 20:12; Dt. 5:16			7:10	Ex. 20:12; Dt. 5:16		
167	15:8-9	Is. 29:13(LXX)			7:6-7	Is. 29:13(LXX)		
179	17:10	Mal. 4:5						
195							7:38	Prov. 18:4; Is. 58:11
195							7:41	Mic. 5:2
209			10:27	Dt. 6:5; Lev. 19:18				
270							10:34	Ps. 81[82]:6
274	19:4-5	Gen. 1:27; 2:24			10:6-8	Gen. 1:27; 2:24		
274	19:7	Dt. 24:4			10:4	Dt. 24:4		
277	19:18-19	Ex. 20:12-16; Dt. 5:16-20; Lv. 19:18	18:20	Ex. 20:12-16	10:19	Ex. 20:12-16; Dt. 5:16-20		
288	21:5	Zech. 9:9					12:15	Zech. 9:9
291	21:13	Is. 56:7; Jer. 7:11	19:46	Is. 56:7; Jer. 7:11				
291	21:16	Ps. 8:3 (LXX)						
293					11:17	Is. 56:7; Jer. 7:11		
298	21:42	Ps. 117[118]:22-23	20:17	Ps. 117[118]:22	12:10-11	Ps. 117[118]:22-23		
301	22:24	Gen. 38:8; Dt. 25:5	20:28	Gen. 38:8; Dt. 25:5	12:19	Gen. 38:8; Dt. 25:5		
301	22:32	Ex. 3:6	20:37	Ex. 3:6	12:26	Ex. 3:6		
302	22:37	Dt. 6:5			12:29	Dt. 6:4-5		
302	22:39	Lv. 19:18			12:31	Lv. 19:18		
302					12:32	Dt. 4:35		
302					12:33	1 Sam. 15:22		
303	22:44	Ps. 109[110]:1	20:42-43	Ps. 109[110]:1	12:36	Ps. 109[110]:1		
310	24:15	Dn. 9:27; 11:31			13:14	Dn. 9:27; 11:31		
324							12:38	Is. 53:1
324							12:40	Is. 6:10
332							13:18	Ps. 41[42]:9
336	26:31	Zech. 13:7			14:27	Zech. 13:7		
337			22:37	Is. 53:12				
342							15:25	Ps. 34[35]:19; 68[69]:4

§§	MT	O.T. REF.	LK	O.T. REF.	MK	O.T. REF.	JN	O.T. REF.
352	26:64	Dan. 7:13			14:62	Dan. 7:13		
356	27:9-10	Jer. 32:6-9; Zech. 11:12-13					Ac. 1:20	Ps. 68[69]:25; 108[109]:8
365					15:28	Is. 53:12	19:24	Ps. 21[22]:18
371							19:36	Ex. 12:46; Ps. 33[34]:20
371							19:37	Zech. 12:10

A Synopsis
of the Four Gospels